BRAVE

Adventures into the

NEW

Uncharted World of Cannabis

WEED

JOE DOLCE

HARPER WAVE

As of publication, cultivating and consuming cannabis are criminal offenses in many states and illegal pursuant to federal law. This book is intended to enlighten and inform and does not encourage or advocate the unlawful use of cannabis. It is not intended to provide guidance for any particular course of medical treatment incorporating cannabis, which should only be pursued under the care of a physician in states where such use is permitted by law. The author and publisher disclaim any responsibility for loss or liability caused as a result of the use or application of material in this book.

A hardcover edition of this book was published in 2016 by Harper Wave, an imprint of HarperCollins Publishers.

FIRST HARPER WAVE PAPERBACK EDITION PUBLISHED 2017.

Design by Fritz Metsch

Library of Congress Cataloging-in-Publication Data has been applied for.

ISBN 978-0-06-249992-9 (pbk.)

17 18 19 20 21 LSC 10 9 8 7 6 5 4 3 2 1

PRAISE FOR
Brave New Weed

"One of the most fascinating accounts of the state of marijuana. A charming, honest look into pot's past—and what that says about its future."

—*Rolling Stone*

"Employing aspects of travel narrative, pop history, journalism, and personal diary, Dolce is a genial and engaging narrator with a knack for breaking down complex science and making it easily digestible for laypeople. *Brave New Weed* will prove popular with cannabis enthusiasts, and will surprise and entertain the general reader."   —*Publishers Weekly*

"*Brave New Weed*, a loving rethink of all things marijuana, is likely to be a trusted hitchhiker's guide to this new universe."

—*New York Times Book Review*

"An expansively researched book that finds the author trekking from Amsterdam to Israel to Colorado to craft an up-to-the-minute portrait of the past and future of cannabis."   —*Stranger*

"An outstanding book."

—Dr. Raphael Mechoulam, award-winning professor of medicinal chemistry and natural products, Hebrew University, and the grandfather of cannabis research

"No matter where you fall on the cannabis debate, this book will surprise you, intrigue you, and make you think. *Brave New Weed* provides a fresh perspective and demonstrates just how little we know about this ubiquitous, multifaceted, and ancient plant."

—Dr. Andrew Weil, author of *Mind Over Meds: How to Protect Yourself from Overmedication by Knowing When Drugs Are Necessary and When Alternatives May Be Better*

"The ultimate 'Just Say Yes!' book. I got a contact high from reading it."

—John Waters

"*Brave New Weed* is a delightful, even joyous, book, filled with fascinating information about the expanding world of new strains, higher strengths, and tasty means of ingestion. Still, it left me feeling regretful about all the years and lives wasted by prohibition—and all the people in pain who remain without help because of archaic laws. Dolce has given us a major brief in the fight for legalization."

—Barbara Ehrenreich, author of *Nickel and Dimed* and *Bait and Switch*

"Part travelogue, part cultural inquiry, part state-of-the-art scientific and medical survey, Joe Dolce's engaging and entertaining book provides an image makeover for cannabis that's long overdue."
—Dr. Julie Holland, author of *Moody Bitches* and editor of *The Pot Book*

"I've always avoided cannabis—watch enough 'dance moves' at your rock icon dad's concerts and you'd avoid the stuff, too. But Joe Dolce has opened my mind to the heart and horticulture of the herb in his pot page-turner. Pellucid science and story. I now want to heal from and exploit it in every way. HIGH-ly recommended."
—Moon Zappa, actor and author of *America the Beautiful*

"A fresh, clear-eyed, and lucidly reported travel guide to the rapidly expanding American subcontinent of medical and not-so-medical marijuana. Gone are the smoke-filled dorm rooms of yesteryear. In their place, bright dispensaries with 'budtenders' and 'cannabists,' and connoisseurs microdosing on the latest batch of 'Bio-Diesel' or 'Super Lemon Haze.' Dolce is our de Tocqueville for Weed 2.0."
—Brad Gooch, author of *Smash Cut*

"A superb book, *Brave New Weed* delivers a sharp, funny, incredibly interesting assessment of modern cannabis. A terrific writer, Dolce examines the scientists and the quacks, the heroes and the hucksters, the cops and the crooks converging in the great game of marijuana."
—Michael Backes, author of *Cannabis Pharmacy, The Practical Guide to Medical Marijuana*

"A thoroughly enjoyable and highly informative romp through the politics, science, industry, and culture of cannabis."
—Ethan Nadelmann, Executive Director, Drug Policy Alliance

"Fresh, engaging, and thoughtful. . . . The finely-tuned prose is infused with a marvelous sense of curiosity and in-depth journalism. Dolce won me over immediately and held my attention from one page to the next, following him around the world as he explored the past, present, and future of cannabis. . . . An engaging, worthwhile read no matter what side of the cannabis argument you happen to be on."
—Green Flower

"Dolce weaves a fascinating tale of the twisted history—and even more twisted pretzel logic—behind marijuana prohibition. . . . Equal parts travelogue, existential discovery, and historical exegesis. . . . A well-spun narrative and a damn fun, breezy read about the ubiquitous weed. . . . Dolce writes with clarity and expertise about the plant and its utility to mankind."
—The Fresh Toast

To my mother, Rose,
another beautiful flower

What is a weed?
A plant whose virtues have not yet been discovered.

—RALPH WALDO EMERSON

Contents

Contents

PART I

THE
OLD
WORLD

Introduction

THE GIRLS IN THE BASEMENT

New England

W ant to see my new hobby?"

It was 8:17 on a crisp Sunday morning in the autumn of 2012 when my cousin awakened me with a cup of coffee and that question. He was standing over my bed, practically panting with an anticipation that made saying no impossible. Little did I know that his new hobby was about to change my life.

I sipped my coffee, pulled on my clothes, and followed him downstairs through the garage, then behind a padlocked door that led me into a foam-insulated antechamber that housed plant food, smelled like Odor-Eaters, and hummed with machine-made white noise. He flashed me a broad smile as he unlocked another door, which led me into a basement grow room and the source of the new hobby: two floor-to-ceiling Mylar bags that, when unzipped, revealed six budding female cannabis plants, all basking in the hot yellow glow of one 400-watt high-pressure sodium lightbulb. The girls oiled the air with a skunky, grassy scent, and they looked very happy—as they should be, living in a cushy, digitally controlled 68-degree climate, bathing in a steady cloud of intoxicating CO_2, and guzzling the finest organic nutrients.

I was impressed by the simple technical apparatus, but I was far more impressed by the fruits of my cousin's labor a few hours later, when I had the pleasure of sampling a strain called Super Lemon

Haze. Finally, after some thirty years of smoking whatever pot came my way, I found something that seemed to complement—no, enhance—my biology. The aroma was citrusy and the taste was smooth enough. And the effect? Let's say that my brain ticked away linearly, laterally, and happily with no soporific slouch. No paranoia. No cloudy thinking. It was energizing yet soothing at the same time, as if my body were radiating sunshine from the inside out. "I need to get reacquainted with this plant," I told myself as we retired to my cousin's man cave, where freshly harvested stalks were curing on wire hangers, and long, sugar-coated "colas" (the top buds of marijuana plants) were stored in Mason jars, as if on exhibit in a museum.

On a website called 420magazine.com, my cousin showed me some extremely cool electromagnified photos of mature cannabis flowers, each tiny leaf carpeted with glistening sacs filled with resins. These sacs are called trichomes, he explained, and they are equally responsible for the plant's survival and its allure. Botanically, they produce the powerful chemicals that repel predatory insects, inhibit deadly molds, and bring humans and some animals intoxicating pleasure. In eight more weeks, the girls in his basement would mature into ladies and their sacs would be bubbling with sticky, stinky, gluey, wet resins—and that's the moment they'd be chopped down and killed. Is it an accident that men have traditionally been the keepers of this ritual, given its unavoidable Freudian connotations?

That comment elicited little more than a shrug from my cousin. Like many growers, he was more interested in talking about plants than my snarky observations on gender stereotypes. The resinous heads of the plants, which are plump with THC, plus powerful essential oils called terpenes, flavonoids, and hundreds of other compounds, are revered by breeders, who have, in the last forty years, created the strongest strains ever known. "You harvest the plants just as the trichomes start to go cloudy," my cousin explained. "That's when they're at the height of their powers."

My cousin, who once told me I couldn't write one word that would ever teach him anything, has never shown any propensity for higher education in the traditional sense. But he has always had a green thumb and a taste for this plant. That, plus his excessive desire for privacy and mistrust of law enforcement, has driven him to cultivate his pursuit in well-guarded secrecy. Even his family is seemingly unaware of what grows below its living room. He once broached the topic with his wife, a religious Christian, and the conversation went something like this:

"I have a new hobby, dear. Do you want to hear about it?"

"Not really."

And that was that.

I hadn't smoked much in the last fifteen years—as with many people in my generation, I found that weed had become too strong, too unpredictable. There were too many nights spent paranoid and unhappy, or asocial and cocooned in self-absorption, or just a blink away from sleep. If I was going to alchemize my consciousness, I wanted to go up, not down, so I moved on to other pursuits: wine, sport, meditation, yoga, single-malt scotch. But that day it struck me: If my cousin in rural New England could learn about strains, obtain the high-quality seeds and the equipment to cultivate them, and then educate himself, mainly through the Internet and in conversations with the guys who ran his local gardening store, about growing prime, organic, pesticide-free bud indoors, then a revolution of sorts had occurred in my absence. Maybe it was time I investigated more deeply.

My timing was auspicious. My great sixteen-year relationship had just ended. We had tried spackling over the problems, addressing, therapizing, ignoring them, whatever it is two people do when they sense things falling, inevitably and irretrievably, apart. We tried because we loved and respected each other, but ultimately we called it quits. It was the same with my career as a magazine editor. For years, I had been pretending to be excited by a profession that once brought me torrents of pleasure; but now it just seemed like work, with all of the drudgery and deadlines and none of the creative charge. I was, for the first time in two decades, adrift, primed for change, ready to dance, drink champagne, recharge my sex life, and reinvent the way I worked. My entire life was in need of a rethink, my vices included.

My headiest pot-smoking days had occurred in college. In the 1970s it was easy to blaze joint after joint and never become too scarily high. When I look back I wonder how it was possible to inhale that amount and still graduate from Northwestern University with a 3.5 grade point average. As it turned out, it was possible because the pot I was smoking then was baby-ass weak compared with today's varieties. The weed I smoked in high school probably averaged 3 to 5 percent THC. By the time I hit college, highly potent sinsemilla had debuted in North America, and the average THC content doubled, then tripled. Today's crops clock in at between 15 and 29 percent THC. That is a significant change, one brought about intentionally by growers and unintentionally by Ronald Reagan. But I'm getting ahead of myself.

Once back in New York, I dipped further into this subject. There are hundreds of blogs and Instagram accounts authored by all types of cannabists (a more refined title than "pothead" or "stoner," don't you think?)—people who devote themselves to the plant and its many mysteries. Endless words are spewed on techniques of growing. Topics range from soil nutrients to the most powerful and energy-efficient lights to use indoors, from the quietest ventilation systems to the ongoing debates over the benefits of sun-grown versus indoor cultivation or soil versus hydroponic. There are sites devoted to the politics of pot, hash making, oil production, rare strains, cooking with cannabis, curing cancer with cannabis, and other obscure corners of connoisseurship. The most arcane are the real-time videos of grow rooms—cameras trained on the plants and just left to run, with no irony intended. *You'd have to be really zonked to watch this*, I remember thinking.

The more I explored, the more I discovered that the world of cannabis was in flux. There were new products that intrigued me: shatter, CBD, wax, the incongruously named butane honey oil. And there were hundreds of strains, some with evocative names like Tangerine Dream and Super Silver Haze, and others with scarier monikers such as AK-47 or Green Crack. I originally presumed these offerings were just new wrappings on age-old products, but that assumption too turned out to be just another indication of my ignorance. I read about medical marijuana, but initially thought it more of a ruse than a legitimate course of treatment that had been used for centuries in Asia and the Middle East. And then there was the surreal history of prohibition and the demonization of a plant. Once I learned that cannabis has accompanied man in his travels for as long as history has been recorded, I began pondering the larger purpose of such a magical, medical substance that grows in the earth. I had a lot to learn.

One truth came through loud and clear: For aficionados, pot is more than just a plant. It's a relationship, a commitment. Certain people—I'm thinking of growers in particular—develop a passion that borders on love for their crop. They don't simply like or revere it, as you might a rose or an heirloom tomato. They obsess over it much the way vintners fixate on their grapes. They test the soil regularly to ensure it maintains the proper pH level, so that the right minerals nourish their plants' roots. Indoor growers monitor the air temperature and humidity levels hourly. They baby their plants, inspecting them for molds or fungi that could decimate months of hard work in just a few hours. Some consult moon cycles to determine the optimal time to plant, feed, water, and harvest, and then they debate whether it's better to chop their plants in the morning or evening. They forgive their plants when a crop isn't up to snuff and extol them when it delivers. It's full-blown plantophilia.

Although I had been in close communion with this plant for

decades, it struck me that I knew almost nothing about it. And I wasn't alone. Most of my acquaintances thought they understood pot, while in fact they knew nothing about how it worked in the mind or body; others blithely dismissed it as a been-there-done-that phase of their youth. Part of me harbored that attitude because I never deemed a mere *weed* to be worthy of respect. Because of its prevalence, I just assumed cannabis wasn't very interesting.

In the ensuing weeks, I continued my halting reacquaintance with the plant, coming to a new acceptance of what I could and could not do in the enhanced state. I enjoyed watching movies but couldn't read, as my mind would wander promiscuously around the page, off the page, and into deep vortexes of thought between the first and last word of a sentence. But music . . . ahhh, music sounded richer, deeper, more textured. Food became a revelatory sensory explosion, and sex deepened to an intimate exploration of my partner's body and, at times, soul.

In those early days of Super Lemon Haze I smoked largely alone, because, as I've come to realize, I was in a cannabis closet of my own making. I guarded my secret exploration for fear of being judged as a pothead, which I was not. I used occasionally and moderately in the same way I drank, and as pretentious as it might sound, I liked to think of my usage as conscious consumption. But gradually I ventured out. I went to parties and other social gatherings where I cautiously invited certain guests to join me in a puff. To my surprise, my offerings were greeted appreciatively by men and women, friends and strangers, most often on my side of the generational divide. I assumed that I would be dismissed by my peers as a middle-aged guy desperately chasing his youth, but I was wrong. These were businesspeople, journalists, lawyers, filmmakers, entrepreneurs, and professionals, and they were delighted to partake. Even those who weren't interested in smoking were intrigued and full of questions. Many recounted a familiar trajectory: they had smoked in their twenties, got paranoid in their thirties, and now that their bodies were falling apart, or their kids had left home, or their material success hadn't delivered on its promises, they were ready to take another look at this plant. Often someone would pull me aside to discuss my rekindled pursuit in detail. Was it causing any harm? Would it help for this or that pain? Was it really an aphrodisiac? *Can you get me some?* To my surprise, almost everyone was curious about cannabis.

One afternoon, over lunch in midtown Manhattan, I was describing this epiphany to my lawyer, one of the best and most erudite in New York City, when, in between bites of my red snapper, he stopped me. "You know, Joe, one of my favorite things to do on a Saturday night is to come home after dining out with my wife and go into my study. I turn on some music, turn down the lights, and smoke a joint." He never cared about single-malt scotch or potato vodka, and he finds the wine snob thing ridiculous. And, he added, the fact that some bureaucrats in Washington, DC, could dictate what substance he used to relax was one of the most flagrant overreaches of policing authority on the books. He told me of a party he had recently attended in LA. Most guests were in their sixties—and all of them were lighting joints or openly sucking on vaporizing pens, talking about strains and percentages of THC. "California is like a different universe," he said. "In LA, everyone is smoking or eating these candies and cookies and it has completely changed the culture."

He was, of course, correct. In 2012, before the Feds cracked down on Orange County, there were more dispensaries in Los Angeles than Starbucks franchises (but fewer than McDonald's). If you weren't cannabis inclined, this proliferation escaped your attention and had little impact on your life; but if you were a user, you could, with a doctor's recommendation, walk into a dispensary and consult a "budtender" about which strains on offer best suited your "condition." Without the stain of criminality, the dispensary system taught customers about the many varieties of cannabis and their unique properties. It was nothing short of revolutionary.

Titillated by all this fresh information, I decided to do something new and different—even if it meant reacquainting myself with something old and familiar: to submerge myself in this brave new— and yet at the same time, ancient—world. Events were unfolding at breakneck speed—the residents of Washington and Colorado voted to legalize and tax recreational cannabis. Dr. Sanjay Gupta aired his cannabis apologia, *Weed*, on CNN and started a national conversation about the medical relevance of the plant. The Obama administration softened its antipot rhetoric, and then–attorney general Eric Holder issued the Cole memo, indicating that the Feds would not be storming the Rockies to stop legalization from going forward. And it wasn't only America that was changing its tune. Uruguay and Spain legalized and Jamaica followed suit. Would, as prohibitionists had claimed for almost a century, the fabric of these societies fray? Would their citizens smoke themselves into stupors and crowd into emergency rooms, or would society adapt more gracefully? What would the world look like once this plant became as accepted as beer?

Before diving in, I decided to establish some ground rules for myself: No stupid smoking myself silly. Be open about what I'm doing with everyone to help tear down the cannabis closet. Avoid politics, as laws were changing too rapidly to keep pace with. And keep my focus on the ways *adults* could use this plant to their benefit. For too long now, the conversation has been hijacked by those who steer it to the harmful effects of drugs on children. I don't believe children should use substances, but experience has demonstrated that ignorance is more dangerous than intoxication and that they should be educated about the harms and benefits of alcohol, pharmaceuticals, and consciousness-altering plants.

My final determination: to see if I could harness cannabis to suit me as an engaged, responsible, and professional adult. Could certain strains or delivery methods better enhance the flow of creative ideas or intimacy in sex or empathy among friends? Could I actually take a certain dose and use it not only for play, but also for work? Could I use this weed to sprinkle a little magic onto a world that is overly reliant on data and thin on enchantment?

One day I called my cousin to thank him for launching me on this great adventure. He was already nurturing his second harvest, which he estimated would yield the equivalent of a few months' rent for a small city apartment.

"I think my wife is having a change of heart," he told me.

"Why's that?"

"The other day she said to me, 'You know that hobby of yours? I hope you do it really big. I think I'd like to plan an early retirement.'"

Chapter 1

BIG BAD SCARY WEED

New York City and Newton, Massachusetts

I had always assumed there was some risk of brain, lung, or motivational damage from smoking pot, but I also knew it was far less dangerous than any other recreational substance, and that the risks could be contained with moderate use. Changing consciousness always seems to involve some risk. Certain thinkers, like Dr. Andrew Weil, have argued that human beings have a genetic predisposition to alter our states of awareness, and that it might be evolutionarily advantageous to do so, helping mankind develop spiritually and psychically. I am familiar with that urge and have always found it a worthwhile pursuit.

But here's what I didn't understand: If pot is as benign as its adherents claim, and such a miraculous and versatile medicine on top of that, how did it acquire such a bad rap? Or more accurately, so many contradictory bad raps? How did it get grouped along with heroin and LSD as a schedule I narcotic, which, according to the government, means that it has no medical benefit and is potentially lethal? And exactly which problems did it cause? Did it kill brain cells, sex drive, motivation, or sperm counts? Did it lead to lung or brain cancer, sexual compulsion, cocaine addiction, violence, or insanity? Did it grow breasts in men? And if it did unleash these horrors, how did I—and most of my generation—escape them?

According to biologists, botanists, and anthropologists, the cannabis plant, a relative of hops, debuted in the Caucasus Mountains, most likely in current-day Kazakhstan (ancestral home of Borat), some ten thousand years ago. The harsh landscape and climate forced the plant to be hearty and, to a certain extent, inventive if it was to survive. It had to grow quickly, before the short summer season ended. Animals and birds loved the seeds (cannabis seeds are still allowed in bird feed, the only cannabis product to escape the US federal ban), and they gobbled them up and then pooped them out while migrating. This is one way the plant used the feet and wings of other species to proliferate.

When humans arrived, they carried seeds out of the Caucasus along the Silk Route, and this is where the first fork in the genetic river occurred. The seeds that moved east into the colder regions of the Himalayas developed into the so-called indica strains, also known as kush strains; the high they produce tends to be more physical than cerebral. It brings on sleepiness and the condition that is perfectly expressed by the term "couchlock," that state of deep stoneyness in which even the thought of getting up to get a glass of water to soothe your parched throat is exhausting and thus unlikely to occur.

Indica plants are short and bushy, with leaves that are round. More crucially, this variety is very productive. Indicas flower quickly, in twelve to sixteen weeks, to contend with their short growing season.

Seeds that went west to the Middle East and Africa eventually became known as the sativa varieties. These warmer-climate plants are more gangly, at times stretching twenty feet tall. They have narrow, finger-shaped leaves and rangy buds that take longer to mature (some can take up to half a year). A sativa variety generally yields a more energetic high—I once heard it described as "my mind on jazz," which pretty much nails it. They stimulate talkativeness, nervousness, and those machine-gun bursts of creative flow. These are the strains I prefer.

It may sound a bit mad to call cannabis inventive or intelligent, but ethnobotanists agree that this plant has astutely inveigled its way into the lives of human beings over thousands of years. When our hunter ancestors were chased by a wild boar, they likely nibbled some cannabis buds afterward to help them forget the trauma, relax, recover, and get up the next day and hit the plains again for another day's supper. When night fell, the plant encouraged our ancestors to fall into the arms of their loved ones. Women munched the sticky flowers to ease the nausea of pregnancy and to numb and then forget the pain of childbirth so they could repeat the experience and help our species proliferate—a miraculous and evolutionarily strategic benefit, when you stop to think about it.

Once humans settled down and began to farm, cannabis seeds not only fed the animals but also yielded an oil that contains the exact ratio of essential fatty acids needed to help children thrive.[1] The stalks provided fiber that was turned into tents and clothes. Burning the flowers in enclosed structures enabled village elders to create rituals that connected the tribe to higher powers and also helped rival factions relax; after a few minutes of sitting together in the smoky tent, they could more amicably sort out their differences. And the plant found its way into the healers' medicinal arsenal. Without healing plants, their formulary, their stature, and not to mention their patients, would have disappeared.

The ancient Chinese considered this wild grass one of the fifty fundamental herbs and were the first to write about the medical and spiritual benefits of it, over 4,700 years ago. The father of Chinese medicine, Shen-Nung, used "ma" to treat a dazzling array of illnesses including gout, rheumatism, malaria, constipation, and absentmindedness. Of the two thousand medicinal plants known in the vast field of Ayurvedic Indian medicine, cannabis is the most important among them.[2] While members of all these cultures occasionally inhaled cannabis as smoke—presumably to get closer to God—it was most commonly used as a tincture or eaten. The

Egyptians used it in suppositories and to relieve eye pain; they buried kings and royalty with pounds of pot, presumably to be presented as a housewarming gift to God once they had moved on to the next life. And the Greeks made wine steeped with cannabis, which they used to treat inflammation and ear problems.

Westerners began to view plant substances with suspicion with the advent of modern Christianity. In its efforts to break the human bond with magic plants on earth and refocus the gaze of its constituents on One God in Heaven, Catholic church elders in the Middle Ages branded plant users pagans, sorcerers, or witches—and reinforced the message through one of the religion's foundation myths: Adam and Eve were tossed out of Eden for tasting the forbidden fruit. It may have been an apple, but it could just as likely have been another plant, possibly cannabis. No matter. The message was clear: partake of a plant's pleasures, God will be displeased, and you will be punished. This realignment didn't extend solely to cannabis, but to all psychoactive plants as well. The Spanish conquistadors massacred hordes of natives in Latin America for using psilocybin, peyote, datura, morning glory, salvia, and ayahuasca, to name but a few.

Europeans remained largely ignorant about cannabis until Sir William Brooke O'Shaughnessy, an Irish inventor and physician, went to work in the hospitals of Calcutta in 1839. While there, he developed a fascination with Indian botanical medicines, primary among them a tincture of cannabis indica, also known as hemp oil. O'Shaughnessy was curious about the ways Eastern cultures, in particular those in hot, crowded regions, used botanicals to prevent diseases before they happened and then to treat them once they struck. He did the first animal studies on cannabis and noted that it effectively eased the pain of muscle spasms caused by rabies, tetanus, cholera, and many other illnesses. So convinced was he of the plant's ability to heal that he brought it back to England, where it caused a sensation. Physicians and small companies began to produce their own cannabis elixir and sell it privately and in general stores. Even Queen Victoria's doctor reportedly—perhaps mythically—used it to ameliorate the pain of her menstrual cramps.

In the following sixty years, over one hundred scientific and medical papers were written about this wonder drug that treated some old-fashioned-sounding illnesses (including neuralgia and melancholy) and many others that are still with us today (including sleeplessness, nausea, and neuropathy). In the United States, physicians began making their own hemp oil tinctures and selling them out of their offices, as did drug companies such as Eli Lilly, Parke-Davis, and Squibb. These companies are now somewhat embarrassed about their association with this maligned weed. When *Fortune* magazine asked Eli Lilly for details on its historical cannabis sales, a Lilly spokeswoman responded, "Due to competing priorities, we . . . are unable to facilitate your query."[3]

The primary problem with this all-purpose plant tonic was not its efficacy but the difficulty of ensuring accurate dosing. When cannabis is swallowed, it takes one and a half to two hours for the effects to come on, so early patients never knew if they had taken enough. Too large of a dose could cause harrowing anxiety, but most doctors worried about prescribing too little.

From 1913 through the 1920s, just as anti-alcohol fervor was beginning to grip the United States, twenty-seven states passed anti-marijuana prohibitions. The meticulously researched 1974 book *The Marijuana Conviction* by two professors, Charles H. Whitebread II and Richard J. Bonnie, examined legal archives and newspaper articles from those states to learn what spurred them to take such drastic measures against a plant that was still little known on these shores. Only about fifty thousand US citizens had ever smoked the plant in the early part of the twentieth century, and this unawareness made the passing of such prohibitions almost effortless, since most people didn't connect the liquid in the brown bottles in their medicine chests with this imported green weed.

Whitebread and Bonnie quickly deduced that marijuana prohibitions were motivated less by hostility to the drug and more by hostility to the immigrants who used it. In 1914, following the Mexican Revolution, immigrants flooded into the Southwest in search of stability and better economic conditions. They labored as beet-field workers and cotton pickers, and they brought with them an herb they called "mariguano."[4] It was easier to carry than bottles of alcohol—and cheaper too, as it could be picked in their yards or along roads for free.

On the floor of the Texas State Senate, one legislator pronounced, "All Mexicans are crazy and this stuff is what makes them crazy." Another legislator from Montana put it this way: "When some beet field peon takes a few traces of this stuff . . . he thinks he has just been elected president of Mexico, so he starts out to execute all his political enemies." Even states in the Northeast, which had almost no Mexican immigrants, prohibited cannabis prophylactically. No one in this state uses it, the logic went, but we should ban it to prevent the drinkers who are being cut off from alcohol from coming here in search of a drug they can use.

Utah was the first US state to criminalize the use and possession of cannabis. Whitebread and Bonnie first presumed that this was due to the immigrant invasion, but further investigation revealed that Utah had only a tiny Mexican population. The antiweed laws were more influenced by that other American intoxicant, religion.

---

*Origins of the antonym "pot" are more obscure. One urban myth says the term came from the Mexican Spanish *potacion de guaya,* or "drink of grief," a sort of wine beverage mulled with marijuana buds and leaves. The problem with this theory is that no one has yet found *potacion de guaya* actually being used in Spanish cultures. A different theory posited by TheWordDetective.com harks back to another slang term for the stuff: "tea." This writer thinks that dried marijuana leaves resemble those of tea and that eventually they became a pun on "teapot." One Wikipedia entry on jive slang says "tea" is a "short name used for the mysterious potted plants that musicians always traveled with in the 1930s and '40s."

In 1910, elders in the church of Latter-Day Saints declared polygamy to have been a mistake and banned it. A number of Mormons were unhappy with this change and emigrated to northwest Mexico in hopes of setting up "traditional" communities that would convert heathen Indians to Mormonism and allow them to take multiple wives. After four years, those plans weren't panning out. The Indians weren't buying Mormonism, and the Mormon faithful were unhappy being separated from their flock. Many of them headed home, and they brought weed with them. The church elders have always opposed stimulants of any kind, including tea and coffee, so when these apostates were discovered taking a puff, Utah's legislature turned a religious prohibition into the country's first drug law in 1915. Other states quickly followed suit, including Wyoming (1915), Texas (1919), Iowa (1923), Nevada (1923), Oregon (1923), Washington (1923), Arkansas (1923), and Nebraska (1927). Despite this flurry of legislative zeal, the majority of Americans still had no idea of what marijuana was. It took an ambitious bureaucrat to exploit that ignorance.

Harry Anslinger was the thick-necked chief of the Federal Bureau of Narcotics (FBN), the predecessor to today's Drug Enforcement Agency (DEA), and the spiritual godfather of America's War on Drugs. Much like his rival J. Edgar Hoover, Anslinger seemed to enjoy steamrolling anyone in his path, and he was very effective at doing so.

During the Depression, tax revenue plummeted, which meant massive government job cuts, Anslinger's agency included. The disastrous economy—27 percent unemployment—plus the influx of two million Mexican laborers who had entered the country illegally provided Anslinger with a crisis he couldn't resist. What if he could tie that foreign loco drug to crime and convince the country that this terrible scourge could be fought only by steady, forceful action from a beefed-up FBN?

Sounds crazy? Just wait.

With financial backing from the beverage industry, which was just recovering from fourteen years of alcohol prohibition, plus the support of the archconservative newspaper tycoon William Randolph Hearst, who owned some eighty national newspapers (and who became rabidly anti-Mexican when Pancho Villa confiscated his 800,000 forested acres in Mexico during the revolution), Anslinger proposed the Marijuana Tax Act to Congress in 1937. The idea was to impose a tariff so stiff and paperwork so burdensome that no doctor would prescribe a cannabis tincture and no company would produce it.

When Whitebread and Bonnie asked the Library of Congress for a copy of the congressional hearings on the Marijuana Tax Act, the librarians couldn't locate a transcript. It took them four months to honor the request because the hearings were so brief that the slim volume containing the transcript had slid behind a bookshelf. The librarians had to dismantle the bookcase to retrieve it.

More surprising still were the file's contents. With no medical or scientific evidence backing him up, Anslinger claimed that "marihuana is an addictive drug which produces insanity, criminality and death." Speaking before Congress, Anslinger called a number of "experts," including Dr. James Munch, a pharmacologist from Temple University, who injected marijuana's psychoactive ingredient into the brains of three hundred dogs, two of which died. When asked if he chose dogs because their reactions mirrored those of humans, he replied, "I wouldn't know, I am not a dog psychologist." Nor was he much of a pharmacologist. THC wasn't discovered until 1964, so whatever the doctor thought he was injecting wasn't what he claimed it was.

Next up was Dr. William C. Woodward, a lawyer, physician, and chief counsel to the American Medical Association (AMA), who testified that his organization "[knew] of no evidence that marijuana is a dangerous drug" and opposed the legislation. To which one congressman replied, "Doctor, if you can't say something good about what we are trying to do, why don't you go home?"*

When the bill passed to the (un–air conditioned) floor of the House at 5:45 on a clammy August afternoon, the debate lasted one minute and thirty-two seconds. FDR signed it into law, and Anslinger later named the dog pharmacologist from Temple the "Official Expert of the Federal Bureau of Narcotics on Marihuana," a position he held until 1962.

His target now clearly in his sights, Anslinger cranked up his attacks. One article, "Marihuana: Assassin of Youth," published in Hearst's countrywide chain of newspapers, famously claimed that "the weed from the devil's garden" caused white women to seek sexual relations with Negroes, and caused whites and black to dance cheek to cheek. He wangled money from alcohol and pharmaceutical companies to make antipot films. *Reefer Madness* is a cult classic today, but it succeeded then in swaying the vulnerable masses that marijuana was a portal to lewd behavior. One puff brought on irreversible insanity.

Skeptics might question how one man could wage such an effective propaganda campaign against a plant. But in the late 1930s and 1940s, five lurid murder trials came to national attention, and in each the defendants pleaded not guilty by reason of insanity from smoking marijuana—an ideal defense, since Anslinger claimed marijuana caused insanity. In the most famous trial, two women jumped on a Newark, New Jersey, bus and robbed, shot, and killed

---

*Perhaps lawmakers were ruder back then, or perhaps this congressman felt Woodward's testimony was a sore loser's response to Franklin D. Roosevelt's 1936 landslide reelection. FDR brought with him two Democrats for every Republican, almost all of whom had pledged to support the New Deal. The AMA, however, had opposed every piece of New Deal legislation since Roosevelt was first elected in 1932, so by 1937 this Democratic-controlled congressional committee was probably fed up with hearing the group's opinions.

the driver. The women claimed marijuana-induced insanity, and the defense called the same pharmacologist from Temple University, who told the jury about his animal experiments, adding that he himself had tried the drug. After two puffs, he said, he turned into a bat and flew around the room until he found himself in the pit of a two-hundred-foot-deep inkwell. "Killer Drug Turns Doctor to Bat!" the next day's Newark *Star-Ledger* howled.[5]

The two suspects got off.

By 1941, the Marijuana Tax Act had succeeded in causing such a burden that doctors quit prescribing cannabis. It was dropped from the *American Pharmacopeia*, and the tincture vanished from the shelves. Two years later, Anslinger, desperate for a few arrests, launched a crusade against jazz musicians. Duke Ellington, Charlie Parker, Billie Holiday, and Louis Armstrong were among the suspects. The jazz drummer Gene Krupa was busted in San Francisco and jailed for eighty-four days. The singer Anita O'Day got six months.

For some reason Anslinger had a beef with jazz. At a 1948 hearing in which he was gunning for another funding bump, one senator asked why he needed additional staff. He replied, "Because there are people out there violating the marijuana laws."

"Like who?"

"Musicians."

The senators' faces must have registered looks of disbelief, because then he added, "And I don't mean good musicians, *I mean jazz musicians.*"

Seventy-six newspaper editorials slammed Anslinger; within three days the Treasury Department received fifteen thousand letters, one of which simply said, "I applaud your efforts to rid America of the scourge of narcotics addiction. If you are as ill-informed about that as you are about music, however, you will never succeed."

Sadly for cannabis users, Anslinger's zeal didn't diminish.

Except for the Beat poets and others on the fringes who extolled it, pot use declined during the cultural dry spell of the Eisenhower era. Once the 1960s counterculture began to send its green shoots into the mainstream, however, cannabis became the fuel that powered the Beatles, hippies, Vietnam War protestors, and civil rights activists. It was once again in the spotlight, but instead of an ambitious bureaucrat railing against it, now it was that most paranoid of presidents, Richard Nixon, who took up the battle and backed it with the full power of his office.

In 1968, the same year Nixon was elected to office, Dr. Lester Grinspoon was being toasted as one of Harvard's golden boys. The then-forty-year-old psychiatrist taught, saw patients, conducted research, and published papers and books—in short, he was an exemplary academic who lent burnish to the Ivy League faculty. On weekends he and his wife, Betsy, would party with fellow Harvard luminaries, including the poet of the cosmos, Carl Sagan, and the anthropologist Stephen Jay Gould. At those parties Harvard's best and brightest were trading in gin for joints, or combining the two.

Sagan jousted regularly with his white-shoe friend, urging him to smoke, assuring him it would expand his splendid but narrow mind, but Grinspoon's reply was always the same: "I'm a psychiatrist and a doctor, Carl, and you shouldn't smoke that stuff. It's dangerous." Sagan would roll his eyes and take another hit. "I'm not one of those fissured ceramics, Lester," he would say, employing his favorite phrase for "crackpot." "It won't harm you. You'll love it."

After a while, Dr. Grinspoon grew weary of sermonizing and decided to launch his own investigation into the brain-addling weed. "I'll write the definitive treatise spelling out the hazards to young people so they will stop destroying their lives," he told himself. It would be his most valuable contribution to protecting America's youth, not to mention a few of his misguided friends.

In the stacks of the Countway Library of Medicine, Grinspoon devoured the poetry of Dumas, Balzac, Baudelaire, and Gautier. He examined dozens of reports on criminality, sex, addiction, and the so-called gateway theory, which claims, with no evidence whatsoever, that "soft" drugs like marijuana are stepping-stones to stronger, more dangerous drugs such as heroin.[*6] He read about the pharmacology of cannabis intoxication and investigated how it affects the brain in the near and long terms.

Midway through his research, Dr. Grinspoon came to an uncomfortable realization: He had been duped. All the "facts" about this plant's dangers had been disseminated by the US government or its drug enforcement agencies without one shred of historical, medical, or scientific evidence to support them. Even worse, he understood how his ignorance was passively condoning the government's jailing of its own citizens for no justifiable cause. "At that time we were arresting 300,000 people a year for using or selling marijuana," he recalls. "Now it's just under 900,000, which is terrible, and here I was being a part of that persecution."

Dr. Grinspoon published his findings in the *International Journal of Psychiatry*, a small-circulation professional review, where they went unnoticed. Among the few who read his report, though, was the editor of *Scientific American*, who reprinted it as the lead article in his magazine in 1969. That attracted a few more eyeballs, two of which belonged to Murray Chastain, an editor at Harvard University Press, who urged Grinspoon to expand the manuscript into a book.

---

*This theory has never been proved, and the evidence indicates that the opposite is more likely the case. According to a 2014 study by the RAND Drug Policy Research Center on national drug use and health, the amount of marijuana consumed in the US likely increased by about 30 percent from 2006 to 2010, while the amount of cocaine decreased by about half.

Though it wasn't his primary area of interest, Grinspoon agreed—provided he could have a finished copy by March 24, 1971. That date was immutable, he explained, because his sixteen-year-old son, Danny, had been diagnosed with acute lymphocytic leukemia, and Grinspoon wanted him to hold the book in his hands before he died.

As is the case with so many marijuana advocates, it was Grinspoon's personal experience with the plant that cemented his change of mind.

Danny's chemotherapy regimen was wreaking havoc in his body and on the entire family. The minute he was off the gurney Danny was overcome with nausea, and the Grinspoons would rush their son home so he could avoid the humiliation of puking in the car. "Once in his room, he'd be vomiting or dry heaving for the next eight hours. It was awful to hear, let alone witness," Lester recalls today. "Chemo made my boy nauseous in every cell in his body. You could see that he was feeling it in his toes."

It was Lester's wife, Betsy, who suggested they try marijuana—his own research showed that it was a traditional treatment for nausea, after all—but the good doctor refused. It's illegal, he reminded her, and besides, he was wary of offending the valiant physicians who were treating his son. "It's a line I regret uttering until this day," he admitted to me.

Betsy was less concerned about ruffling the feathers of Lester's colleagues, so en route to treatment one day she stopped in the parking lot of Danny's high school and asked one of his friends to find her some pot. Once the boy overcame the shock of selling grass (as it was quaintly known) to his friend's mother, he handed her a few hastily rolled joints, which she and Danny shared.

When Lester walked into the treatment room that day he was surprised to find Danny and his wife laughing. After chemo, Lester was further startled when Danny stood up and said, "Hey, Mom, can we get a grinder on the way back to school? I'm sort of hungry."

Lester had witnessed firsthand the plant's healing capacities. "Doctors in the nineteenth century knew more about cannabis than we did in the 1970s," he recalls. "They knew nothing about its chemistry but they knew it stopped nausea and that it was not toxic."

His professional and personal insights gelled into the most famous of Grinspoon's ten books, *Marihuana Reconsidered*, which was published on schedule in March 1971. His son didn't survive the cancer, but he did live long enough to see the book's dedication: "To Danny."

Betsy still believes it's the best line Lester has ever written.

Lester didn't sample cannabis for two more years. He suspected he might be called as an expert witness before the courts and legislatures if the book gained traction, and he didn't want to impugn his professional credibility.

Grinspoon's hunch was correct, and at one hearing in Massachusetts, an especially aggressive state senator challenged him about his personal use. "Senator, I'd be glad to answer that question if you'll tell me if an affirmative answer makes me a more or less credible witness," Grinspoon replied in his Boston Brahmin accent. The senator huffed, "You, sir, are being impertinent," and stormed out.

That night the doctor went home and lit the joint that he had stashed in his bedside table. "It was clear that it made no difference whether I did or did not smoke," he recalls. He and Betsy had a wonderful evening together, and Grinspoon has been smoking unapologetically ever since.

Marihuana Reconsidered was an instant classic. The book was reprinted around the world in fourteen languages and sparked a tidal wave of discussion, primarily among the chattering classes. Lester became a hero in Cambridge; his photo occupied the entire front window of the Harvard bookstore.

But other countervailing winds were blowing at the time. Richard Nixon, who hated marijuana as much as he despised the hippie leftie pinko commies he associated with it, was determined to eradicate pot from the country's shores. He launched the first war on drugs to intercept drug shipments on land, sea, and air, and he simultaneously ordered a national study on drug abuse that he hoped would once and for all prove the dangers of the evil weed.

Nixon named Raymond P. Shafer, the conservative Republican governor of Pennsylvania, to lead the National Commission on Marijuana and Drug Abuse. He knew Shafer was itching to be appointed to the Supreme Court, so he was the ideal candidate to do his bidding. He also instructed his aides to ensure the report packed a wallop. "I want a goddamn strong statement on marijuana," Nixon instructed his chief of staff, H. R. "Bob" Haldeman (the discussions were recorded by hidden microphones Nixon had installed in the Oval Office). "Can I get that out of this sonofabitching, uh, Domestic Council?"

Haldeman reassured him (and, ever the obedient lieutenant, he didn't correct him on the name of the commission that he had appointed).

"I mean one [statement] on marijuana that just tears the ass out of them," Nixon continued. "You know. . . . Every one of the bastards that are out for legalizing marijuana is Jewish. What the Christ is the matter with the Jews, Bob? What is the matter with them?"

Nixon feared pot was becoming a white suburban problem that would lead America to ruin. No one cared if black musicians or a few poets used it, but voting parents seeing their kids lighting up—that was cause for alarm. "Do you think the Russians allow dope?" he asked Haldeman and John Ehrlichman, his domestic policy advisor. "Homosexuality, dope, immorality . . . these are the enemies of strong societies. That's why the Communists and the left-wingers are pushing the stuff. They're trying to destroy us."

Shafer's commission fanned out across the world, conducting over fifty national studies and visiting countries as wide afar as Holland, Morocco, Afghanistan, and Jamaica to study cannabis and the effects it had on societies. The final report, over four thousand pages long, was published in four volumes. It cost $4 million in 1971 dollars ($23.5 million today) and was, and remains, the most comprehensive government study of cannabis in American history.

When released in early 1971 under the title, *Marihuana: A Signal of Misunderstanding*, the report wasn't what the White House was expecting. It concluded that the punishment for marijuana was more harmful than the drug itself and recommended decriminalizing personal possession and moving it from the restrictive schedule I category into schedule III, alongside synthesized testosterone, estrogen, and acetaminophen, and other drugs that carry "less potential for abuse." "Considering the range of social concerns in contemporary America," wrote the Shafer Commission, as the group that authored the report came to be known, "marihuana does not, in our considered judgment, rank very high."

Nixon was apoplectic. He disavowed the commission's findings and ignored its every recommendation. As a result, it received scant media attention, and the silence surrounding its findings solidified the previous forty years of disinformation, scholarly works by Harvard professors notwithstanding. Most damningly, Nixon disregarded the report's advice and kept cannabis and all of its constituents, whether psychoactive or not, shackled as a schedule I narcotic. This meant that THC and CBD, the other unsung chemical hero of cannabis, were preposterously designated along with heroin, LSD, and Ecstasy as the most dangerous drugs in existence, with a high propensity for addiction and no medical benefits. Cocaine, methamphetamine, and OxyContin are schedule II.

Needless to say, Raymond Shafer was never named a judge. And as seen in the following chart, cannabis is still classified as a schedule I narcotic, despite the fact that it has never been cited as causing one death from overdose.

US OVERDOSE DEATHS, 2001-2014[7]

Drug	Schedule	Total Overdose Deaths from 2001-2014	Percent Increase from 2001 to 2014
Prescription Drugs	II or III	25,760	242%
Opioid Pain Relievers	II	18,893	369%
Benzodiazepines	II	7,945	600%
Cocaine	I	5,415	42%
Heroin	I	10,574	439%
Cannabis	I	0	0%

Dr. Grinspoon was eighty-six when we met at his home in Newton, Massachusetts. He suffers from "a host of medical disasters" that he has little interest in discussing, but he is one of the few medical professionals in America who is eager to talk honestly about marijuana, a subject that has captured his imagination for the last four decades.

Although he's largely homebound, his friends in the medical marijuana community stay in contact, emailing him so frequently that he can't keep pace, and sending him gifts to ease the torments of his ailing body. Amid the stacks of books on the shelves and tables in his study is a large portrait of Danny and two smoking devices that Sagan sent him while filming *Cosmos*: an ancient opium pipe and an Egyptian hookah. His favorite new invention is his slim vaporizer pen filled with hash oil that he wears nerd style in his shirt pocket. A puff or two offers relief from the host of symptoms that plague him.

Most popular histories blame ambitious lawmakers and paranoid presidents for sounding the death knell for cannabis. But Dr. Grinspoon, a consummate researcher, told me that two other medical advances played an important role in sidelining the herb as a medicine. In 1900, *Cannabis indica* was most often prescribed for pain and insomnia. But in 1898, Bayer created aspirin from birch bark, and shortly thereafter the first barbiturates were also synthesized. Today we take for granted the inexpensive manufacture of precisely dosed, easy-to-swallow medications, but the invention of pills and capsules that could be precisely measured in milligrams was groundbreaking at the time. Tincture of *Cannabis indica*, which varied in strength depending on the crop from which it was derived, and was vexing to dose, suddenly seemed very old-fashioned.

Pharmaceutical companies have since tried to synthesize a drug that mimics cannabis, but they have come up short. Because the plant contains upwards of seven hundred compounds, eighty of which are thought to be therapeutic, and all of which combine synergistically to produce both the high and the healing, extracting just one compound in a lab has never proved as effective as the whole plant is. In 1985, the US government supported Unimed Pharmaceuticals in developing Marinol, a chemically derived THC, which authorities hoped would stanch all cries for legalization. "With Marinol the government was saying, you should stop pressing for legalization because we're going to have a single-bullet drug soon," which would make smoking marijuana unnecessary, says Grinspoon.

To spur sales, the government classified Marinol as a schedule II drug, which allowed doctors to legally prescribe it. When it still wasn't catching on, it was placed in schedule III in 1992. But today we know that it isn't simply THC in cannabis that causes the high and delivers therapeutic effectiveness. Hundreds of other compounds—CBD, terpenes, phytochemicals, flavonoids, and other so-called minor cannabinoids—all work together to create an ensemble, or entourage, effect.

"My experience is that the people who use Marinol are doing so because they don't want to smoke anything or they're afraid of the law," says Grinspoon. "I've yet to have a patient who smokes and prefers Marinol. Cannabis has other benefits, of course. It's the best recreational drug—you get more bang for the buck and you don't wake up with an awful hangover like you do with alcohol and [despite the unfounded claims over the last eighty years] you're not damaging liver or brain cells."

Grinspoon still smokes daily for enjoyment too. "It stimulates the frontal lobe and ideas come out of my brain like darts at a dartboard. You get more bad ideas too, but you also get more good ones. That's why I like to consider things both stoned and straight."

Throughout our conversation, Dr. Grinspoon repeatedly hit his vape pen. He let slip that he is suffering from cancer, diabetes, hemophilia, and a stomach condition that has enervated the vagus nerve that controls digestion, among other functions. He hates speaking of his own illnesses and will be cross with me for revealing them, but his vape pen is a lifesaver when his digestion goes awry.

He also swallows a high-CBD, low-THC cannabis capsule every night, sent to him by a cannabis practitioner in California. "Just like everyone took vitamin pills in the sixties and seventies, I believe that in the future cannabis will be treated equivalently. THC with CBD is a powerful antioxidant and anti-inflammatory. There's no way of proving it and it's not a scientific or medical claim, but I think it has slowed down these diseases I've been burdened with."

In 2013, Grinspoon published a lengthy article calling for the creation of a new discipline that he termed "cannabinopathic medicine." Because the safety of cannabis has been chronicled for over fifty centuries by millions of people across cultures, and because the

National Institute on Drug Abuse (NIDA) has conducted hundreds of studies over forty years attempting to prove the harmful effects of cannabis, without any success whatsoever, he advocates forgoing clinical trials and perhaps reclassifying the drug as a nutraceutical (a product derived from foods or plants that is presumed to support health). These are heretical words for a scientist, but Grinspoon correctly insists that cannabis doesn't fit within the confines of traditional medications and should be treated akin to aspirin or penicillin. Neither of those medications went through clinical trials in their day, as their safety and efficacy were established before the Food and Drug Administration set up those protocols. In fact, since one thousand people a year die from aspirin-related deaths and no one in the history of recorded time has ever died from cannabis, it is, strictly speaking, safer than aspirin.

Even today, most doctors, who learn about drugs primarily from pharmaceutical companies and can still lose their licenses if caught prescribing illegal medications, remain silent, skeptical, or downright hostile to the plant. Is their silence justified in light of the legal consequences?

Though often praised for his early scholarship, Grinspoon's courage on behalf of medical cannabis is rarely acknowledged outside cannabis-centric circles.

"I didn't try marijuana until after publication, because I wanted to keep objective, but once I did try it I was honest about it," he recalls. "I was on the Barbara Walters show in 1974 with Norman Zinberg, the former head of NIDA, and Robert DuPont, the first drug czar, who now owns a lot of urine-testing patents—he makes a lot money off of that and is doing well.

"Barbara asked if we had used marijuana, and DuPont, the drug czar, said no, which I knew not to be true. He trained at my place, and while I never smoked with him, he spoke about it. Zinberg also said no, which also wasn't true, because I smoked with him the week before at his house.

"When she asked me, I replied, 'Not only have I smoked it, but I do smoke it.' Her mouth dropped open. She was not prepared.

"But I believed then, and still believe firmly, that coming out is crucial to changing the stereotype of the cannabis smoker. That was one of Carl Sagan's major contributions and regrets. He would tell me, 'I wish I could help you in this fight, Lester,' but there was no way he could come out. He was testifying before congressional committees in 1969. It would have destroyed his career, no question about it."

And what about Dr. Grinspoon's career? Did coming out as an unrepentant cannabist negatively affect his career trajectory?

"It didn't destroy it, but it sent me down a different path. In 1975, I was put up for early professorship. I had published two books, *Schizophrenia* and *Marihuana Reconsidered*. The dean called me to his office after a promotions committee meeting and told me they didn't give me the professorship. 'They loved the schizophrenia book but they didn't like *Marihuana Reconsidered*. They said it was too controversial.'

"I said, '*Controversial?* We're in the academy! What about the scholarship?' People moved away from me at Harvard because of my outspokenness. But I stuck to my guns and I think I made the right decision."

By the late 1970s, it appeared that pot was well on its way to being decriminalized. Media on the left and right were calling for it, thirty states had reduced penalties for possession, and in 1977 President Jimmy Carter announced his intention to stop arresting people carrying under an ounce. The prospects for reform looked promising until Dr. Peter Bourne, Carter's drug policy advisor, attended a Christmas party thrown by the National Organization for the Reform of Marijuana Laws (NORML) in 1977. Many guests were shocked when Bourne was offered cocaine and then took two hits from a small glass vial. Though Bourne denied taking the snorts, the incident was widely witnessed and it hit the press. Bourne resigned a few months later, and Carter dropped the reform effort once his political fortunes began flagging.*[8]

When Ronald Reagan swept into office in 1980, he distinguished himself from his "soft" predecessor by declaring drugs to be America's number one scourge. He not only revived Nixon's drug war but turned it nuclear by funneling billions of dollars away from treatment and into the police and prison industries. Within one year, law enforcement jobs at every level rose 36 percent and prison-related jobs jumped 86 percent. By 1984, his administration had upped the penalties for possession, cultivation, and sale of cannabis. Nancy took her "Just Say No" show on the road (this despite the fact that she was a chronic user of prescription tranquilizers, according to her daughter Patti Davis).[9] The DARE (Drug Abuse Resistance Education) program indoctrinated American youth about the dangers of illegal drug use and further blurred the distinction between "hard drugs," such as heroin and crack cocaine, and pot.†

Reagan also took the drug war into the skies. US spy satellites hovered above Central and South American countries to pinpoint grows, while crop dusters sprayed deadly paraquat over Mexican fields. At home, the effort centered on the breadbasket of cannabis cultivation: Humboldt, Mendocino, and Trinity Counties in Northern California, a remote area with abandoned logging sites

---

*Some claim that Bourne's bust was singly responsible for the change in pot's legal fortunes, but that is as simplistic as crediting the television show *Will & Grace* for the acceptance of gay marriage. Carter had many reasons, among them gasoline shortages, high inflation, and the Iran hostage crisis, to steer clear of another difficult battle.

†The results of the DARE effort were, at best, mixed. In 1992 researchers at Indiana University found that DARE grads had significantly higher rates of hallucinogenic drug use than those who hadn't entered the program.

that attracted growers because of its heavy forestation and often-impassible roads. In a matter of years, the so-called Emerald Triangle had become the world capital of sinsemilla ("without seeds" in Spanish), and strains like Big Sur Holy Weed, Maui Wowie, and Kona Gold acquired legendary status. With its new-found potency and flowers the size of fists, North American cannabis entered its golden age of cultivation.*

The wily genius of those early breeders was in part born of necessity. Rather than cultivating the twenty-foot-tall sativa strains that were native to the Americas but grew so large they might as well have been wearing a neon sign that flashed BUST ME!, these New World growers combined North American strains with shorter, heartier indicas smuggled in from Asia. Years of studious crossbreeding enabled them to create more potent varieties that could be packed into tight spaces and that flowered in three months, not five, thus doubling their annual yield. In an indirect "fuck you" to the War on Drugs, an estimated thirty thousand citizens in all states began to grow, launching what has rightfully been called the largest underground breeding experiment in agricultural history. One of Reagan's least heralded but most enduring legacies is this: as the ferocity of the Drug Wars intensified, so did the potency of pot.

But the DEA was not deterred. Narcs in camouflage established checkpoints on roads, buzzed homes in helicopters, raided private grows, hacked up gardens, and seized property. For all intents and purposes, Northern California "rejoined, operationally speaking, the Third World," as Thomas Pynchon wrote in *Vineland*, his novel set in the area during Reagan's rule. Of course, local cops loved it, as a river of money flowed nonstop from Washington,

---

*According to DrugScience.org, cannabis is still the United States' number one cash crop—despite the $51 billion the DEA spends each year prosecuting the drug wars. Revenues for cannabis are greater than that of all other US-grown commodities, including wheat, soy, and corn. It is one of the few remaining products that is truly made in America.

providing jobs and expensive equipment for their small-town forces.

October 26, 1989, is the day that changed the plant and growers' entire operation forever. Operation Green Merchant was the brainchild of one FBI agent, Jim Stewart, who two years before had noticed the number of ads in the back pages of *High Times* placed by hydroponic equipment stores, garden centers, light companies, and Dutch seed banks. He organized hundreds of FBI agents to pose as growers and fan out across forty-six states to visit the advertised shops. After two years of under-cover ops, the FBI pounced, confiscating mailing lists and sales receipts in what most legal scholars now term a gross breach of privacy laws. Then, often with TV cameras and reporters in tow, federal agents swooped down on unsuspecting private citizens, many of whom were (legally) growing orchids or tomatoes in-doors to (illegally) search their homes without warrants. From 1989 to 1991, over 400 citizens were arrested, 50,000 plants were killed, 358 indoor grows busted, and $10 million in merchandise seized.*[10] From then on, growers doubled down their efforts to move indoors.

George H. W. Bush kept the drug war going full tilt, but Clinton—he who never inhaled—spent more money on drug war activities than Reagan and Bush combined. The Clinton admin-istration got creative about the way it drove home its antipot/anti-drug messages.[11] One covert program sponsored by the Office of National Drug Control Policy (ONDCP) offered about

---

*Some of that merchandise was never to be seen again. George Warren, who owned six hydroponic stores in the Northeast, was never arrested or associated with any crime, but still had over $200,000 in lighting equipment confiscated. When he inquired about having it returned, FBI agents told him that it was going to be sold at auction. "You mean they confiscate my merchandise because they *think* some people are going to grow pot with it and then they sell it to someone else?" he asked in astonishment. "That's how it works," he was told.

$25 million each year to the five major television networks to shoehorn antipot messages into the plots of their most popular prime-time shows.[12]

Here's how this neat little scheme worked: ONDCP selected the shows most valuable to its mission, secretly vetted scripts, and then paid the networks for instituting the script alterations they suggested.

In the original script of one episode of the WB's *Smart Guy*, two substance-using kids were depicted as cool and popular; after the drug office's input, "we showed that they were losers and put them in a utility room," said one ONDCP contractor. Other programs that had antidrug subplots woven into them included *ER*; *The Practice*; *Beverly Hills, 90210*; *Home Improvement*; *Sports Night*; *7th Heaven*; *The Drew Carey Show*; *Sabrina, the Teenage Witch*; *Boy Meets World*; and *General Hospital*. Bill Kovach, a media watchdog and then the curator of the Nieman Foundation at Harvard, called this sub rosa propaganda campaign a "venal . . . form of mind control."

While some of the plot switches were understated, others were as subtle as a brick through a window. *The Wayans Bros.* featured a career-devastating, pot-induced freak-out of angel-dust proportions. *Sports Night* showed a death behind the wheel due to alcohol and pot combined. *Cosby* showed kids caught with marijuana being pressed to name their supplier. The White House denied trying to influence content; its officials insisted that it was only trying to achieve an "accurate portrayal" of drug use. Most networks also denied collaborating with the government. But those denials rang hollow once a CBS spokesman admitted that his network "is proud to be working with the government in regard to the war on drugs."[13]

Forty years after Lester Grinspoon realized he had been duped, I had reached the same conclusion. Now that I'd stripped away the fictions about this dangerous weed, it was time to find the facts.

Chapter 2

THE DUTCH MASTERS

Amsterdam, the Netherlands

Operation Green Merchant forced growers in the United States into three different directions. They went either (1) into early retirement, (2) indoors and out of sight, or (3) to Amsterdam to ply their trade in relative peace. Ever since 1976, when the Dutch government decriminalized cannabis, Amsterdam has lured aficionados. But the escalation of the American drug wars crowned Amsterdam as the center of the pot universe, and exiles flocked there, just as literary exiles once flocked to Paris in the 1920s. I thought the Dutch capital would be an ideal place to see how that culture had flowered, as it were— but like so many aspects of cannabis and the place it occupies in modern life, so much of what I thought I knew turned out to be wrong.

My arrival in Amsterdam in November 2012 coincided with the twenty-fifth anniversary of the Cannabis Cup, the oldest such festival in the world. Since 1987, when the editors at *High Times* magazine* inaugurated the event, "the global ganja community"

---

*The magazine has become to old-school cannabis lovers what *Playboy* once was to past generations of men: a dying standard-bearer, courageous and provocative when it began, but a bit of an artifact today. It regularly includes centerfolds of "nug porn," magnified buds and calyxes, dripping with juicy resins that dedicated readers pore over, cut out, and tape to their walls as if they were forbidden carnal pleasures.

has made the pilgrimage to the Cup with the same reverence as Muslims making their Haj to Mecca.

The Cup lures thousands of fans to sample and crown the best strains of cannabis and hashish grown each year. A $350 entrance badge gives participants access to the exposition hall and the "right" to purchase the strains in competition at designated coffee-houses. The badge also turns attendees into judges, allowing them to vote for their favorite strain, plus other categories including "Best Glass," "Best Booth," and "Best Concentrate." Winners receive the accolades of the cannabis community, which isn't worth all that much, and a serious marketing lift across the world, which is worth a whole lot more. A Cannabis Cup win has turned many a well-grown strain into a global superstar.

The premise of the judging baffled me—how can anyone who has inhaled several strains in an hour distinguish differences in flavor, not to mention the quality, of the highs? I was apparently alone in my concern. Few of the three thousand people in attendance seemed to question this. Most were grateful for the opportunity to simply light up in public without having to look over their shoulders.

When the Cup debuted, it was a select, invitation-only affair—or perhaps just an excuse for *High Times'* editors to escape the office and ply their trade in a more exotic locale. In the Cup's early days, the editors invited the founders of the four biggest seed companies—the so-called Dutch Masters—to share the fruits of their harvest with the community of celebrants. Those early Cups were reportedly huge fun, involving lots of smoke plus wacky "spiritual" rituals that honored the plant's ceremonial roots.

Today's Cups are as much about cash as they are about hash, a five-day trade show thinly disguised as a celebration for seed sellers, hemp clothing makers, twenty-first-century farmers, and a lot of hopefuls looking to make a buck. Each vendor pays $4,500 for a booth that is housed in a damp, barely heated shipyard warehouse.

In addition to the expo, there is a daily lecture series on topics ranging from "A Historical Perspective on the Emergence of the Cannabis Industry" to "Cooking with Cannabis." *High Times* now sponsors just under a dozen spin-off cups in cities across the world, including Medical Cannabis Cups in California, Michigan, and Oregon. It has also spawned a circuit of competing industry events, which include CannaTrade in Switzerland, Spannabis in Barcelona, the London Hemp Fair, and Hempfest in Seattle, which in 2013 drew about 85,000 participants a day.[1]

I arrived just as the 2012 event was kicking off, and from the crowd gathered outside I thought I had been dropped into a refugee camp for Woodstock exiles. Groups of men huddled around fires burning in oil drums, warming their hands, drinking coffee, and puffing up, or they were hunched over mounds of tobacco and pot, rolling and sparking spliff after spliff. When the purple "cannabus" unloaded another squadron of revelers in Rasta hats, dreadlocks, and tie-dye shirts, I sighed and wondered if the 1960s would ever be over. Just three weeks prior, the citizens of Colorado and Washington had voted to legalize pot, and news reports were claiming that four in ten Americans had smoked at least once in their lives. The press was painting pictures of legal weed being sold as openly as wine and implying that parents would soon be smoking at PTA meetings, but I was having difficulty reconciling the scene before my eyes with the bright vision of normalization that I imagined to be just around the corner. A vision that includes the absorption of this ragtag group into a larger legal market that makes room for people (like me) who like pot but haven't made it their lifestyle.

It wasn't until I stepped inside the hall and inhaled that fragrant secondhand smoke that I was able to loosen my guard and see past the bad fashion and unkempt appearances. In fact, some of the activities were strangely futuristic, such as people attaching five-foot-long clear balloons to Volcano vaporizers and then sucking down the clouds inside them. This method of inhalation makes smoking a joint look positively old school. Buds are ground up and placed into a bowl atop the Volcano, which resembles the bottom of a blender. A gust of hot air heated to the ideal temperature, 368 degrees Fahrenheit, melts the oils into a milky vapor that inflates the giant balloon. Once filled, the balloon is passed around and the crowd sips from the joyous cloud it contains. At about $600, this German-made digital instrument is the Maybach of vaporizers. Patients in enlightened dispensaries around the world use Volcanoes to take in the psychoactive and healing oils without irritating their lungs with plant matter. Vape pens, which sell for a fraction of the price, are an increasingly popular but far less effective delivery system.

In another booth a wide-smiling Canadian cannapreneur who called himself "Bubbleman" was holding forth with a frenetic energy largely absent in this heavy-eyed crowd. In one hand he brandished an enormous glass bong. In the other he held a pillbox of "bubble hash," small clumps of golden powder that he had produced. After a colossal hit that sent him into spasms of coughing, he wiped a tear from his eye and tilted the pipe to anyone who showed interest, which was everyone but me. It was afternoon, I was pleasantly enhanced, and I didn't want to spend my first day in a fog thicker than the mist that had blanketed the canals that morning. "I'm a lightweight," I said lamely, prompting a look of perplexed pity. What he had just sucked down was the purest, most concentrated form of THC ever created, Bubbleman told me. Most pot clocks in at 12 to 20 percent THC; his is a thonking 60 to 70 percent THC. One hit and you're up, up, and away.

"If it's so pure, what's making you cough?"

"Oh, that's just the oils expanding in my lungs . . ." *Hack, hack.* "You know what they say, 'If you don't cough, you don't get off.'"

Like many of the career enthusiasts in this hall, Bubbleman, aka Marc Richardson, was only too happy to give me a primer on his product, which is also known as "full melt" or "water hash." The plant's resins are contained in tiny glands or "bubbles" encased in a wax that sit atop skinny stalks, just as golf balls sit on tees. Magnified under a powerful close-up camera lens, the trichomes, bracts, and calyxes—the different structures that make up the flowering buds—resemble trippy and colorful underwater seascapes. When the bubbles are decapitated from their stems, collected, and pressed together, they become hashish.

For centuries, hash was traditionally collected by placing plants on screens, sieves, or silk cloths and shaking them until the glands fell off. The concentrated green, amber, or red powder was then formed into cakes, balls, bricks, or cubes, stamped with place of origin, and transported around the world. At some point in the 1980s, an American named Sadhu Sam noticed that the glands could also be dislodged by submerging whole cannabis leaves in icy water, then straining, drying, and pressing them into "water hash."

Bubbleman has taken this technique to the next level. He makes hash with his very own Bubble Bags—a twelve-bag kit that is marijuana's answer to microbrewing. They have made him a wealthy man.

To make bubble, Marc soaks about ten pounds of "trim," the lower-grade leaves that are removed before a bud makes it to market, in a tub of ice water. The cold bath freezes the waxy coating on the trichomes, knocking them off their stalks. The resins sink (oil is heavier than water) and the wet plant matter is strained through a series of filter bags with increasingly smaller holes. Ten pounds of trim yields one ounce of bubble hash.

If you're enterprising, as Marc obviously is, you might press the hash through a laminating machine. If you're adventurous (reckless?) you might then mold it into the shape of your credit card and slip it into your wallet. Plastic-coated hashish is virtually odor free and is essentially invisible to customs agents. Note to all would-be smugglers: Be sure to place your wallet in your jacket, not in your trousers, or your body heat might leave you with a gooey wad of bills and a tarry stain on your seat.

"What you have here is the ideal marijuana product for the twenty-first century," Marc announces to no one in particular. He has clearly used this line before. "It answers health, purity, and security concerns all at once. The cleaner it is, the fewer residues it leaves behind. That's why it's called full melt." He sparks up another bowl and invites me to inspect it close up. The hash froths mightily, but once inhaled there's nothing but a black smudge remaining.

Some minutes later a half dozen cops as wide as Sub-Zeroes come charging down the center aisle of the hall, which prompts a few vendors to scurry behind the curtains of their booths, grab as many duffel bags as they can shoulder, and hurtle toward the door. This year the police have capped the amount of product that one can possess at five grams, and this show of force is their way of demonstrating that they mean business.

Low attendance and increased police presence are but two indications that things are tougher today in the Dutch cannabis trade than they have been since the mid-1970s, when the Health Ministry instituted the "Tolerance Policy" that decriminalized soft drug use.

Based on research showing that young people typically find their way to harder drugs through dealers, the Dutch allowed a designated number of shops to sell cannabis and decriminalized the possession of small amounts. (Bafflingly, they made growing the plant illegal.) It has eliminated all arrests for possession but also discouraged drug use among the young. Dutch youth today use fewer drugs than those of any other European country, most likely because the familiar is always less alluring than the forbidden.

When it comes to drug policy, politics often trumps facts, even in sensible, pragmatic Holland. In 2011, locals from the more conservative, Calvinist southern counties began complaining about weekend traffic jams caused by "cannatourists"—smokers who drive across the border to purchase a week's supply and then head home. These counties passed laws that limited the amount tourists could buy to three measly grams, which hardly justified the gasoline used to make the journey. They also tried to force buyers to register their names and addresses, scaring off anyone with even the slightest mistrust of authority.

The mayor of Amsterdam signaled that he too was contemplating instituting the same "Weedpass" laws until coffee shop owners and their (unionized) workers did something unusual—they organized themselves into a coherent opposition. Some business owners, including Arjan Roskam, Amsterdam's self-anointed "King of Cannabis," argued that visitors to the Dutch capital were not coming for the weather (among the dampest in Europe, with 214 gray days a year), the food (mayo on everything), or the famously grumpy Dutch service (keep reading). They were coming for the cannabis and depositing some $2.6 billion in revenue (and approximately $500 million in taxes) into the Dutch economy for the privilege. After a pitched seven-month battle, the mayor backed off. By the summer of 2011, Weedpass in Amsterdam was dead.[2]

Things quieted down in the intervening years, but I sensed the Dutch cannabis industry was still recoiling from the realization of just how fragile its existence is. The Tolerance Policy is, after all, nothing more than a dispensation—it's not a law—and it can be revoked as easily and quickly as it was put in place. When a group of Belgian growers turned their back on me as I entered their booth— did my short hair or open notebook finger me for a narc?—I began to question if Amsterdam was indeed the new world of cannabis or the old world in decline.

On day two I skipped the Cup to immerse myself in the city's other cannabis attractions. The first stop: The Hash Marijuana & Hemp Museum in the city's informally christened "Green Light District,"

just beyond the famed Red Light District (though Amsterdam is slowly scrubbing this area, replacing storefront brothels with expensive bakeries, cafes, and organic food shops. The items on display in these shop windows are far more tempting than the women flogging their flesh in street-facing brothels). The museum is a bit tatty and in need of some love, but still, the hodgepodge of smoking instruments, medicine bottles, and ephemera from around the world demonstrates just how much human ingenuity has gone into the pursuit of getting high.

The museum is owned by Ben Dronkers, who also owns SensiSeed, one of the oldest and largest seed banks in the world ("We were authentic before it was hip" is its tag line). Dronkers got into cannabis early and began collecting seeds and growing illegally. He was arrested many times for his "criminal" activity, though lenient Dutch jail sentences of two or three days for fifty pounds of pot are in stark contrast to the severe American penalties. Still, it was tiresome, so to pass the hours of incarceration Dronkers studied the Opium Act (the Dutch precursor to the Marijuana Tax Act) and learned that the seeds were excluded from the ban because they contain no psychoactive material. Dronkers went to court and won permission to grow plants for seeds, a legal loophole that allowed him to quietly produce seeds for over ten years.[3] He cultivated plants in greenhouses on farms in the south of Holland, paying farmers twice what they earned growing tomatoes, and Sensi became the go-to source for growers around the world. Buyers today can still choose from dozens of classic strains based on price ("most affordable" to "premium"), yield ("medium" to "XXL"), plant size ("compact" to "high"), and climate ("sunny" to "cool").[*]

---

[*] In fact, many companies got away with selling seeds by stating that they were for "collection purposes only." They were to be held and not sprouted until the laws changed.

Today Dronkers is the most established cannapreneur in Holland. His family-run enterprise owns several buildings on the museum's block, not to mention a resort in Thailand, a home in Malaysia, and an eighteenth-century villa forty miles outside Amsterdam called the Cannabis Castle, a "marijuana Mecca" where gawping tour groups can "take photos and touch any of the 2,000 plants exhibited."

I spent days pursuing Dronkers in hopes that he might give me his perspective on the future of cannabis—after all, he's been in this game longer than most—but he was tough to pin down. Only after leaving messages at his shops, tacked to his front door, and on his voice mail, did he reluctantly invite me to visit him in the penthouse office of HempFlax, his two-decade-old enterprise dedicated to growing and processing cannabis's sober cousin.

I was on time for our appointment but no one answered the buzzer. I inquired in the Hemp & Hashish Museum but the kids in the ticket booth said they didn't recognize the owner's name, which was either indicative of their "I don't give a hoot" service ethic or Dronkers's skill at maintaining an unassuming profile.

Finally, after buzzing and calling, the door creaked open to reveal a Botticelli blond boy—one of Dronkers's sons. He led me upstairs to his father, a handsome man who could have passed for a politician but for the fat spliff wedged between his fingers. His minimally furnished penthouse overlooks some of central Amsterdam's most valuable property—the view from the windows a charming jumble of crooked rooflines and weather vanes. The sounds of scooters and bike bells were interrupted only by the cawing of seagulls perched atop gables. But it was the bud the size of a small sex toy lying on the table that gripped my attention.

Dronkers was polite, but not terribly interested in recounting his checkered past for some writer. He threw out a few canned lines—the SensiSeed bank "is as important as the rainforest" because it preserves old seeds. The museum "is one of his greatest gifts to cannabis culture." Its new sister museum in Barcelona is a beautiful way to show that "hemp is the crop of the future—it can save the world." Hemp fiber is more absorbent and durable than cotton and no pesticides are needed to grow it. It makes great paper—better than trees, so it can help end deforestation. It's used for soil remediation, as it helps refresh toxic land by sucking pollutants out of it. When compressed, it's tougher than metal and won't split like plastic, which is why Bugatti, Jaguar, and Bentley use it to make car doors.

In restoring hemp to the country that profited from it so mightily four centuries ago, Dronkers is completing his metamorphosis from criminal to entrepreneur to humanitarian. Like the Bronfmans, who smuggled whiskey into the United States in defiance of Prohibition during the 1920s but who later rehabilitated their family name, Dronkers appears to be focused on his legacy. Or maybe he's just sick of talking about weed.

In this way the Dronkers and Bronfman families have much in common. The Bronfmans of Montreal emerged from the dark days of dryness with a reliable brand that people trusted. Other bootleg scotches were often an unholy concoction of grain alcohol, prune juice (for coloring), and creosote (to lend the smokiness). Some fakes were spiked with embalming fluid, bleach, or even paint thinner for "kick," which had the unfortunate consequence of killing people. But Seagram's was always reliably pure, not to mention tasty.

Following Prohibition, Seagram's was first in line to secure US import licenses and go legit in order to slake our national thirst. The brand also employed a marketing tactic that tomorrow's cannapreneurs should bear in mind—they ushered in the notion of "social drinking" and encouraged intelligent, rather than uninformed, consumption by adding the phrase "Drink moderately" to their labels. Those two sobering words, plus millions of dollars donated to charities over the years, helped the Bronfmans shift from gangster bootleggers to responsible capitalists, to benefactors of the arts, to model citizens.

Perhaps it was the soggy November miasma that shrouded the city, but the coffee shops I passed by were mostly grim-looking affairs. Sparsely populated, underdecorated, neglected, and unloved, they were yet another signal that Amsterdam and perhaps the entire country was retrenching from its open embrace of cannabis.*

I decided that evening to visit one of the Green House coffee shops that are favored by a global cast of celebrities and boldface names. I walked to a shop on the south side of town, but when I arrived around nine p.m. I was surprised to find myself the lone visitor. While waiting for the party to get started I studied the menu, which was printed on laminated sheets the size of placemats. Categories included Herijuana, whatever that is, HydroWeed (grown hydroponically), Neiderweit, (low-strength Dutch home-grown), and a number of different "extractions." I had been trying to navigate the Dutch strains but I found the classifications as confusing as the terroir system for wine. At least the terroir system, which characterizes and categorizes French wines by the soil and climactic conditions of a particular region, is based on something tangible—geography. With cannabis, the names generally come from the whim and sometimes questionable judgment of the breeder. Take the highly vaunted and terribly named strain AK-47. One myth says its name is derived from the grower's initials (AK) and the number of days it takes to mature (47). Wrong! The original breeder, Simon from Serious Seeds, said he christened

---

*This may, in fact, be the case. Today, Holland has about 750 coffee shops, half the amount of a decade ago.

it after a machine gun because it delivers a powerful high that qualifies it as a true one-hit wonder.[4] A marketing genius he is not.

"Why is this one called Blueberry Cheese?" I asked the bud-tender, who was robotically weighing and bagging bud behind the bar. "Cuz it must smell like cheese," he grunted. (Actually, *dude*, it smells more like blueberry. But this sort of begrudging service was typical of what I encountered that autumn. Unlike New York, where waiter-actors frothily treat you to a thirty-second soliloquy on the family history of the cow your hamburger came from, diffidence here is the norm.)

A few stragglers wandered into Green House, bought some goods at the bar, and promptly left. I bought a plump pre-roll of Silver Haze, took a few pleasant hits, and moved inside to the main lounge, where I sank into a velvet couch and scanned the photos of famous visitors on the wall, Woody Harrelson, Pink, Quentin Tarantino, Miley Cyrus, and, puzzlingly, David Hasselhof among them. Silver Haze was pleasant enough but nowhere near the soaring high that came from the stuff that my cousin had produced. Many cannabists contend that decades of interbreeding the same seeds and strains has rendered Dutch weed unremarkable, or "one big mongrel bucket of crap," as Robert Connell-Clarke, one of the world's leading ethnobotanists on cannabis, put it.

Finally I asked the grumpy budtender if I was in the right place. Could this be the famous Green House I'd heard so much about? This is a local's spot, he said, shaking his head in disbelief about the dumbness of my question. Most people here just take away. If you want the scene you need to go to the Green House near Dam Square. "Rihanna was there a few nights ago," he offered. "She was a real mess."

The Dam Square locale was a hive of activity. An aggressively young crowd was jostling to inspect the buds and hashishes dis-played below the glass-top bar, and the half-dozen smiling bud-tenders, mostly Spaniards, were struggling to keep up. I bought another pre-roll of something called Arjan's Super Haze #1, found a seat, and ordered a cup of peppermint tea. This was more like it. The crowd was a handsome mix of men and women. (That was unusual; the cannabis circuit is about 70 percent male today and could benefit from more female presence.) A "Strain Hunters" video was playing on the flat screen. This is a vanity project by Green House owner Arjan Roskam, the aforementioned King of Cannabis, who travels to remote lands in search of rare strains that haven't yet been imported to the West.

To my mind Arjan is a modern spokesmodel for the new world of cannabis. While Dronkers is touting hemp as a cure for what ails the planet, Arjan is trying to drag the Dutch cannabis industry out of the 1980s and into the mainstream with well-designed shops staffed by friendly, enthusiastic servers. In his own way he's a disrupter—someone who does things differently, or so he claims. When he began cultivating indoor sinsemilla in the 1980s, all the coffee shops sold hash exclusively. The cannabis in Europe was, at the time, of low quality—it often came packed in bricks—and it was so rarely found that smokers referred to it as spinach. Seeing he faced an uphill battle, Arjan gave his cannabis to coffee shops for free and urged them to give it away to customers.

The freemium marketing model didn't work. Dutch smokers shied away from bud, so Arjan struck out on his own, launching the Green House shops in 1992. Obviously born with the PR gene, he invited the mayor and the chief of police to one opening. He still has a copy of that letter and mentions it frequently as a point of pride. He also ensured that *High Times'* editors were always greeted by a few ounces of his latest strains when they checked into their hotels.

Since then, he has racked up nearly thirty Cannabis Cup prizes. He claims that companies in California are wooing him to share his strains. Even his language is evocative and gauged to sell. "Have you tried our Sharkberry Cream?" he asks me. "It's really

flowery, like spring and summer. The Lemon Haze Crystal? It's
super strong. We suggest you smoke it at night."

But this well-groomed *High Times* cover boy is more than a
marketer. He's also trying to inject some new juice into a loosely
aligned industry that is now facing real competition from abroad.
He is a spokesperson for the Cannabis Retailers Association,
which serves as a trade group for coffee shop owners. He claims
the Green Light District was his concept to attract celebrity smokers
from the United States. When they do show up, Arjan is first in
line to snap a photo with them, which he duly posts on Facebook
and Instagram.

In trying to turn cannabis from a plant into a brand it's useful to
have a king, even if he is self-crowned. The Strain Hunters films—
which have aired on the National Geographic Channel and on
Vice TV—burnish his media profile, while his retail operations,
seed company, and plant-nutrient company signal that his business
is in growth mode rather than in decline. I suspect this is why he,
in the midst of this dark moment for the Dutch industry, sees
opportunity. "In the past we couldn't do anything because it was
illegal everywhere. But now, the Czech Republic, Spain, Uruguay,
even Albania . . . it's all changing. I think the best ten years are
ahead. The feds and the police are finally getting tired of us."*[5]

On the last day of the Cup I met an American in a porkpie hat with
a bushy beard the size of a small animal on his face. Adam Dunn
was one of those drug war refugees who moved to Amsterdam in

---

*In the Albanian village of Lazarat (population 7,000) farmers last year sowed
300,000 cannabis plants on 60 acres. The haul was estimated to yield 500
tons, which was on track to earn the town $6 billion. When the cops attempted
to burn the crop a few colorful reports claim they were met at the village gates
by grandmothers taking aim at them with machine guns and antitank missiles
to protect their harvest.

the late 1980s and ended up developing an award-winning strain called SAGE (Sativa Afghani Genetic Equilibrium). In 2001, SAGE took second place at the Cup and elevated Dunn to a top-tier grower. Now, twelve years later, he was here trying to interest buyers in his hemp clothing line, HoodLamb, which is worn by the surfer Kelly Slater, Chuck D. from Public Enemy, and Snoop Dogg, and thus carries A-list celebrity cred.

It was nice to be back in Amsterdam to see friends, Adam says, but he's grumbly about the heightened paranoia and the sparse crowds. This was the lowest attendance in years and Adam finds the Dutch scene depressing. The place in Europe for popping seeds these days is Spain, he tells me, and the clubs in Barcelona, he hears, are especially nice. As far as growing is concerned, well, he moved to Denver last year. "There's no energy here anymore. Colorado, man, it's wide open. There's places with three thousand plants, places with two thousand lights legally. There's potential to do all the things we wanted to do in Holland but couldn't because there was no infrastructure, no space or even air conditioners. And no one wanted to invest the money.

"The lights, they're going off in Amsterdam. Denver, man, that's the future. I swear it's so much easier there," he said, white smile cracking through his facebush. "You should come to see what's going on there, man. We can hang out."

Adam was on point. With US states now going legal, what exactly would normalization look like once the fearmongering and criminality were taken away and cannabis was sold as openly as beer? That was the big question, but other questions were percolating in the back of my mind, especially regarding the medicinal side of this much-disputed weed. Namely, what exactly is the difference between medical marijuana and the stuff that people use for recreation, inspiration, or simply to get high? And what healing properties does the plant actually possess?

Chapter 3

THE MARTYR AND THE MILLIONAIRES

San Francisco, Oakland, California

The father of medical marijuana in the United States was . . .

A: Thomas Jefferson
B: Sanjay Gupta
C: Dennis Peron
D: George Soros

S toners might guess Jefferson. They'll cite his diary entries and the laws he passed exhorting American farmers to plant hemp. They incorrectly use those facts as proof that the founding fathers may have enjoyed a puff in between starting a revolution and establishing a country. Not true. All countries at the time cultivated hemp for fiber, which they used to make sails, clothing, and paper.

American television viewers would likely vote for Gupta. His 2013 documentary, *Weed*, helped convince Americans that the plant is real medicine and showed them how it could ameliorate symptoms of severe and rare diseases, such as Dravet syndrome.

The correct answer, however, is C and D, Dennis Peron and George Soros. This proxy marriage of a Vietnam vet, pot dealer, gay activist, and onetime Republican candidate for governor of Wisconsin, and this billionaire supporter paved the way for California's Proposition 215, the world's first-ever medical marijuana law. Peron almost single-handedly reframed the plant—and the debate around it—from a reckless drug of rebellion to a botanical medicine, but his mission would likely have imploded without the deep pockets and deeper convictions of a few unwavering backers.

Until Peron, pot advocates in the United States were spinning their wheels, arguing that citizens should have the right to intoxicate themselves in any way they see fit. While this argument is valid, it's not all that persuasive: fighting for the right to get stoned never resonated with soccer moms (or dads) who didn't want their kids exposed to yet another temptation, no matter how safe or natural it was. Peron tectonically shifted the paradigm, but outside of a small coterie of California activists, his story is little known.

I tracked down the self-proclaimed "fairy godfather of medical marijuana" (MMJ) in San Francisco, where he lives in a hulking Victorian pile known as the Castro Castle. I rang the doorbell at noon as we had arranged the day before, but the gentleman who answered apologetically informed me that Dennis had to unexpectedly take his brother to the airport. He invited me into the kitchen, where I watched a bear of a chef in an apron cooking lunch for a group of men seated around a table in various states of undress, speaking different languages. The walls were a shrine to the king of this castle. There were photos of Dennis with Harvey Milk, Dennis in bell-bottoms addressing a rally, yellowed newspaper clippings of Dennis running for office. Was this a gay bordello? A commune? I didn't ask. Instead, I retired to the back garden to await my audience.

I sat myself near a grotesque mural of Brownie Mary (née Mary Jane Rathbun), one of Peron's best friends and a local legend who was known as the city's Florence Nightingale for distributing "magic brownies" to AIDS patients in city hospitals. With her gray hair and unfashionable eyewear, Mary may have looked like a kindly grandmother, but her scabrous remarks made her a cause célèbre. "If the narcs think I'm going to stop baking pot brownies for my kids with AIDS they can go fuck themselves in Macy's window!" she announced to deafening cheers at a rally following one of her several arrests. With Mary's image smiling insanely over my shoulder, I was handed a mug of tea by a handyman who informed me that the Castro Castle is in fact an inexpensive B and B frequented by travelers hungry for a taste of old-school San Francisco life.

Two cups of tea later, Peron joined me. With his short, neatly combed hair and button-down shirt, he looked more like a priest than a firebrand, and he sounded rather subdued as well. A stroke in 2010 had reduced his voice to a raspy whisper, but the impish twinkle in his eye signaled to me that this guy could still cause trouble.

Peron's infatuation with pot began, as it did for many, in Vietnam, where his Air America unit was dispatched to the Thai border to spy on the Ho Chi Minh Trail for the CIA. The Vietcong learned about the mission and rained mortar shells on Peron's unit every night for a month. Constant bombardment taught Peron two things: (1) that sleeping could be fatal—this is one reason so many Vietnam vets suffered debilitating insomnia once they returned from war—and it was safer to lie awake at night; and (2) that he was gay. It was in the trenches that he first had sex with a man.

Tour of duty over, Peron returned home with a duffel bag full of Thai Stick. He grew out his crew cut, moved to a commune, and dedicated himself to the vague goal of "helping America come to peace with itself." (OK, it was the early 1970s.) Pot was the instrument through which he hoped to execute that unlikely reconciliation.

In the late 1970s Peron flouted the law to open the Big Top pot supermarket in San Francisco, which quickly became the country's largest cannabis retailer. It was so successful that Peron had $1 million in twenty-dollar bills stashed in a closet. Just as large bundles of cash make dispensary owners vulnerable to robbery and paranoia today, they also did so back then, so when a horde of plainclothes policemen knocked down the door, Peron assumed he was being burgled. He hoisted a five-gallon water jug over his head to hurl down the stairs at his invaders, but the cops fired first, landing a bullet in his leg.

Given the looser laws of the Carter era, the 199 pounds of pot on the premises should have landed Peron in the clink for a few years. But when Officer Paul Makaveckas was asked at the trial to show the court how he fired the shot, he stood up in the witness box and aimed his pistol at Peron for a long thirty seconds. Then Makaveckas audibly lamented his faulty aim. A hit to the heart would have meant "one less faggot in San Francisco," he said within earshot of lawyers.

That untoward remark won Peron a reduced seven-month sentence in county jail, an unyielding hostility to law enforcement, and instant stature in the small but growing movement to legalize pot. Once out of jail he authored Proposition W (for "weed"), which directed the district attorney to stop arresting San Franciscans for possessing, transferring, or growing marijuana. The largely symbolic city ordinance passed overwhelmingly in 1978 with 63.7 percent of the vote.

After Mayor George Moscone and Supervisor Harvey Milk were gunned down by Dan White, a former cop who later somehow convinced a jury that an overdose of Twinkies had caused his diminished mental capacity, AIDS began its rampage and gay men began dying. The desperation was palpable. No one at the time knew what caused the scourge (it was still being misidentified as GRID, Gay-Related Immunodeficiency Disease) and there was no treatment for the Kaposi's sarcoma (KS) that scarred people with purple lesions, or the PCP pneumonia that drowned them to death in their own sputum. When Peron's partner, Jonathan West, was diagnosed in the late 1980s, there were always a few ounces of weed on hand to ameliorate his suffering.

One evening, just before midnight, ten plainclothes narcotics officers in rubber gloves showed up at Peron and West's home with a search warrant. The cops ransacked the apartment and forced Jonathan facedown onto the floor, bootjacking his neck. "Know what AIDS stands for?" one of them asked. "Asshole In Deep Shit."[1] The cops arrested Peron for possessing four ounces of Humboldt green with intent to sell. At his 1990 trial, West—ninety-eight pounds, face mottled with purple KS lesions the size of grapes—testified that the pot was his. The judge dropped the charges and scolded the arresting officers. West died two weeks later and Peron channeled his fury into writing Proposition P (for "Peron"). It was the country's first medical-marijuana initiative, and Peron was on a roll.

Activists (and politicians and actors) are typically blessed—or cursed—with a messianic self-belief that powers them forward despite good sense and the overwhelming odds against them. Their vocabularies are absent the word "compromise." Peron, impetuous and at times bombastic and utterly uninterested in the formalities of law and regulation, is no exception. Provocation turned him on. But compassion was also a part of the equation—it's no exaggeration to say that people with AIDS had been abandoned by the medical and political establishments and were left to fend for themselves. Peron's next move was to rent a five-story building on Market Street and set up the Cannabis Buyers Club, the country's first dispensary. Tacked to the wall of the office was a sign: THIS IS A FREE-DRUG WORKPLACE.

The top two floors of the club were decked with comfortable, if raggedy, furniture. Meals cost one dollar, and liquid nutritional supplements were served to those who couldn't hold down food. But it wasn't décor or food that did the healing. George Zimmer, the founder of the clothing retailer Men's Wearhouse and an early visitor to the Buyers Club, recalled that his strongest impression was the support the patients offered each other, since so many were pariahs, shunned by their families and isolated in spheres of loneliness. Even Peron's parents supported the work he was doing. "My parents would get calls saying: 'Your son is on TV! He is selling marijuana to AIDS patients,'" Brian Peron, Dennis's younger brother, recalls. "My mom would say, 'Good, they need it.'"[2]

By 1995, the Cannabis Buyers Club had four thousand members; the following year, membership tripled. The locale became a popular stop on the tourist circuit, and Peron kept the rules for admission loose. Anyone over fifty-five was automatically accepted—Dennis defended this practice by asking, "Don't you think people that age have the right to decide what they want to treat their aches and pains with?"

Later that year Peron altered the course of history by drafting another ballot initiative that allowed anyone suffering from any ailment for which marijuana provides relief to buy or grow the plant. The wording was intentionally vague—it allowed doctors to "recommend" cannabis for any condition they saw fit. (If the initiative had used the word "prescribe," it would have been on a collision course with the federal policy that barred doctors from prescribing any illegal substance.)

There were 433,000 obstacles to turning Proposition 215 (aka the "Compassionate Care Act") into law—that was the number of signatures needed to get it onto the California ballot by April 1996. By January, with only three months pending before the deadline, the situation was looking dire. Peron's ragtag band of volunteers was woefully behind; they claimed to have accrued 250,000 signatures, but in fact they only had 35,000, and most of them were fakes, copied out of the telephone book.

Enter Ethan Nadelmann, a Harvard-educated lawyer who had been eyeing the flailing effort from New York. Funded by the business magnate George Soros, Nadelmann's organization—then called the Lindesmith Center and today called the Drug Policy Alliance—had a goal even more quixotic than Peron's: ending the War on Drugs. And this is how the unlikely marriage between the martyr and the moneymen began, a quiet but necessary affiliation that has propelled the movement forward until this day.

In the chaos of the California ballot initiative, Nadelmann saw an opening to score a win in the big leagues of American politics. Polls showed that a majority of Americans on the West Coast agreed that the drug war had gone too far and that addicts should be treated rather than jailed. With public opinion on his side he called on Soros, who had recently earned $1 billion by short-selling £10 billion during the 1992 UK currency crisis, to get the ball rolling.

"At the time George was more of a Rockefeller Republican than liberal Democrat, but there were always a few issues he felt strongly about," Nadelmann recalls. "I was walking him through our [group's] national agenda, which included expanding access to methadone maintenance, needle exchanges to reduce the spread of AIDS, rolling back mandatory sentencing laws, and finally, medical marijuana. 'Medical marijuana?' George interrupted. 'I like the sound of that.' It was the intersection of two areas he cared deeply about: drug policy reform plus dying with dignity."

Soros ponied up $550,000, but he was hesitant to become the effort's sole backer, as he lived out of state and didn't want the Daddy Warbucks stigma of buying an election. Nadelmann dug into a few other deep pockets; George Zimmer, an Oakland resident, chipped in $250,000. Peter Lewis, the founder of Progressive Insurance, anted up $500,000, and John Sperling, whose Phoenix, Arizona–based Apollo Group owned eighty-eight private colleges, kicked in $200,000. Gail Zappa, the wife of Frank Zappa, and Larry Flynt, the publisher of *Hustler*, chipped in more. Laurance S. Rockefeller, a brother of New York governor Nelson Rockefeller, who passed the country's first mandatory prison sentences for all drug offenses, topped it off with $50,000 at the behest of the spiritual teacher Ram Dass.[3]

Though Soros and Sperling had sampled cannabis, legalizing

the plant was not their primary aim. They were far more aggrieved by the 1.5 million US citizens arrested yearly for drug crimes, over half of which were—and still are—marijuana related.[4] Eighty-eight percent of these arrests were for mere possession. Despite roughly equal usage rates, blacks were 3.73 times more likely than whites to be arrested for marijuana. Most shockingly, the total number of cannabis-related arrests in 2010 exceeded arrests for violent crimes, including murder, manslaughter, forcible rape, robbery, and aggravated assault.[5]

Over the years, Soros has remained one of pot legalization's strongest backers, contributing an estimated $25–$30 million to the cause since the mid-1990s. Zimmer and Lewis were, on the other hand, both smokers and had a more personal stake. Of the two, Lewis was more outspoken about what the plant added to his life. "Marijuana being illegal is a tragedy I want to correct," he said in one of the last interviews he gave prior to his death. "I feel deeply that helping to achieve this objective is one of the best contributions I can make to the well-being of our great country."[6]

Nadelmann understood that Proposition 215 couldn't succeed without Dennis Peron, but he also knew it couldn't succeed with him either, so he offered the money with strings: Peron had to submit to the authority of Bill Zimmerman, a pollster whom Nadelmann had appointed campaign chief. Peron agreed nominally, and in the next three months Zimmerman's army collected the necessary signatures. But Zimmerman and Peron got on like chalk and cheese. The activists thought that the politicos were shunting them aside, and Zimmerman judged Peron to be an untrustworthy liability. "His statements too often turned out to be intentional lies," he says today.

Zimmerman ordered Peron to stop speaking to the media and publicly excoriated him as a pot dealer whose chicanery would contravene the seriousness of the medical issue. But his attempts at stifling Peron only created more resistance. After months of putting out fires, Zimmerman opened the *San Francisco Chronicle* to see Peron puffing a fat doobie, and proclaiming that "all use, whether you know it or not, is medical." Opponents of 215 had a field day. This was the logic of an addict, they screamed, more proof that medical marijuana was nothing more than a stalking horse for full legalization. "I think the medical marijuana movement has more to fear from Dennis Peron and people like him than from law enforcement," Zimmerman fumed publicly.

Whether MMJ was a ruse or not, Peron's statement was both true and confusing. It's partly due to semantics, but also due to the narrow definition of medicine that has dominated the twentieth century. Take, for instance, people who smoke pot to ease anxiety. Are they medicating? If they were to visit a doctor, they'd get a prescription for an antidepressant or Xanax, which would attack the problem from a different route. Is an antidepressant more of a medicine simply because it comes in a pill? Many would say no.

Vitamin C is another example. Most of us take it to prevent unspecified illnesses, such as colds. But if you have scurvy, a fatal condition that is annihilated by vitamin C, you bet it is medical. Perhaps the most succinct definition of medical marijuana comes from Dr. Amanda Reiman, the California policy manager of the Drug Policy Alliance: "Medical marijuana treats a specific symptom or disease. Using it more generally, say, to change your mood, is adult use."

In the lead-up to the election, Drug Czar Barry McCaffrey, plus Senators Barbara Boxer and Diane Feinstein, predicted disaster if this "dangerous" bill were to pass; they were soon joined by Presidents Ford, Carter, Clinton, and George H. W. Bush in calling for its defeat.

Doonesbury, it turned out, was more in touch with California voters than those officials. Garry Trudeau, the creator of the comic, ran a two-week series poking fun at the storm 215 had whipped up. In one installment, Zonker's friend Cornell says, "I can't get hold of any pot for our AIDS patients. Our regular sources have been spooked ever since the Cannabis Buyers Club in San Francisco got raided . . ." In response, California's attorney general Dan Lungren held a press conference to rebut the cartoon. "Sure it's a comic strip, but what's the difference between advocating drugs in a comic strip or in a rap video or on the street corner?" he fulminated. "Zonker's a real person in our society. He is not fictitious. And we should put Zonker behind bars where he belongs!"

On November 5, 1996, over five million Californians voted to pass Prop 215—56 percent of voters—and, in a twist that must still have Peron smiling, his fiercest opponents were then charged with enforcing the measure.

Proposition 215 was intentionally loose. It created medical cooperatives between growers and patients and allowed anyone with a doctor's recommendation and a California ID to purchase pot. But it made no mention of distribution, sales, or taxation, and these gaps have caused a storm of confusion, lawsuits, and disagreements ever since.

For years, rumors circulated that the original bill included regulations about how to distribute medical marijuana and that the duplicitous Peron had erased the language from the ballot initiative. But 215's author, Bill Panzer, laid that rumor to rest. "We thought, 'Let's just start out with growing your own,'" he told me. "We didn't think that people were ready for distribution and that it would be going too far.

"In retrospect, I have more respect today for how Dennis read the electorate than I did then. I used to pooh-pooh the idea that all use can be medical, but he turned out to be right. And I have to laugh. You see the commercials for prescription medicines on TV and at the end they say all this or that can kill you or give you suicidal thoughts, and you realize that cannabis doesn't do any of this stuff."

When 215 became law, social apocalypse was predicted in California. Workplaces will be overrun by pot smokers! Crime will skyrocket! More drug babies will be born! Philip Morris will buy up Humboldt County! Today, twenty years after partial legalization, the results are in, and they should be examined with a hard gaze, no matter how inconvenient they may be.

Polling data show that younger adults are now substituting cannabis for alcohol, and their parents approve. California parents believe the herb is less harmful to their children's health and safety, especially when driving. Some cities have struggled to regulate the sudden explosion of dispensaries, but the fears that the pot shop on the corner would attract unsavory lurkers, traffic, and declining neighborhoods never materialized. Nor has imposing a local tax on medical marijuana, such as Oakland, San Jose, and other cities have done, driven consumers to the black market in search of cheaper prices. Buyers have demonstrated that when they are given the opportunity to purchase high-quality, clean marijuana legally, and when the experience is welcoming and respectful rather than furtive, they will return for more.

Cultivation has sparked a modest boon in some rural northern communities, creating tax revenue and cottage industries that service the cannabis industry. The old adage that the gold rush made some people like Levi Strauss, who sold pickaxes to miners, richer than those who found gold, seems to be holding true: testing labs, gardening centers, and software developers are all alive and well. Even political conservatives running for election in Riverside County were counseled by consultants that being a prohibitionist was to be on the wrong side of history.

But the biggest changes have occurred through education. People across generations, professions, and classes are reframing cannabis, not only as a promising botanical medicine, but also as an integral part of the state's economy and culture, not all that different from wine, almonds, and earthquakes.

In one tony San Francisco restaurant, I spied a party discreetly passing around a pen vaporizer between courses. Because these e-joints emit barely a hint of odor, they make public enhancement as easy as drinking a beer. At a cocktail party in Vancouver, British Columbia, seniors sucking on Pax vaporizers were discussing literature and debating the aesthetic differences between sun-grown and indoor varieties of cannabis. Indoor grows were deemed cleaner and less prone to mold, but the consensus was that pot grown under the sun has a wider spectrum of tastes and effects. "I think of indoor guys as the bodybuilder who builds his torso but still has skinny legs," one guest said. "Sun-grown flowers are looser, leafier . . . happier." A Hollywood studio head told me he has replaced sleeping pills with low-dose edibles and relies on them to ease the wear and tear of red-eye flights between the coasts. "A low-dose cannabis chocolate-covered coffee bean an hour before the plane takes off and I wake up in New York refreshed and with no hangover. It's better than Xanax."

In spite of the 1996 victory, George Soros continued to waver on legalization. He thought that decriminalization—simply removing the penalties for possession but not regulating or allowing pot's sale—was the safer route to travel. Despite the evidence that pot is less addictive or physically destructive than tobacco or alcohol, he was concerned about the mayhem that might ensue if citizens were allowed open access to "a drug." He maintained that ambivalence for over a decade but continued funding the effort to reform state laws nevertheless. By 2010 it had become obvious that decriminalization was insufficient to stop the massive number of arrests of young men of color for possession, and Soros made the case for legalization in a measured and logical opinion piece in the *Wall Street Journal*.

"Regulating and taxing marijuana would simultaneously save taxpayers billions of dollars in enforcement and incarceration costs, while providing many billions of dollars in revenue annually," he wrote. "It also would reduce the crime, violence, and corruption associated with drug markets, and the violations of civil liberties and human rights that occur when large numbers of otherwise law-abiding citizens are subject to arrest. Police could focus on serious crime instead."[7]

Soros had finally awakened to what middle-class white kids like me have always known: When we are caught snorting a line of cocaine or smoking a joint, we get a slap on the hand, maybe a fine. A black kid gets a ticket to orange.

Nadelmann described Soros as possessing a soaring intellect, of which I have little doubt. But his writing was dispassionate and impersonal, and I was curious about the inner journey that caused him to revise his opinion. His PR man rebuffed my request for an interview, so I was left to assume that he was either tired of being associated with this disreputable plant or that he was more interested in the issues that result from pot's illegality—that is, the multibillion-dollar prison-industrial complex that he cited in the *Journal* opinion piece. The situation has only worsened in the intervening years.

Over 2.3 million inmates are currently residing in state, federal, and private prisons throughout the country. That's a half million more people locked up in the land of the free than in China, even though the People's Republic has a population five times as large.

Ten years ago there were only five private prisons in the United States, holding 2,000 inmates. Today, there are one hundred for-profit prisons, with 62,000 inmates, and that number is projected to swell to 360,000 in coming decades. Why? Because for a state to contract a private prison, it must guarantee an 80 to

90 percent occupancy rate, and the drug wars provide a steady stream of occupants.[8] As Soros wrote, "The roughly 750,000 arrests [local law enforcement] made each year for possession of small amounts of marijuana represent more than 40 percent of all drug arrests. This amounts to one arrest every 42 seconds and 120,000 more arrests for pot each year than for violent crimes."

Local law enforcement has also developed its own drug dependency—on pot in particular—thanks to something called asset forfeiture. Each year, the Drug Enforcement Agency funnels some $10 billion in grants to local cops, incentivizing them to seize the property of anyone suspected of producing or selling illegal substances. No proof of guilt is required—a cop's suspicion is enough to seize property. The cops tally up the value of the seized items—a house, a car, an iPad—and submit it to the DEA, which takes a 20 percent schmear off the top and then returns 80 percent in cash to the local forces, which use the boondoggle to buy advanced weaponry, new cars, or office furniture. Asset forfeiture is little more than a program of perks for cash-strapped local forces, which turns America into a giant Walmart for law enforcement. Between 2002 and 2012, marijuana arrests yielded them $1 billion, according to Justice Department data.[9] Property owners have no recourse to the courts; even if they did, the legal costs to get back their property would often exceed its value.

Even while polls indicate that beat officers favor reforming marijuana laws, institutional forces go to the mat to maintain the status quo. In Florida, the state sheriffs' association, led by Polk County sheriff Grady Judd, became the public face opposing the medical marijuana referendum on the 2014 ballot. Judd rattled off the familiar and largely fact-free arguments against reform: the dangers of driving while high, increased workers' compensation claims, teenage addiction, and the imaginary increase in respiratory illnesses. But the annual strategic plan his office submitted to the Polk County Board of Commissioners tells a different tale, one that has nothing to do with public health. In it, Judd says that his force is "doing more with fewer resources" and that he's had to cut seventeen deputy sheriff positions due to a lack of funds. He describes seizures from marijuana grow houses as a significant revenue source, assets that help "meet eligible equipment or other non-recurring needs that could not be met by local funding, thereby putting forfeited and unclaimed funds to work in crime prevention, for the taxpayer." A Florida law enforcement newsletter describes the state's marijuana-eradication program, which nets about $1 million a year, more concisely: It is "an excellent return on investment."[10]

Like Soros, Peter Lewis, the founder of Progressive Insurance, the nation's fourth-largest insurance company, also concluded that the drug wars are little more than a $51 billion-a-year jobs program for cops, prison guards, and piss-testing companies. "On its face, based on examination of any set of facts, the War on Drugs is a gross waste of money," Lewis observed. "Its only practical rationale is to imprison certain segments of the population so the jailers can make a living." But Lewis had a more intimate relationship with the plant, and he opened up about it toward the end of his life. His thoughts are worth recounting, as such personal revelations from the mouths of the rich and powerful are so rarely expressed.

Lewis's reign as CEO of Progressive lasted thirty-five years. Until the mid-1990s, the insurance magnate aimed his philanthropy at cultural institutions, universities, and museums. But following Lewis's divorce from his first wife, one of his sons handed him a joint to help him cope with his emotional upheaval. He took to it instantly and continued smoking unrepentantly for the rest of his life.

From all accounts, Lewis was an unusual executive, a seeker of the "unconventionally possible, a boundary breaker," in the words of his friend and former Princeton classmate Ralph Nader.

He hung Andy Warhol's Mao portraits at Progressive's Cleveland, Ohio, headquarters and delighted in the anger they aroused in some employees, noting that at least the art stimulated them.[11] Lewis felt that the legalization movement and the plant itself could benefit from reimagineering. He wanted to torch the walls of the cannabis closet to liberate pot from the constraints of its stoner image and argued for a national coming-out day, when professionals, family members—even strangers—would publicly share their experiences with cannabis.

Lewis's own coming out, however, wasn't his choice. In 1999, a former employee snitched about his smoking habits to a reporter from *Fortune* magazine. In a prime example of mainstream media boneheadedness, the reporter patronized Lewis as a "functioning pothead," but praised his bottom-line business acumen, as if the two traits couldn't coexist in one brain. The following year, while Lewis was passing through the Auckland, New Zealand, airport, drug dogs sniffed out 1.7 ounces of pot and 2 ounces of hash in his luggage. Lewis pled guilty to the charge of importing drugs and spent one night in jail, but the charges were dropped after he agreed to "donate" $53,000 to a drug rehab center. The judge subsequently invited Lewis to stick around New Zealand to watch the challenger for the America's Cup yacht race and "enjoy the fresh air."

In 2001, at age sixty-four, Lewis's left leg was amputated below the knee because of an incurable infection. Confined to a wheelchair and in excruciating pain, he smoked constantly. "It didn't exactly eliminate the pain, but it made the pain tolerable—and it let me avoid those heavy-duty narcotics that leave you incapacitated," he said.

Like a modern-day Howard Hughes, Lewis dispensed vast sums of money to causes close to his heart. Waging his own "War on Drug Laws" was high on his list. "Our marijuana laws are out-dated, ineffective and stupid," he wrote in *Forbes*. "Everything that has been done to enforce these laws has had a negative effect, with no results."[12]

It's the rare CEO of a public company valued over $14 billion who speaks about the value of emotions in business, but in doing so Lewis initiated a conversation that needs to occur more audibly if weed is ever going to assume its rightful position alongside alcohol as a socially sanctioned intoxicant. His refreshingly candid comments reveal the ways the plant wove him into the wider fabric of life. "Running a business turns out to be a pretty lonely thing to do," Lewis said. "Marijuana would help me commune with myself. It would turn my daily collection of information into some kind of understanding of what was really going on—what the key components were, what the emotional components were. It made me better at my job. Except for activities that require physical dexterity like playing tennis, I think it basically helped me be better at almost anything I ever did."

Pot, he concluded, enabled him to stay "open to craziness, to new ideas, to stuff that no one ever thought about before. It kept me open to doing things that everybody else said you shouldn't do. . . . [It] helped me to accomplish what I set out to do, made me easier to be with and easier on myself. It allows me to be more accepting of, and caring for, other people."

Graham Boyd, who administered Lewis's philanthropy, told me that Lewis donated over $40 million of his personal fortune to marijuana reform. That money underwrote ballot campaigns, research, polling, and legal defense, and it enabled twenty-three states to enact medical marijuana laws by the time of Lewis's death in November 2013.

The movement to legalize weed is often compared with the effort to legalize gay marriage. The two have many surface commonalities. Both took root in the 1960s and waged a half-century-long battle. Advocates of both groups were vilified by pseudoscience and an unquestioning media. Before they became poster boys for Baby

Bjorns and Chinese newborns, gay men were largely pictured in lipstick or in leather. Similarly, cannabists are still hampered by Harold and Kumar portrayals. Few mainstream businesspeople other than Lewis or Sir Richard Branson have spoken out about their personal use. That gaping silence allows otherwise intelligent and influential pundits, like the former *New Yorker* editor Tina Brown, to peddle tired stereotypes without being held accountable. "Legal weed contributes to us being a fatter, dumber, sleepier nation, even less able to compete with the Chinese. Will pot be our nation's downfall?" she tweeted after the presumably fatter and dumber voters in Washington and Colorado legalized marijuana.

The thoughtful *New York Times* columnist David Brooks climbed high onto his horse the very same day to issue this peroration: "In legalizing weed, citizens of Colorado are, indeed, enhancing individual freedom. But they are also nurturing a moral ecology in which it is a bit harder to be the sort of person most of us want to be." It's not difficult to picture him sipping his eighteen-year-old single-malt scotch when finishing that little disquisition.

While coming out about marijuana may not win elections or change the smug opinions of the chattering classes, it will demonstrate that pot is used far more widely and interestingly than is currently presumed. As Ted Trimpa, a lobbyist who worked on both gay marriage and Colorado's legalization efforts, observed: "When pot becomes not just the kid with long hair and skateboard or the guy in the beat up VW van . . . when it's the investment banker, the doctor . . . that's when things will change."

Here's a little secret: It already is the banker and the doctor. They're just not talking about it openly yet.

Lewis passed away before we could speak. So I was pleasantly surprised when George "I guarantee it" Zimmer agreed to meet. I was even more surprised because I had contacted him just after the board of Men's Wearhouse, the company he had founded in 1972 and that had grown to be the largest men's retailer in the United States, had booted him. He'd left without a struggle.

Zimmer was called "the most interesting man in fashion," in part because his interests reached far beyond suits, sales, and spreadsheets. A member of the board of the Institute for Noetic Sciences, he has been a student of consciousness studies for decades. He practiced a form of compassionate capitalism that centered around one tenet: happy employees attract happy customers. Make no mistake, I'm not attributing Zimmer's success to cannabis, but by his own account, it guided him to becoming a more effective leader.

One way he did that was by traversing the country to spend face time with the rank-and-file employees at their holiday parties. He wouldn't talk to the executives but spent the night on the dance floor with the troops. "It made them feel great," Zimmer told me. He also banned background checks and drug testing. Eighty-four percent of large American companies subscribe to this form of chemical McCarthyism, but Zimmer viewed drug tests and background checks as serious infringements on personal liberty, both of which are weighted unfairly against cannabis.[13]

"If you want to have trust, you need to be trustworthy," Zimmer explained when I asked him to expand on his position. We are sitting in the bland offices of his new enterprise, Montclair Venture Partners, perched above a shopping strip in one of Oakland's wealthier suburbs. His office is impersonal and generically appointed, but two objects stand out among the drabness. One is a framed front page of the *Houston Chronicle* announcing "Nixon Resigns!" The other is a chessboard set up with a game that he is playing remotely with a partner named Chris.

"Asking an employee to do a drug test or a background check is like saying, 'I don't trust you at all.' Besides, what am I going to find out? That some guy was stopped for a few joints when he was fifteen?" Zimmer, who has an affinity for conspiracy theories, points out that one of the largest urine-analysis companies, Bensinger, DuPont & Associates, was cofounded by Nixon's former drug czar Robert DuPont. It's a multibillion-dollar industry centered on piss, paranoia, and the fiction of a drug-free America. Lobbying for the industry is supported by Jim Beam and Anheuser-Busch, among other liquor companies—further evidence that conspiracies are typically more than theories when the subject is pot.[14]

I wasn't sure how Zimmer would respond to personal questions about cannabis, but unlike the other, tighter-lipped members of the millionaires' club, he was loose and relaxed. He has never taken an outspoken public stance but has voiced his opinions when asked. In a 1999 article in the *San Francisco Examiner,* he proclaimed his support for the 55 percent inheritance tax and his opposition to the War on Drugs. He also recounted how he offered his mom medical marijuana when she was undergoing chemotherapy. "She looked at me like I suggested that she blow up a building," he recalled. "She said, 'Absolutely not,' and I said, 'OK.'"

His board of directors greeted such remarks with displeasure. "They would say, 'George, there's no benefit from speaking out [about pot] and there may be harm.' I would say, 'Actually, there's no harm and there may be benefit.' The rank and file loved my ability to speak truth to power."* And apparently they liked that the boss smoked openly, which he did with employees off the clock. "After a [sales] training, sitting around a fire pit, I'd take out a joint

---

* There's no doubt that pot fosters irreverence toward authority. Nixon sensed this, and if he had been a student of literature he would have known that it had been mentioned for centuries. *The Arabian Nights* recounts the tale of a king who dressed as a commoner and went to town to ask people what they thought of his rule. He ran into a few hash smokers and peppered them with questions. In response, one stood up and imitated the king giving a pompous speech. The king realized that to be loved by the common man, he should speak to them more directly. Somehow pot pulls back the curtain on authority: It's "I am you and you are me and we are all together" in this human endeavor. Authority senses that; insecure authority fears it.

and say, 'Since most of you had to fly here you probably couldn't bring any pot, so I'm going to light a joint.' Not everyone smoked, but you can be damn sure that a myth developed concerning my open use of cannabis."

Pot, says Zimmer, helps him "shut out noise. As long as you're not totally fucked up, pot enables you to have a sense of the small picture and macro at same time. I've always thought that being a successful businessperson is the ability to balance that focused financial statement analysis with the panoramic right brain way of thinking." It also made him more willing to collaborate while softening some of his aggressive edges. At one time, he recalls, he was type A competitive. Pot didn't make him less of a fighter. It simply provided an awareness that aggression isn't the only route to crossing the finish line first.

While his management style may be modern, Zimmer's smoking habits are defiantly old-school. He smokes three joints a day and finds it therapeutic to roll his own. The nuances of edibles, strains, and concentrates hold little allure. When I show him a menu from Harborside Health Center, the world's largest dispensary, located just a few miles down the road in Oakland, he laughs at the epicurean list of categories. "Supermelt? Shatter? Amber? Sun-grown? *Strains?* I've never noticed the difference between strains," he says. "I've never tried to notice. The only thing people look at is the price."

"What, you'll smoke whatever comes your way?"

"Including my own roaches! I won't throw roaches away any more than I throw away my change. There ought to be a way to tip with roaches."

I am looking at this gray-haired gent being swallowed by a black leather couch, realizing again that this forthrightness is precisely what's missing from today's cannabis conversation—an American icon openly discussing rerolling his roaches. By talking about it honestly and personally, Zimmer is nudging cannabis into acceptance. It's what Peter Lewis suggested in a 2011 editorial he published in *Forbes*: "If everyone who used marijuana stood up and said, 'I use this; it's pretty good,' the argument would be over."

I mention this to Zimmer and he smiles. "The latest polls show that fifty-eight percent of America thinks pot should be legal. As data comes out from Colorado and Washington, we'll see that the only real changes are auto-accident deaths going down and tax revenues going up. When you factor in the changes it will bring to the criminal justice system, it's enormous."

His gaze moves toward the chessboard. "It's like chess when you're up a knight. After twenty years, we're finally in a winning position. We just shouldn't fuck it up."

PART II

THE
NEW
WORLD

Chapter 4

WIDGETS AND DABS

Denver, Colorado

Samuel R. Caldwell's gravestone in the Mount Pleasant cemetery in Erie, Colorado, is a sad sight. Few people in the Denver area know the name of this hapless drifter and occasional bootlegger, who, on October 6, 1937, became the first US citizen to be arrested for selling a handful of "marihuana cigarettes." Justice was swift and harsh back then. Just five days after the Marijuana Tax Act was passed, Caldwell was fined a staggering $1,000 and sentenced to four years' hard labor in Leavenworth, then the country's largest maximum-security prison. "I consider marijuana the worst of all narcotics—far worse than the use of morphine or cocaine," the sentencing judge said. "Marijuana destroys life itself. I have no sympathies with those who sell this weed."

Caldwell paid the fine with his life savings and was confined to a cramped cell on murderers' row. Less than a year after completing his sentence, he died isolated and alone. His gravestone, on a wind-scraped hill, is sinking on one side. Down the hill, a larger road is being built beside the cemetery, and dirt movers have cleared the land for new construction.

It's early 2013, and Denver is in the beginning stages of its frothy green rush—in the last election, more Coloradans voted for legalizing marijuana than voted for Barack Obama—and a new economy is being built in some part on the anticipated fortunes that marijuana will bring. But no one is naming a strain after Samuel Caldwell—the state's first marijuana martyr is long forgotten.

My first trip to Denver occurred just six weeks after medical marijuana was legalized and a year before recreational sales were to begin. Until this point, the state had fuzzy regulations that authorized some dispensaries to operate, but also allowed local governments to shut them down willy-nilly without warning or explanation. The cannabis industry was operating in the so-called gray area, which meant that operators who one day thought they were within the law found themselves out of business the next. It was a mess—until the voters decided enough was enough.

It's not outwardly obvious at this early stage that Colorado is the first fully legal medical marijuana state—people aren't gathering on street corners puffing up. But there are clues, some obvious, others more subtle, that changes are in the offing. The double-story stacks of HVAC units on the roofs of warehouses along I-70, the city's main artery, indicate that they have been converted into massive indoor grows. Billboards along downtown Denver's newly christened "Green Mile" show a man passed out with a bottle and a football on the ground. The caption reads "Marijuana: Safer Than Alcohol . . . and Football," a swipe at the NFL for its strident anticannabis stance. Where ads for sex and escorts once filled the back page of *Westword*, the Mile High City's alternative weekly, there are now ads for dispensaries announcing daily specials. The *Denver Post*'s "The Cannabist" is the country's most insightful blog on the business and culture of pot, stoners coyly refer to themselves as medicators, and the city that was once the healthiest in America now has the highest percentage of chronic-pain patients. Seattle can't be far behind.

The rapid birth of an industry this large makes all of Denver feel like a start-up. Businesses large and small are springing up, and if the players adhere to the laws, which they appear to be doing, Colorado could be the model that is replicated throughout the country. Pain-management clinics, "glass galleries," clone bars, hydro houses, and yes, the country's first Bud 'n' Breakfast—the range of products and services is expanding so quickly that there is a shortage of plant in the market.

I arrive at Adam Dunn's hemp clothing shop, HoodLamb, at one p.m., as agreed. The sign indicates that HoodLamb is open at noon, but the doors are locked. There's a very cool vintage Cadillac hearse parked around back but no one in sight. I call Adam, but his voice mail is full and not accepting messages. I text. No response. I'm now used to this—stoners share a notable disregard for time. Amotivational syndrome? "Atemporal syndrome" more describes my experience.

Adam finally pulls up in a beaten-up car, unaware or unconcerned about his tardiness. He hands me his card, which reads: "I may not have friends in high places but I have high friends in places," which instantly washes away any hint of annoyance and makes me smile. His beard has grown to an epic ZZ Top length since we met in Amsterdam, and I'm transfixed by the quarter-size discs in his earlobes. They are so big I could pass my forefinger though the holes.

Adam leads me through a wide aisle of loosely arranged racks of hoodies and outer jackets, stacks of old-school graffiti paintings, and a small display of Dr. Bronner's Hemp Oil Soaps into the back office.* This is the inner sanctum and it is crammed with two gold velvet sofas, a minifridge filled with IPAs and ales, a washing machine (used to wash trim), and monitors showing the security camera view of each entrance. The coffee table—the centerpiece in all stoner décor—is strewn with the remains of last

---

*David Bronner, a grandson of the founder of the liquid soap company, has been an outspoken supporter of hemp and legalization efforts.

night's adventures: anthills of ground cannabis flowers, massive pipes, and blowtorches of varying sizes. One glass vial contains a substance that looks like crumbled wax. It's called "budder," or "earwax," Adam explains. It's a hash concentrate that still contains the waxy trichomes that envelop the resins. (If there were more women in this industry, I guarantee that no product would ever be named after the secretions and dead skin that accumulate in the outer ear.) There are also small packets of what looks like amber candy wrapped in white paper just like cocaine used to come, called "shatter." I'm curious about every one of these new-world products, but Adam has other things on his mind.

It's official. What the car is to Detroit, what digital technology is to Silicon Valley, cannabis is to Denver—and every grower is ramping up to meet the demand. One friend was actually storing his car in his garage, Adam tells me, until he realized it would be so much more profitable to turn it into a grow. *Duh!* His landlord agreed and helped him rewire the garage with additional amperage for lights and ventilation. Another has quit her day job as administrative assistant to the state senate majority leader to lobby for the legal cultivation of hemp. The regulatory, legal, and political structure is finally in place to do big things here. This is why growers cannot be dismissed—without growers there are no plants, and without plants there is no industry.

Adam is modest, charmingly ironic, and authentically hip without any hipster artifice. He defines himself as a "lifestyle guy." He was born in Woodstock in the summer of 1969—"How fitting, right?"—and was raised by his single mom, Adrienne, who has recently moved in with him, his wife, and their young son, Nyc. Adrienne does grandma duty while also tending to a few plants. She and Adam have been growing partners since he was a teenager, and they are thisclose. "She grows better than I do," he confides. "In Amsterdam, all of the Cannabis Cups I won, it was her work. I was the one out there on the front lines."

Back in Amsterdam, Adam's marketing formula was "grow it and know it before you sell it." At harvest time he'd invite people around to evaluate several new crops: How does each one smell, taste, and burn? What are the effects? What is the bag appeal (appearance)? But to discern a truly great strain, all he had to do was wait to see which sample disappeared first. "It's like food," he tells me. "It doesn't lie."

And it's the route to his success here too. "I'm looking for customers for life, so I can't separate myself from weed. Our clientele, the people who want hemp clothing, are smokers, and you can't turn your back on those people. *We only grow hemp, but we don't smoke? You kidding me?* You're turning your back on the people who love cannabis. One thing I've learned, if you have great cannabis, everyone loves you and you'll have a great business."

Dunn envisions the day when the warm Colorado sun will be shining over fifty thousand acres of hemp. "But right now [until it becomes legal to grow hemp] we'll take an eighth of an acre of hemp and produce enough seed for five hundred acres. Next year we can produce a thousand acres. Within four years we'll have fifty thousand acres from an eighth of an acre. That's kinda nice. We'll be completely self-sufficient from a handful of seeds.

"The thing about growing is that when you produce something you get such a good high just knowing you did it all yourself. If I can say 'I was part of that,' I would feel complete."

Until that rapturous day arrives, Adam is content to occupy an almost saintly position among growers. His skills at what were recently regarded as fringe criminal activities are making him suddenly, and highly, employable. He and his buddies are the R&D guys of an emerging market.

Derek Cumings, for example, is a hotheaded, foulmouthed "hash consultant" in high demand. Besides being a proficient hash oil producer, he has devised recipes that mask the oil's bitter taste, which he is now licensing to five different edible companies. Steve is a horticulturist who last year made over four million cuttings of orchids and other noncannabis plants (in true stoner fashion, he counted). He's anticipating a busy career once recreational cannabis comes online. Educated horticulturists are valued because their knowledge of plants and plant diseases is more comprehensive than homeschooled pot growers. Chris is a trimmer in a vast industrial grow, but he's eyeing a career change. Trimming leaves off plants all day is as dull as factory work. It's making his fingers stiff with early-onset carpal tunnel syndrome, so he's gunning for a job with the twentysomething founder of Evo Hemp bars. Working in the cannabis trade is to this generation what waiting tables was to mine.

There are a few unspoken rituals that all celebrants observe here in the cannabis chapel. There are no introductions or formalities. New guests float in, exchange a nod, and park. Rarely are they acknowledged by name.

It's what they pull from their backpacks that identify and confer status on them: large glass jars of freshly cured flowers that are passed around for everyone to savor. The lone woman in the crowd has come with her husband to replenish the hash oil cartridges she uses in her vaporizing pen. She doesn't rate the prepackaged oils as highly as what she obtains here, either in taste or effects. Derek painstakingly injects them with some of the top-quality goo he manufactured that day. Not a penny changes hands.

The other rule of the windowless room seems to be: speak of nothing but pot. There is no mention of women, sex, politics, sports, love, philosophy, or food.* Cannabis is the single shared

---

*Not once in the four days I spent here did anyone mention food. I plan my dinner over breakfast but these smokers were utterly uninterested in eating, which is odd, given pot's well-established connection to the munchies. These guys also drank very little alcohol—water, energy drinks, and the occasional Corona Light were the mainstays. Serious smokers know that pot and gallons of alcohol don't mix.

obsession. Derek has achieved a sort of hero status for keeping one citrusy smelling strain, Tangerine Dream, alive for eleven years. A while back he spread the seeds among these growers and tonight one has returned with his first harvest. Cracking open a jar of finger-length "Tanj" buds, he passes it around for inspection. Steve, the horticulturist, dunks his nose in the jar and closes his eyes, inhaling. "Aromatherapy," he utters to no one in particular.

As I'm observing these goings-on, it strikes me again that this plant holds a uniquely powerful sway over certain members of the human race. People who grow cannabis don't just like it. They love it (to the same extent that its detractors detest it). When not growing, they long for it. Another grower I know has maintained a grow in his bedroom closet for years. He doesn't smoke that much and he doesn't sell—he gives it away, because money isn't the point. The sheer act of nurturing the plants, knowing that they are in his closet sucking up electricity and doing their thing, provides the same comfort as a dog or cat, he told me.

Perfectly sane people from all walks of life have a deep, abiding emotional relationship with this plant.

I initially compared pot aficionados to wine snobs, but I'm revising that analogy. These guys are more like early Silicon Valley geeks, holed up in their garages, diddling with motherboards and circuits in near isolation. No one—maybe not even they—knew what they were up to, yet they were fueled by the conviction that they were creating something new, possibly revolutionary. Their (initial) motivation wasn't money; it was more a desire to upend the established order with something of their own creation. Both groups had questionable social skills, but their dedication was unfettered and the momentum they launched unstoppable.

Once night falls, the dabbing begins. Dabs (as in "a little dab'll do ya," Jimmy Buffett's 1970s ad for Brylcreem) are a wholly new way of taking in stratospheric amounts of THC that has taken the weed world by storm. Although hash oils have been made in the West for fifty years, they were formerly difficult to produce, messy to use, and never really caught on.* Now, with modern extraction methods and a new generation of smokers in search of cleaner superhighs, dabbing is so popular that some breathless headline writers are heralding it as "The Future of Getting High."

It's also marijuana's biggest public-relations nightmare. Even if you believe that the plant is harmless and creates only good in the world, watching someone dab may cause you to rethink your position. It makes smoking a three-foot-tall bong look old-fashioned.

Adam demonstrates. Because oils burn at a higher temperature than flowers, he first aims a blow torch—the type I've used to make crème brûlée—at a titanium nail that sits in the bowl of his giant glass water pipe called a rig (as in "oil rig") until the nail is glowing orange. With a dab stick, a metal instrument that resembles the device a dentist uses to scratch plaque from teeth, he slices a poppy seed–size dab of hardened hash oil, the aforementioned "shatter." The dab hovers above the heated nail and *whoosh*! As it melts, a lush plume of smoke swirls into the pipe. Powerful pot is 20 to 25 percent THC. A dab is a mind-stinging 70 to 90 percent THC.

That evening, Adam hits a dab every hour or so and never misses a beat. His conversation is steady, coherent, and sharp; he must have the tolerance of a giant.

Cannaoisseurs claim that concentrates are the sous vide of their evolving culture—the closest thing to a psychedelic experience

---

*Cannabis oil (aka hash oil) briefly spiked in popularity in the 1960s, when hippies painted it on joints to boost highs. We now know that that application was an utter waste of material because oil burns at a different temperature than flowers. What's more, the goo was messy to use and stuck to clothes like tar, so it fell out of favor.

one can wrest from cannabis. They also claim, perhaps rightfully, that smoking concentrates constitutes "harm reduction," as all the lung-irritating plant matter is removed, so it delivers the strongest, purest high with the lowest amount of toxins. And while dabbing is still largely an insider thing, it is filtering into the mainstream. At one cannabis fund-raiser at Bill Maher's compound in the Hollywood Hills, there was a margarita bar on one level, and upstairs, a seventy-foot dab bar with a half-dozen rigs lined up and loaded. Cannabis quenchers in grape and lemonade flavors were also served to soothe parched throats.

Critics—who range from Robert Connell-Clarke, an ethnobotanist and one of the world's experts on the plant, to anti-marijuana mothers' groups—are less sanguine about dabbing. Many articles, and far too little research, malign dabs as "a dangerous new drug" (fact: dabs are simply another form of marijuana or hashish), "the crack of marijuana" (fact: dabs are powerful but not addictive), or "increasing risk of overdose" (questionable: "overdose" is a loaded word that generally implies death; this can't happen with cannabis, but other weird and inexplicable things can, as I was soon to learn).

Armchair critics typically fail to realize that there are two ways of extracting these concentrates: with CO_2 or water, like Bubbleman's bubble hash, or with more toxic solvents, such as butane. The latter category is called butane honey oil, or BHO, and herein lies the true nub of the controversy.

To make BHO, marijuana leaves are packed into a long glass tube. Liquid butane, the same solvent used in cigarette lighters, is pushed through the leaves, stripping them of their oils. This produces a green puddle of solvent and cannabinoids, which is then baked to theoretically evaporate the remaining solvent. The result is "pure" concentrated THC. The length of bake time determines if the resulting concentrate takes the form of a gooey oil or the hard candy-like substance known as "shatter."

One doesn't need a PhD in chemistry for several concerns to spring to mind.

First, butane is extremely flammable. Some amateurs may accidentally strike a match and blow themselves up, which makes the comparison to meth cooking unavoidable, but also brings with it other, more immediate dangers. YouTube is sprinkled with videos showing houses being rocked off their foundations. This is serious. Camy Boyle, the associate nurse manager for the burn unit at the University of Colorado Hospital, told the *Denver Post* that in 2011 and 2012 he saw only one injury that could be traced to hash oil production. In 2013 the hospital's burn unit saw ten. It's not difficult to see why people don't want their neighbors or their neighbors' kids toying with this.[1]

Second, even though baking theoretically evaporates the solvent, chances are that traces remain. This means that humans who smoke BHO are inhaling a substance that contains some quantity of benzene, a hydrocarbon refined from crude oil that has been linked to diseases of the liver, kidney, and central nervous system, not to mention cancer. Although some extractors claim to use the world's cleanest butane, even that, according to Connell-Clarke, "is full of contaminants, some present due to inefficient butane collection and others added for their odor so the butane has an easily detected smell. Some impurities and additives are slow to evaporate, become trapped, and can readily contaminate butane-extracted oils."[2]

Third, the allure of powerful highs is undeniable, as is the need for strong medicine to treat serious illnesses, but steady dabbing strikes me like taking morphine for a headache when aspirin will do the trick. There is no research about what a constant infusion of supersize doses of THC does to the body. Unless such high doses are prescribed for specific medical conditions, their repeated use seems like an unnecessary risk until more is known.

States are now debating whether to ban concentrate production or at least limit legal production to cleaner CO_2 or cold-water extraction methods in proper labs with security features. That's a sensible compromise, a far better idea than prohibiting concentrate production altogether. As the last eighty years have shown, prohibition is a superhighway to increased desire.

The following day, Adam takes me on a nickel tour of some of the start-ups fueling the cannaboom. We visit the kitchens of Incredibles, makers of cannabis chocolate bars. The company is owned by a former chef who was struggling to make ends meet behind the stove. His fortunes have changed almost overnight—his main struggle now is finding enough oil to meet the ever-increasing demand. Later we drop into a community discussion being held in the cavernous back area of a neighborhood saloon. Lawyers, former cops, and policy makers are onstage discussing how to avoid arrest for driving under the influence. The issue is a thorny one because THC stays in the body for some thirty days. Even if you haven't smoked in a month and are stone-cold sober, a urine test could still yield a positive result and you could lose your driver's license.* A lawyer reminds the one hundred attendees that the police can't force suspects to take a DUI test, and that drivers should refuse if asked. Ditto if they insist on searching the car without a warrant. These are thorny issues, ones that won't be solved overnight, but it's rather thrilling to see a group with different agendas hammering them out together. It's the way grassroots democracy is supposed to work, and it left me feeling discontented that I live in a state where such discussions are not even on the horizon. Same country, different world.

---

*The law has since been rewritten. If THC is identified in a driver's blood in quantities of 5 milligrams per milliliter or higher, "such fact gives rise to permissible inference that the defendant was under the influence."

The excitement in Denver wasn't restricted to Adam's small world of craft cannabis growers and makers. If these independent operators are the cannabis equivalents of microbrewers, other ambitious players are gunning to be Coors. Dixie Elixirs is the king of cannabis-infused edibles and drinkables in Colorado and possibly the country (it's impossible to know, since there is no Dun & Bradstreet of the industry yet), and edibles is the market's fastest-growing segment. "Not everyone wants to smoke a joint," Vincent "Tripp" Keber, Dixie's cofounder and CEO, tells me as we inspect his 27,000-square-foot factory. "Some people may have had a bad experience with marijuana in youth. Others have kids and they may not necessarily want to be lighting up. We have over one hundred SKUs representing twelve different delivery systems. Our widgets allow you discretion."

Keber actually used the word "widget" to describe his goods, as if the anodyne language of manufacturing proves his claim that he holds no particular attachment to the plant. "I'm not suggesting I never inhaled, but we started this company to make money," he said. In fact, distancing his company from the pot of old is one of the routes he's taking toward legitimacy. When television crews visit the facility they're shunted away from the plants. Dixie's packaging is wisely absent the green cannabis leaf. Nor is Keber the predictable face of a cannapreneur. With his Palm Beach sports jackets and salesman's smile, he has been pegged as the Gordon Gekko of Ganja, a distinction he relishes. Being the straight man in a stoner world is radical in its own way.

Keber and company were real estate developers who hit it big by building "intergenerational resort communities" in southeast Florida. In 2009 they smelled opportunity and became passive investors in Dixie Elixirs. They'd supply the capital, hire the "talent," and then sit back and watch the business explode.

Or so they thought, until the reality of turning a crew of hobbyists into an industry hit home. In its first year, production at Dixie began to lag. When Keber stopped by one day to deliver another $250,000 funding bump, he found that his top four lieutenants were "more interested in medicating than manufacturing." He axed them and jumped in as CEO. And while his coiffed appearance may win him credibility in the business community, it didn't help him with suppliers, who viewed him with suspicion. On one early expedition to procure "raw plant material," he was instructed to meet his contact in a junkyard. Keber was wandering through the debris when the grower slinked out from behind a pile of scrap metal, spooking the hell out of him. "Couldn't we just have this meeting in an office?" he remembers thinking.

On another buying trip he was blindfolded and shoved in the backseat of a car, bookended by two Russian thugs. The GPS on his phone was disabled, he was driven in circles for thirty minutes and shunted between different cars. Upon arrival he was led into a room where the table was stacked with cash and his hosts were all packing guns. An Armenian with a long-filter Russian cigarette dangling from his lips commanded him to sit.

"You vant coffee?" Keber doesn't drink coffee, but the Czech translator tipped him off: "Whatever he offers you, accept. In our culture it's rude to refuse."

Keber drank the coffee. "I'm trying to show the soccer mom in Ohio that what we're doing is legit, that there are people who wear jackets to work and don't have dreadlocks and who are building companies that you can monetize. It was the Wild West then.

"Thankfully, I haven't heard a Russian accent in a long time."

Today, Dixie is Colorado's premier industrial-scale cannabusiness, churning out candies, sodas, chocolates, and skin creams. It has impressively fine-tuned its manufacturing to punch out one thousand brownies an hour that are consistent in dosage and flavor. It owns the intellectual property to its processes, which ensures no oil blebs or plant detritus in the formulations. Its packaging is now child resistant and tamper proof, and it's got the labeling, ingredients, and nutritional facts ready to go, so "if the FDA decides to regulate the industry, we'll be prepared."

For what, exactly? "Once eight states legalize adult use, I believe unequivocally that Big Alcohol or Big Tobacco will be asking, 'Who do we make the check payable to?'" Keber said. "And saying this makes me unpopular, but we're building a company to be attractive to the alcohol model. It's something they can absorb into their group, turn into a division, and then expand upon with their distribution."

Die-hard cannabists contend that this desire to sell out to Big Bad Corporate America betrays their decades-long struggle for legitimacy, and there's evidence that that sentiment taps a deep vein. Many consumers want to know where their products come from, if it's clean and locally grown. They want to know it's connected to their community. But surely there is room enough for both big and small in this emerging world. Mass marketers will never be able to stamp out innovative small-batch producers like Adam and his merry band of growers. Just as with chocolate, coffee, or beer, it's easy enough to envision the day when Marijuana pre-rolls are sold in a supermarket-size dispensary and Adam Dunn's more artisanal goods are for sale inside his shop and at other specialty stores.

Samuel Caldwell must be doing double flips in his grave.

"You ready to try one?" Adam is firing up a nail, goading me to relinquish my dab virginity. It's my last night in Denver. The boys have been extremely gracious about not pushing anything on me, but after days of watching these guys consume inordinate amounts of dabs, curiosity has overcome my apprehension. These guys are doing dab after dab and are energetic and focused, so I accept the offer before Adam and I head out to dinner.

Adam picks off an apple seed–size piece of shatter and hovers it above the Ti nail. An apple seed is twice the size of a sesame seed, but the distinction is so minute I think nothing of it and suck it down. It hits hard and fast. In seconds my entire being is teeming, every cell a vibrating tightrope of sensation.

The car ride is magic—I'm flying miles above the slight feeling of enhancement I've grown used to since this journey began. Once at City, O' City, the hottest vegan restaurant in Denver at the moment, we drift through the crowded dining room and land two seats at the bar. Adam is telling me about how people all over the world are using cannabis oil to treat skin cancers and I'm thinking, *Yeah, right. Tell me more when you haven't hit the bong.* But then I glance at the menu and see that the words are dancing on the page, off the page, refusing to come into focus. Within seconds the room is swerving, the floor tilting and buckling like a boat in crashing waves. Before I can identify what's happening, my skin goes clammy and I feel the color drain from my face. This isn't going to end well.

I stumble outside in hopes of the cold air slapping me straight, but it's too late. A heave rumbles in my gut, kicking its way up into my throat and out of my mouth, ending in a full Linda Blair exorcism. I can't understand how this can be happening. Cannabis is supposed to be antiemetic, and I'd eaten nothing all day.

After what seems like hours, but was more like twenty minutes, I slouch inside and explain the sidewalk disaster to Adam. Humbled and embarrassed, my mouth rancid, I ask him to deliver me to my hotel, which he does graciously, but not without two pit stops in a snow-strewn gutter along the way. My last memory of City, O' City was seeing a busboy outside unhappily mopping up my mess with a few pitchers of hot water and a broom.

Inside my room I lay on the bed in the dark for minutes or maybe an hour. In a lone corner of my mind I recall reading that drinking cold lemon water and taking hot baths are antidotes to extreme drug discomfort, but I can't muster the energy for either. I topple into an indistinct dream, fully clothed and shoes on.

What the hell happened? It would take months of searching to find out.

BRAVE NEW WEED WORDS

Old	New
Amsterdam	Denver
Pot	Meds
Stoner	Cannabist
Blasted	Dosed
Joints	Dabs
Hashish	Full melt; bubble
Wrecked	Enhanced
Bong	Rig
Buds	Flowers
Sinsemilla	Strains
Dealers	Dispensaries
Scoring	Weedmaps
Maui Wowie	Blue Dream
THC	CBD
Brownies	Edibles
Pipes	Glass
Golden Triangle	Emerald Triangle
420	710 (read upside-down, "710" spells oil, as in "hash oil")

Chapter 5

THE ENDOCANNABINOID SYSTEM:
THE BODY'S SUPERCOMPUTER

Jerusalem, Israel

The Denver disaster, as I've come to think of it, put a damper on my unbridled enthusiasm for cannabis. No matter what anyone says, too much pot can create feelings of deep discomfort. You can't stop the anguish—you must simply wait it out for what seems like a lifetime.

After a merciful sleep I woke up shaken but fine, except for a throat frayed from stomach acids flowing in the wrong direction. Still, the upheaval was a stern reminder that no plant intoxicant, benign or otherwise, is 100 percent predictable. Pot has always been known as a fickle woman. If this relationship was to continue, I needed to get a handle on her capriciousness.

The last time pot had smacked me that hard was in San Francisco in the summer of 1976, when a lover twelve years my senior told me she was pregnant with my child the very night I had planned to tell her that I was gay. We had smoked a fatty of some Hawaiian strain, and my knotted-up and confused body reacted to this emotional shock with the same testicle-squeezing retching that felled me in Denver. I always presumed that the stonking amount of THC in that Hawaiian weed had sparked the convulsion, but now I wondered if something else, such as the compound that produces the dark-green civety smell prevalent in so many of the Colorado superstrains, was to blame.

Once my head cleared from Denver, I began Googling for answers. One search turned up "cannabinoid hyperemesis syndrome," a spurt of cyclical vomiting that extends for days and is accompanied by the compulsive need for warm showers. Chronic smokers who light up six times a day complain about this, but it doesn't appear to be my problem. Message boards were dotted with amateur hypotheses about "greening out" from overeating, but the Denver dabbers never even snacked, so my stomach was consistently, and unhappily, empty. One post on Weedmaps, a strain directory and the nearest thing to WebMd for cannabis, suggested that violent coughing might have thrown my stomach into reverse peristalsis. Unlikely. Another post echoed my own confusion: If pot allayed nausea, why did it induce vomiting?

I was facing a common problem in the new world of cannabis: a dearth of consistent reliable information. Much of the "expert opinion" on the Web is produced by self-anointed experts or backyard chemists, which makes it suspect, tinged by wishful thinking, or fiction masquerading as fact. There have been an avalanche of experimental studies—over twenty thousand to date—but few definitive clinical trials. As a result, the science can seem like a thicket of contradictions. Cannabis cures cancer! It causes it! It protects the brain! It causes schizophrenia! It's addictive! It helps alcoholics wean themselves off booze! The only drug that treats *everything* is either snake oil or a miracle, and I don't believe in miracles. So what's the truth?

My confusion, it turned out, was not unwarranted. The international prohibitions and unrelenting anticannabis propaganda, much of which is generated in the United States, has been remarkably effective at blurring the line between truth and myth. This has not happened by accident.

Not only does the schedule I classification restrict access to the plant, it also makes researching it exceedingly burdensome. It's no exaggeration to say that studying cannabis in the United States today is as politicized as studying genetics in the USSR under Lysenko was in the 1960s. Rather than send resisters to the Gulag, which is what happened to any scientist who bucked Trofim Lysenko's wacky theories, the US government uses red tape to strangle most meaningful cannabis research. That may sound like an overstatement, but it is, in fact, easier to test a known poison such as arsenic in human beings than it is to test cannabis, primarily because access to the plant has been so tightly controlled by three federal agencies—the National Institute on Drug Abuse (NIDA), the Drug Enforcement Agency (DEA), and the Food and Drug Administration (FDA)—for over forty-five years.

Here's how it works: The feds control the supply of marijuana by growing their own crop at a plantation at the University of Mississippi, where until 2014 the total production was limited to a meager forty-six pounds a year.* Scientists seeking access to the Mississippi crop must first apply to NIDA for permission. If NIDA gives the go-ahead, which it rarely does, researchers must then secure approvals from the DEA and FDA. (Until the Obama administration loosened the rule in 2015, a third approval from a public health service review board—composed of unspecified "health professionals"—was required.)

"The American study of cannabis is light-years behind the rest of the world in terms of what's been done and published," says Dr. Ethan Russo, a neurologist, ethnobotanist, and one of America's leading researchers into medical cannabis. "We have an echelon of official oversight that doesn't apply to any other drug."

A case in point was Dr. Donald Abrams's 1992 attempt to examine the effects of cannabis on what was at the time called "AIDS-related wasting syndrome," which was wiping away thousands of lives a year. In the 1990s, ten thousand skeletal AIDS patients in San Francisco were already smoking pot to maintain their

---

*Production was increased to 1,433 pounds per year in 2014.

appetites and weight, yet no American science was evaluating its effects.

Abrams, who is currently chief oncologist at San Francisco General Hospital, had originally planned to secure medical-grade cannabis from Holland for his study. His application went to NIDA, where it sat for nine months unanswered, until it was rejected for poor experimental design. After several revisions the application finally made its way to the DEA, which demanded Abrams scratch his plan to obtain cannabis from abroad and use the Mississippi stash instead. He complied and resubmitted his application, but it fell into a black hole until 1996, when he received two troubling letters from the independent review board. One reviewer questioned his reason for wanting to investigate such a "toxic" substance; another worried that AIDS patients might develop high cholesterol from smoking pot. In what has to be the understatement of the decade, Abrams told me that the reviewers seemed to "miss the point."

Abrams was so disheartened by the years-long obstructions that he eventually met face-to-face with the then head of NIDA, Alan Leshner, who explained that his organization was the National Institute *on* Drug Abuse, not *for* drug abuse, and that his congressional mandate forbade him from funding any investigation seeking to uncover any benefits of cannabis. With that in mind, Abrams recast his study yet again, this time to examine the ways cannabis might *interfere* with the antiviral drugs that fight HIV. That won him the green light in 1997. The evidence showed that cannabis was perfectly safe for use with retrovirals; moreover, the recipients gained more weight and maintained better health than the control groups using a placebo or Marinol.[1]

When Abrams told me this story, I thought it might have been an isolated incident. But after forty-five years and some 1,800 studies, NIDA, which allots $66 million a year to ferreting out the harms of cannabis, has failed to conclusively prove any health-threatening

dangers of the plant.* That hasn't stopped it from regularly issuing studies correlating cannabis use with brain "changes" in kids,
long-term memory deficits, addiction to more dangerous drugs,
and increased incidence of psychosis or lower IQs. The media
regurgitates these results without question.

The often-repeated claim that cannabis causes permanent
damage to brain cells is equally specious. There is little doubt
in my mind that sustained overuse can produce a certain dull-
ness of thought—the bleary eyes of someone who oversmokes
are a window into a blurry mind. But long-term studies show
that there are no differences in brain activity between heavy and
light users over time. The same goes for the endless studies on
what has come to be known as "cannabis-induced psychosis."
Of course smoking or eating too much pot can trigger extreme
discomfort or a state that some describe as akin to a temporary
psychotic episode, but the symptoms typically disappear and leave
no permanent damage.

The same holds true for schizophrenia. While studies from
NIDA and other groups have found that cannabis users are more
likely to be at risk for schizophrenia, no study has ever established
a causal relationship. It's just as likely that people prone to schizophrenia tend to self-medicate with cannabis. What's more, the
incidence of schizophrenia in the United States has held steady at
about 1 percent since the 1960s, while pot use has risen from 33 to
39 percent. This indicates that from the Dean Martin era through
the Chris Martin era, three generations of adults have used the
plant without the predicted rash of mental illness occurring.

---

*According to the NIDA budget office, the total budget for NIDA in 2015
was $1.016 billion, and the marijuana research budget was $66 million. When
asked to clarify the precise numbers, the National Institute on Drug Abuse
told me, "Please keep in mind that this is for the NIDA budget. NIDA is one
of 27 Institutes within the National Institutes of Health. There are other
institutes who conduct marijuana research."

The United States is the largest funder of medical research in the world. But until Congress releases cannabis from the confines of schedule I, American science in this area will always be viewed as second-rate and subject to doubt. The research blockade also explains why the most groundbreaking cannabis research comes from abroad—primarily from Israel. That tiny country of eight million is, in fact, the capital of cannabis science. It's where Dr. Raphael Mechoulam, the scientist who cracked the chemical code of cannabis a half century ago and then discovered the endo-cannabinoid system (ECS) in the human body with which it inter-acts, is still hard at work.

Oh, you've never heard of Mechoulam or the endocannabinoid system, the largest receptor system in the human body, even though it was discovered over twenty-five years ago? Don't feel uninformed. Ninety-five percent of American doctors haven't, either.

Hebrew University sits high above the tiny village of Ein Kerem, just west of Jerusalem. This large institution is where Mechoulam has worked for almost half a century, beginning shortly after he dis-covered THC in 1964. At that time, the plucky thirty-four-year-old biochemistry grad student had been researching plant medicines at Israel's Weizmann Institute. It struck him then that morphine had been isolated from opium about 160 years prior, in 1804, and cocaine had been extracted from coca leaves in 1850, but the chem-istry of cannabis, which was used much more widely for health and high, remained a mystery.

The Israelis have always taken a hard line against cannabis, due in some small part to anti-Arab bias (Muslims favor canna-bis over alcohol) and because a nation on permanent military alert is incompatible with what Baudelaire called the "silent, lazy, soft benevolence" of pot. But science, when not dictated or restricted by governments, knows no political boundaries, so Mechoulam forged ahead until he hit a roadblock: there was no way for him to legally obtain plant material. He asked the administrator at Weizmann if he had a contact in the police. "C'mon! Just go and pay your parking tickets!" came the response. When Mechoulam explained the nature of his inquiry, the director called in a favor from an old army pal who was number three on the force. "There are some advantages to living in a small country," the professor told me.

At the police station, Mechoulam collected five kilos (eleven pounds) of primo brown hashish, molded into two-hundred-gram bricks, shaped like shoe soles, wrapped in linen, and stamped with their place of origin: "Stambul."* Mechoulam carried his bounty to the lab on a bus in a plastic bag. The smell was very noticeable, he recalls, and very pleasant.

He and another scientist, Yehiel Gaoni, employed a new separation technology that allowed them to isolate and determine the structures of the two major components in the plant: cannabidiol, or CBD; and the psychoactive molecule delta 9-tetrahydrocannabinol, or THC. No one was terribly excited by their discovery, so the team spent the next months scrounging for additional funding to carry on. (Scientific research in Israel is funded just as it is in the West: a scientist gets an idea and must then hunt for money to support his inquiry.) They applied for a US National Institutes of Health grant but were rejected by the head of pharmacology, Dr. Dan Efron, who explained in a polite but patronizing way that "cannabis is not an American problem. It is used in Mexico and by some jazz musicians in the US, but that's about all." The NIH would consider supporting Mechoulam's research when he found another, more relevant topic.

---

*Even smugglers, whose identity relies on not being known, identify place of origin. Why? Branding!

One year later, Efron was on the phone to Mechoulam with an urgent message. A US senator's son had been found smoking pot, and the senator was desperate to know if it could damage his brain. Mechoulam extended an invitation to discuss the matter, and Efron showed up in Jerusalem the next day. By the conclusion of their meeting, Efron had packed most of the world's supply of THC—ten grams—into his suitcase. Presumably he smuggled the drug past US customs, since no official at the time knew what it was.

The NIH has funneled money into Mechoulam's lab ever since. This has allowed his team to become the uncontested world authority on the chemistry of the plant and the endocannabinoid system with which it interacts. Mechoulam himself has published over four hundred papers, edited four books, owns twenty-five patents, and has received twenty-seven honors from six countries. His findings have earned him the respect of scientists, policy advisors, doctors, politicians, growers, and other researchers around the world. Yet prohibition has effectively kept his findings and his name hidden from public awareness.

The discovery of THC solved the mystery of the high, but the more important discoveries were still to come. In 1988, an American chemist, Dr. Allyn Howlett, located a network of receptors in the brain that respond to THC. The densest concentration of these receptors—the Milky Way, as it were—is in the brain areas that coordinate movement and control emotions, memory, pain, pleasure, and reproduction.

Cannabists take this connection between THC and brain receptors as further proof of the symbiotic link between the plant and the human body. But Mechoulam doesn't think the plant has any abiding interest in the grand order of the universe. It may appear coincidental that the cannabis plant generates chemicals similar to those produced by our bodies, but such a coincidence is not without precedent. The human body also manufactures its own opiates, the endorphins, which mimic the pleasure-producing secretion from the poppy flower that becomes heroin. To Mechoulam's evidence-based mind, all plants produce tens of thousands of compounds that both attract bugs and animals to carry their seeds and also protect them from hostile insects, grazing animals, and harmful UV radiation. Cannabis very cleverly "pleasures our minds in order to use our feet," as Michael Pollan put it.[2] These many compounds constitute the plant's immune system, and the fact that they also affect humans is little more than a happy accident.

More important, Mechoulam also knows that the human body doesn't manufacture receptors to respond to random substances found in plants. So he and his team began hunting for a compound like THC that the body itself produces to stimulate these receptors.

In 1992, Bill Devane, a postdoctoral student, and Lumir Hanus, a Czech chemist, both part of Mechoulam's lab, found a brain chemical that mirrors the effects of THC. They named this THC analogue "anandamide" after the Sanskrit word *ananda*, for bliss (that naming convention probably wouldn't fly today). Just like THC, anandamide is thought to radiate a golden, sunny pleasure, intensify sensory experience, stimulate appetite, and temporarily blot out short-term memory.* When I asked Mechoulam why he didn't give the molecule a Hebrew name, he smiled and said, "Because in Hebrew there are more words for sorrow than happiness. . . . Jews don't like being happy." Before long, Mechoulam's lab found another brain chemical that mimics CBD, 2-arachidonoylglycerol, which they named (rather uninspiringly) 2-AG.

Shortly after Dr. Howlett located the brain receptors, other scientists in Britain discovered a galaxy of receptors that snakes throughout the entire body into every organ, gland, immune cell,

---

*This is the assumption, at least. Anandamide has never been administered to a human being due to legal restrictions, so there is no proof.

and connective tissue.* Further exploration revealed this endocannabinoid system (ECS) to be the largest signaling system in the
human body. Let me be clear: this is not a theoretical system that
exists in the minds of a few wishful thinkers. Scientists have found
endocannabinoid receptors in all vertebrates and even the most
primitive invertebrates—sponges—which suggests that the system
has been around for thirty-four million years.

The next inevitable question was: What the hell does it do?

Because they are invisible, neurotransmitter systems are difficult
to picture and comprehend. Think of them as cell phone networks,
but rather than beam signals through the air, the brain sends
chemicals and electric impulses that command cells to communicate
with each other. We are more familiar with other neurotransmitter
systems because they were discovered first—dopamine, serotonin,
histamine—but the ECS is the largest and possibly the bossiest of
all. It has been called "the body's supercomputer" because one
of its functions is to keep every other bodily system in balance.
What's more, it is the only neurotransmitter network that com-
municates with cells in two directions.

Not only do commands emanate from the brain outward, but if
an organ is in trouble, the endocannabinoid neurotransmitters act
like an early-warning defense system, sending a cry for help back
to the brain.

In the last thirty years, an entirely new class of pharmaceuticals
has been formed from the basis of receptor systems. Antihistamines
initially targeted receptors in the nasal passages, for example, but
additional histamine receptors were later discovered in the digestive
system, and that discovery gave rise to medications such as Zantac
or Prilosec that treat all manner of gastric disorders. What's more,
under- or overproduction of neurotransmitters is now linked to

*Receptors in the brain are known as CB1 receptors; receptors in the body's
other organs are called CB2 receptors.

illnesses that have eluded science for decades. Too little dopamine is connected to Parkinson's disease. Overproduction is related to schizophrenia. Serotonin, which mimics the psilocybin found in magic mushrooms, mitigates depression.

As the body's supercomputer, the ECS steadies the "temperature" in every room in the body's house. It appears to regulate the flow and balance—the chi—of all of the organ systems, as well as regulating blood sugar, immune function, muscle and fat tissues, hormones, pain centers, reward centers, and metabolic functions. It maintains the heart's steady beat, the stomach's digestion, the lungs' bellows, and even the rate at which bones heal. It rewards us for eating and having sex, two activities essential to keeping the species thriving. It enables us to forget pain. And it warns the body when trouble is afoot by sending out chemicals to protect troubled areas from further damage. If you're thinking, "Wait, I thought the immune system did that!" remember that not all illnesses involve microbes, viruses, or infections. When you break a bone or bang your head, endocannabinoids act as the body's first responders by sending signals back to the brain. According to Professor Mechoulam's qualified thinking, "They may function as a parallel immune system. Maybe." At the very least they form a cellular bridge between body and mind.

I first greeted this wealth of information skeptically. How was it possible that the largest neurotransmitter system in the human body had escaped my attention? As it turns out, my ignorance is well justified. Even though a global cadre of scientists has been exploring the endocannabinoid system for two decades, prohibition has slowed the enterprise.

Studying and understanding the relationship between cannabis and the endocannabinoid system is burdensome; everything from obtaining raw plant material to sharing information to securing funding is difficult. The mainstream media, rabidly anticannabis until very recently, has passively collaborated by casting a derisive eye on the science. Mechoulam has been called "Dr. Pot," and has been described as holding "a PhD in getting high." Bill Clinton's drug czar, Barry McCaffrey, once maligned cannabinoids as "Cheech and Chong medicine." His ignorance can almost be forgiven, since most Western physicians are also unaware of the ECS for the simple reason that it isn't taught in medical schools. This is in part due to the medical profession's anticannabis bias, but also because it's impractical for medical schools to educate students about a bodily system that can be treated only by illegal compounds.

At the same time, the US government has owned patent number 6,630,507 on cannabinoids as antioxidants and neuroprotectors since 2003. These unstudied compounds are so promising that Julius Axelrod, the Nobel Prize–winning biochemist who discovered dopamine pathways in the brain, is one of the patent's three signatories. The logic of the US government owning a patent on a schedule I drug, which it defines as having *no therapeutic value*, is beyond tortured. When it comes to cannabis, science and government policy exist in parallel universes.

Mechoulam, now in his mid-eighties, is gracious about this lapse of logic, and he recognizes the larger concerns and political pressures at hand. "When insulin was discovered in the early 1920s, it was in the clinic within six months. When cortisone was discovered some 70 years ago, it was in the clinic within two years, and it became very successful. No one has given anandamide or 2-AG to a human because the toxicology research—which costs millions of dollars [and is the first step in all clinical trials]—hasn't been done yet. I've asked the National Institute on Drug Abuse many times—I begged them actually, please do it—because a [pharmaceutical] company will not, and obviously an academic cannot do it. It's a technical thing. It's something that quite obviously should be done, yet it has not been done."[3]

How long will it take to do safety trials on a compound that has been used without incident for thousands of years by millions of people and which mimics a compound produced by our own bodies? I wondered aloud.

"Another decade."

Science has done a good job of describing how these endogenous brain chemicals communicate with receptor cells on the microscopic level. But science has not effectively conveyed what cannabis's ability to mimic the chemicals naturally produced by our brains might mean for medicine or for humanity—poets and philosophers traditionally do a better job at that. This is another reason I've come to Israel: to get a handle on the big picture potential of this plant. Among the handful of scientists who understand these compounds on the molecular and macro levels, Mechoulam heads the pantheon.

Researchers in this small field agree that cannabinoids regulate five basic functions of existence: relaxing, eating, sleeping, forgetting, and protecting our organs. But there is more to this picture than meets the eye, and Mechoulam is beginning to weave the various strands into a coherent theory of how cannabinoids differentiate human beings from every other species.

Take, for example, forgetting. While most people view forgetting as a memory lapse, Mechoulam points out just how important it is for our brains to edit the torrent of sensory data that assaults us daily. Think about a simple task such as driving on a highway. If we couldn't block out the sights, sounds, smells, and sensory input coming at us from multiple sources, we'd be paralyzed by overstimulation, unable to drive—and miserable. Similarly, forgetting is crucial to treating incapacitating illnesses like post-traumatic stress disorder (PTSD), in which painful memories seem to lodge in the mind and haunt sufferers, often for the rest of their lives. In Mechoulam's view, certain chemicals lock in memories, but cannabinoids help unlock them. Informal studies with Holocaust survivors, plus dozens of my own interviews with Vietnam War veterans, indicate that cannabis effectively eradicates harrowing memories that turn sufferers into zombies. No other medicine does this.

Without anandamide we might not ever be able to get over trauma, phobias, neuroses, or chronic pain. Pain is one of the most difficult experiences to recall. It's impossible to remember pain the way you re-create other emotions, and that's for an evolution-arily adaptive reason—think about how many single-child families there would be if women couldn't forget the agony of childbirth. Cannabinoids allow us to forget and move on.

There are other ways that cannabinoids may enable human beings to thrive. This is an odd concept for many of us because it doesn't fit contemporary health-care models in which medicines are used only to treat illnesses; instead, cannabinoid molecules appear to be crucial to maintaining health and wellness. The distinction is profound, and further clues were unearthed in a 1990s study on the effects of cannabis on newborns by Dr. Melanie Dreher, the dean of nursing at Rush University Medical Center in Chicago.

Dreher traveled to Jamaica to investigate how the Roots Daughters, a group of rural and largely impoverished Rastafarian women, use ganja to maintain appetite, help them rest, and allay nausea when pregnant. These women also serve a mild ganja tea to their families as a daily health tonic—when you're poor (or just smart), forestalling illness is less expensive than treating it once it hits.

Dreher followed thirty Roots Daughters and their babies for five years, until the children were old enough to enter school. Her results showed that infants whose moms smoked ganja socialized and made eye contact more quickly and were also easier to engage than the babies of nonsmokers. The ganja kids were not developmentally disadvantaged. In fact, the five-year-old children of smokers scored higher on tests for verbal ability, and for motor, perceptual, and quantitative skills, and memory and mood.[4] "Given what everyone else was finding at the same time, we thought [our findings] were pretty darned interesting and a little counterintuitive," said Dreher.

Dreher's findings, while confined to a small sample group, contravened everything that "experts" had pronounced about the plant's deleterious effects on kids. Yet they were published in 1994 to resounding silence. In the wake of that silence, Dreher applied to the National Institute on Drug Abuse for additional funding to return to Jamaica to follow the same children at age ten, but her request was denied. Instead, NIDA continued to commission more studies on rats, from which researchers concluded that exposure to excessive quantities of cannabis (up to sixty joints a day) in the womb might harm the brain, lower IQ, and damage "executive function." The same dire warnings are still being trumpeted today, all of which Dreher calls "red herrings that drag us from more important findings. Why not look at school performance, social interaction, prenatal examinations, or if these kids are participating in sports or using more alcohol than their peers?" she asks. "This is the ultimate outcome—how we live our lives— not some red herring called 'executive function.'"[5]

A few years later, and completely independently, Dr. Ester Fride found physiological corroboration of Dreher's findings. Fride, a neuroscientist and colleague of Mechoulam's who died in 2010, was investigating the ways cannabinoids affect a newborn's development by testing them on rats that had had their endocannabinoid systems "knocked out" genetically. Her science showed that without functioning endocannabinoid systems, newborns failed to suckle or begin maternal bonding. Further investigation showed that endocannabinoids are essential to a baby's ability to thrive as it grows.[6] Even more surprisingly, she discovered that cannabinoid receptors develop extremely slowly in babies, which is why young children don't experience psychoactivity when they take cannabis. This observation had been anecdotally reported in nineteenth-century medical reports, which noted that children could tolerate mighty doses of cannabis that would have left their parents reeling.[7]

Dreher asks: "Is it an evolutionary accident that the two activities necessary to sustain life and perpetuate the species are eating and sex and that cannabis makes both things more pleasurable?" Or, as Dr. Allyn Howlett put it to Michael Pollan: All the things endocannabinoids do "are exactly what Adam and Eve would want after being thrown out of Eden. You couldn't design a more perfect drug for getting Eve through the pain of childbirth and helping Adam endure a life of physical toil." In other words, cannabinoids are chemicals that enable us to cope with the human condition.[8]

The more science uncovers about endocannabinoids, the more it seems that they are responsible for functions we once mistakenly attributed to other receptor systems. Those happy feelings known as a "runner's high," for example, were for decades assumed to be generated by endorphins flooding our brain. Today, researchers know that the runner's high results from endocannabinoids beaming signals to the brain's reward centers. Evolutionary biologists suspect that these pleasure responses are also adaptive: they guide us innately to knowing that aerobic exercise is beneficial.

In 2012, three American biologists examined how exercise influences the endocannabinoid levels of two naturally athletic species, humans and dogs, and then compared the results with studies of more-sedentary creatures, ferrets. Blood samples taken after a brisk run showed that concentrations of anandamide spiked in the dogs and humans, while the ferrets showed no changes at all. In humans, higher levels of anandamide also correlated with the runner's high.

Why? One explanation comes from Greg Gerdeman, an evolutionary neurobiologist at Eckerd College in Florida. Exercise was not an option in the fields and forests where our hunter-gatherer ancestors lived. Daily life required sweat: walking for hours to gather fruit, nuts, and roots; foraging for firewood; and running miles a day in pursuit of prey. In prehistoric times, hunters were, in fact, endurance runners. Before they invented spears or weapons, our predecessors pursued prey on foot until the animal gave out. The spike of anandamide that encouraged our ancestors to pursue dinner and stay active was an evolutionary advantage that allowed them to survive.[9]

Gerdeman hypothesizes that specific exercises might help activate particular cannabinoid receptors to alleviate depression or shift one's mood.[10] Another study indicates that some lucky people may be less prone to anxiety because their brains produce higher levels of anandamide. Think about that: resilience to anxiety may have nothing to do with the vague and perhaps mythical qualities we call being "strong" or "tough." It may have more to do with winning the genetic sweepstakes.

For fifty years, Mechoulam has sidestepped the moralistic debates about the benefits or harms of using cannabis and has avoided adjudicating on the wisdom or folly of legalization. Legalization "is a social decision, not a medical one," he has said. "Our society says 'yes' to tobacco (although millions die of it), or high alcohol drinks (although millions die of them or become addicts), or high-stakes gambling (although it may ruin families). When our society says 'yes' to recreational cannabis it will join the above, irrespective of anything."[11]

To him, cannabis is a brilliantly packaged factory of compounds that raise all sorts of questions that can be answered only through deeper investigation. Of the five basic functions the ECS performs, Mechoulam's researchers are largely focused on using cannabinoids to help the body protect itself from injury and repair itself more quickly after damage occurs. Before he and I met, he introduced me to his A-team, many of whom are over sixty-five, have been studying cannabinoids for decades, and are the most respected experts in this field. Most of them have never seen, touched, or smelled the plant. I tell you this because it's commonly assumed that people who study cannabis are stoners or, at the very least, advocates. Be assured that this is not the case with Mechoulam's team.

Professor Itai Bab leads a ten-person team that's investigating the ways cannabinoids heal broken bones.* When we meet in his cramped and dark office surrounded by towers of books, I explain that I've come to Israel because American cannabinoid research is so impoverished—few doctors in the United States know of his work.

"That's because the US in general doesn't know much about the rest of the world," he tells me. "Americans read American journals and go primarily to meetings in the US. And it's not only in the cannabinoid world."

Bab is by nature a skeptic—a fine quality in a scientist, especially one who is working in the politically charged realm of cannabis science. Even though his very first presentation to the International Cannabinoid Research Society won him a five-minute standing ovation, he is less convinced than his colleagues of cannabis's great promise. "This is a small, noisy field," he warns, "full of big, hot political pressures." The half smile on his face indicates that he enjoys a certain amount of friendly opposition.

Bab's investigations of animals show that CBD doesn't hasten the healing of broken bones, but it does help them heal more strongly. It also protects the skeleton against age-related osteoporosis. "It's too early to know when to administer CBD or what the correct dose is," he says. "We injected it daily starting one day after a fracture for eight weeks. At the eight-week point we saw this bone-strengthening effect."

* Sadly, Professor Bab died shortly after my interview with him.

Is it possible that CBD can possibly fortify the brittle, withering bones of the two hundred million women around the world
stricken with osteoporosis?[12] As if he can see the cogs in my brain
churning, the professor moves to dampen my enthusiasm. He's
been down this road before.

"Yes, it was all very exciting at first, but journalists always take
this one step too far. There are two big gaps in our knowledge to
date. One is dose. So many different strains of cannabis make it
difficult to know the [exact] constituents, and this makes it difficult
to prescribe." This is true with any plant-based medicine, but it's
especially problematic with cannabis, which manufactures, at last
count, over seven hundred compounds. Nor has there ever been
a large-scale study that addresses adverse reactions. To illustrate,
he walks me through an abbreviated history of another so-called
miracle cure.

Rimonabant was a drug that was developed when one clever
scientist had the idea to synthesize a THC analogue to block the
receptors that ignite the munchies. A drug that reduces appetite
and helps overweight patients shed pounds? The French company
Sanofi-Aventis recognized the appeal—and the enormous profit
potential—and rushed the drug to trials.

Rimonabant worked—for a while. In trials that lasted two years,
people's cravings for food, not to mention alcohol, cigarettes,
and cocaine, all diminished, and the drug was approved for use
in Europe. But once people began using it for a longer period,
they reported feeling morbidly depressed or plagued by suicidal
thoughts. It was eventually discovered that while Rimonabant
makes you eat less, it also blocks receptors in all of the brain's
pleasure centers. Rimonabant had the opposite effect of cannabis:
it was a joy killer and a profit killer, and Sanofi-Aventis quickly
made it go away.

I take Professor Bab's point, but other qualified researchers
have confidently told me that the long-term effects of whole-plant

cannabis are about as worrisome as those of caffeine. "Overdosing" on pot isn't deadly, nor has it ever been linked to any long-term illness. I repeat Lester Grinspoon's contention that, in very practical terms, cannabis has passed the largest human trial ever with flying colors.

"I think this argument is based on romantic reasoning," Bab counters. "It's nice to get a little stoned. Food, music, sex are better . . . it's a terrific world . . . you don't die immediately. But it's lack of knowledge that contributes to this romantic attitude. Who knows what happens after ten or twenty years of use? Maybe all that euphoria turns to depression. Who knows why you vomited? What I'm saying is that in the twenty-first century, we should not use anything where we're not sure of the long-term effects."

Spoken like a scientist who believes that false hope is the enemy of truth. Indeed, many pro-cannabis folks who proclaim pot a panacea for every illness would do well to employ some of his skepticism. But my concern is different: What happens to those who are suffering while science grinds on? Shouldn't they at least have access to a plant that, to the best of our knowledge, has never caused any long-term complications?

"Look," he says, "we know it's anti-inflammatory. It doesn't have the highest potency, which is good because potent drugs have potent side effects—and we are just starting to understand that inflammation is the beginning of many age-related diseases.

"But let's put everything in perspective. There are many important systems in the body, and this is a small portion in the scientific world. At the American Heart Association, thirty thousand people show up for meetings. In neuroscience, twenty to thirty thousand. Bones are small, about four to five thousand. The main cannabinoid conference, the ICRS, has four hundred attendees. So cannabinoids are very, very small. They're not that important in medicine or in life. The benefits are OK, but not earth shattering.

"Even if my dreams come true it will not change the world."

After a half hour, the skeptical professor admitted that can-nabinoid research could maybe lead to important drugs or medicines—"A few, not many." Other scientists, most of whom have never used the plant with patients, have been similarly in-credulous. Because cannabis doesn't fit neatly into established scientific paradigms, they mistakenly suspect it is little more than a placebo that fools patients into thinking they feel better because they're high. That argument baffles me for two reasons: One, CBD isn't terribly psychoactive; it doesn't make users so high that they misread their bodily sensations. Two, most medicines, with the ex-ception of antibiotics that kill infections, are supposed to make you feel better. Isn't that the point?

The one exception to this, Bab granted, could be the way CBD ameliorates traumatic brain injury. "Esther will tell you more about that."

Professor Esther Shohami has published 244 papers on the ways cannabinoids protect the brain from injury in sports, war, car accidents, and strokes. Even though one botched clinical trial indicated otherwise, her research demonstrates that cannabis may be an excellent guardian of our gray matter, probably the best pro-tection we have to date.

Estimates show that 1.7 million Americans suffer traumatic brain injury, or TBI, each year. Of them, 125,000 are left in a sort of cognitive purgatory, in which some brain functions work nor-mally and others go dangerously haywire. When cannabinoids are injected into the bloodstream immediately after a brain injury, they have been shown to lessen paralysis, memory impairment, and all manner of cognitive defects. "The improvement is not marginal, it's significant," Shohami says.

Here's why: When the head sustains a blow (and it need not be one violent whack; a series of concussions on a football field can be just as injurious), the brain rattles against the skull. This jangling sets off a tsunami of glutamate, a toxic substance that wipes out neurons, leaving slurred speech, shaky movements, and dementia in its wake. This toxic surge occurs one to four hours after injury, and if left unchecked it is more harmful than the initial physical blow. Until the advent of endocannabinoids, there was no way temper the glutamate release.

Shohami has shown that cannabinoids injected within this four-hour window diminish the glutamate flood and stop the body from attacking itself. More remarkably, they stimulate healing by recruiting new stem cells to become brain cells. This last finding is crucial. Until recently, scientists believed that the brain stopped generating stem cells at birth. But today we know that they lie dormant, on alert, as it were, waiting to be marshaled into action. "Endocannabinoids direct the stem cells to become brain cells and contribute toward recovery," Shohami says.

In 1998, the Israeli pharmaceutical company Pharmos injected a synthetic CBD into the bloodstreams of sixty-seven Israeli soldiers shortly after they had suffered head trauma. Recovery rates were impressive, so Pharmos expanded the trials to other countries. But when researchers in Poland tried the same experiment, they couldn't replicate the results. What happened?

One of Shohami's key insights was that cannabidiol must be administered shortly after injury to prevent the glutamate storm from rampaging. In Israel, geographic distances are tiny, so getting the drug to the patient quickly was simple. But in places where the distance between the accident and hospital was larger, the glutamate reaction had advanced too far by the time CDB was administered. "Some of the patients were treated eight hours after the damage, and that was too late," Dr. Manuel Guzman, a biochemist at Complutense University in Madrid and a leading cannabis cancer researcher, told me. "It is essential with trauma to get to the hospital soon. If the wait time lasts longer than two or three hours, then damage is usually irreversible." Many other cannabinoid researchers have echoed his conclusion.

When the results couldn't be replicated, Pharmos pulled the plug on the trial. One failed clinical trial typically scares away other companies from investigating new drugs—the expense, insurance, and red tape are formidable—even if the flaw is in the design of the experiment and not the drug.

Shohami maintains her belief in the protective power of cannabinoids. "These compounds are very potent with TBI, and at the moment there is nothing else for this injury. If cannabidiol is taken for development by a company, I believe it would benefit these patients. Besides," she adds, "I think it is amazing that the body has the ability to protect itself and that we can give it something to enhance that mechanism."

At the moment, cannabinoids are potential wonder drugs for treating other illnesses, including diabetes and certain forms of heart disease—"potential" being the operative word.

Early-stage research shows much promise. But until the large double-blind, placebo-controlled studies that are the gold standard of pharmaceutical research are conducted, no proof can be established. Cannabinoids have never failed the test of proof; the test of proof has never been applied.

The potential to stanch the flow of traumatic brain injuries is especially significant for soldiers and other types of modern warriors, such as professional athletes. Shortly after I returned from Israel, five thousand retired players sued the US National Football League for $1 billion in damages because of the brain injuries they had sustained during their careers. They accused the league of hiding the dangers of repeated concussions and the harrowing degenerative brain diseases that result from them.[13] Repeated head blows leave one in three football players eight to fourteen times more vulnerable to early-onset Alzheimer's and dementia than the general population, and symptoms set in as early as age forty.[*] One player was discovered supergluing his rotten teeth to his gums to hold them in place. Another was found urinating into an oven thinking it was a toilet. Yet another was zapping his back with a Taser gun to quell his relentless pain.[14] The issue was thrust into the spotlight when a former Chicago Bears defensive back, Dave Duerson, committed suicide by shooting himself in the chest so he could leave his addled brain to science for dissection. His goal was to force the NFL to recant its long-standing denial about this illness.

Concerned coaches have called for a more-protective helmet design, but this is no more effective than wearing high socks to prevent a broken leg. The league also toyed with fining players who play too rough, but that caused a backlash among fans who enjoy watching their heroes going head-to-head. Cosmetic fixes won't solve the problem. Nothing can repair a brain that has turned to mush.

There has been some Internet chatter about the NFL backing research into cannabinoids to protect players. But at this point such research sounds more like fantasy football than the pro leagues, who are unlikely to challenge the status quo by suggesting that a treatment based on an illegal substance might actually help their wounded warriors.

But Dr. Ethan Russo suggests that CBD could be given as a low-dose preventative medicine, if, of course, it weren't illegal, especially as it has no side effects. "Could low doses of CBD on a regular basis significantly blunt this problem?" Russo asks. "The answer is yes, quite possibly"—but until it is removed from schedule I, we'll never know.

---

[*] Until 2012, the league denied that any brain injury resulted from football.

WHY IS CBD ILLEGAL?

The United States is pretty much alone is placing CBD in schedule I, and this is the result of a historical aberration rather than science. In 1969, Dr. Timothy Leary won a lawsuit against the government that basically threw out the legal underpinnings of the 1937 ban on cannabis. For one year there was no federal law that deemed cannabis illegal. It made no practical difference, however, because by then every state had its own law.

In 1970, Nixon appointed the Shafer Commission to determine what to do about cannabis. As a placeholder until the report's findings were released, Congress passed the Controlled Substances Act and put cannabis (and all of its constituents, whether psychoactive or not) in schedule I. When Shafer recommended decriminalizing pot and making it available for medical use, Nixon rejected the findings even before the report was printed. So the schedule I placeholder was grandfathered into law even though the scientific basis for that classification was refuted at the time and multiple times since.

If you are under the misapprehension that science occurs in gleaming white labs with sleek, modern equipment, let me assure you that Mechoulam's beige world hasn't seen a decorator, let alone a paint job, in forty years. My conversation with the father of cannabinoid research was sporadically drowned out by electricians tearing out the ceiling in the hallway to replace decades-old wiring. I had expected more distinguished surroundings for such a highly decorated researcher, but science is a painstaking affair, not a showy one, and scarce pennies are rarely spent on shiny surrounds. Most scientists would probably be suspicious of showy digs anyway.

Once the banging subsides I kick off our conversation by explaining my journey through the new world of cannabis. "Yes, it is a new world," he says. "Four or five thousand years. Not too old." Gentle admonition noted.

"But for a plant that's been around so long we seem to know so little about it."

"We know quite a bit about it," he counters. "It was used in the black populations and by jazz musicians who said that they couldn't play their jazz unless they were under the effect of cannabis, which probably has some truth. What we don't know, what no one has looked into, is whether it causes any change in the *emotions* that make it better for musicians."

At the time that statement washed over me. Only when later reviewing my tapes did it became clear that he was talking about the potential power of endocannabinoids to affect the emotional center from which artistic expression arises. Instead, I moved on to the less savory topic of my own vomiting and asked: If cannabis is so effective in treating nausea, why can it sometimes trigger the opposite reaction?

It has a lot to do with dose, he explains. A large amount can cause an entirely different response than a small one, "and it is probably individually determined." Everyone has a different susceptibility, probably because our endocannabinoid systems vary. "The first and only time we gave it to people about fifty years ago, my wife made a cake and put ten milligrams of THC in each piece of cake. Five of our guests took the cake with THC and five took the placebo. The placebo had no effect, but all of those who took THC reacted differently. My wife felt a little bit high. She sat in her chair. Another said he felt nothing but every fifteen seconds he started talking, *pa pa pa*. Another didn't stop talking for two hours—he was a member of Parliament so it accentuated what he knows—and the fifth one had an anxiety reaction. So same dose, five different reactions."

Every few months, it seems, new reports come out associating overuse with schizophrenia. Is this fact or is this propaganda?

It depends on what part of cannabis you're talking about, Mechoulam responded. "We gave CBD to a schizophrenic girl in Brazil who displayed no psychotic symptoms as long as she got CBD orally. We couldn't do clinical trials—it takes a lot of money. In 2012, a German group reported that CBD is an extremely good antischizophrenic compound, as good as the drugs being administered today, with one exception: the potent antipsychotics given today cause nasty side effects and CBD does not. In large doses they found that CBD enhances anandamide concentrations in the brain. There are a lot of things anandamide does, all of them essentially positive."[15]

As he's speaking, Mechoulam prints out a chart that lists the dizzying number of illnesses in which the ECS system is somehow involved. In addition to the obvious suspects, the list includes stroke, morphine dependency, Parkinson's disease, Huntington's disease, neurodegenerative disorders, epilepsy, cancer, diabetes, osteoporosis, inflammatory bowel disease, psoriasis, arthritis, and seizure disorders. It also includes so-called untreatable illnesses such as chronic hiccups, a torturous affliction that can persist for months, and Tourette's syndrome, a neurological disorder characterized by repetitive, involuntary movements and weird vocal tics.

My face must indicate incredulity because Mechoulam interrupts himself to ask, "You don't believe me?

"George Kunos, one of the heads of the National Institutes of Health in Washington, recently wrote that the endocannabinoid system is apparently involved in almost *all* major diseases of the body.[16] This is a very strong statement because Kunos is an excellent scientist—Hungarian, you know—and because there are very few compounds that act on everything."*

What I'm thinking is, *Pharmaceutical companies are tripping over themselves to find new drugs that heal without killing people.* But what I say is, "If anandamide or other cannabinoids do all of these marvelous things, why haven't you patented a synthetic version?"

"We did. But by the time we got people interested the patent was ten years old, and then it was too late. A patent is only good for twenty years, and by the time a pharmaceutical company completes trials they'll have just a few years left to make back their investment. And so, there we are."

If I were Mechoulam, I'd probably feel like a lone man screaming in a forest whom no one hears. Isn't he frustrated, I ask, by the political and legal hurdles that have caused his field to progress so slowly?

His warm, questioning eyes greet me with a gaze as if to say, you poor, naive layman. "Why should I be frustrated? It depends on where you start. I'm a pessimist. I didn't expect anything to happen. The first prize I got was for best publication by a young scientist at the Weizmann Institute in the 1960s. A committee made that decision, but the chairman of the academic board thought I should be doing something else and did everything to kick me out."

I don't believe he's a pessimist. Mechoulam's investigations and

---

*In May 2013, George Kunos and Pál Parcher wrote in the *FEBS Journal* that "modulating endocannabinoid system activity may have therapeutic potential in almost all diseases affecting humans, including obesity/metabolic syndrome, diabetes and diabetic complications, neurodegenerative, inflammatory, cardiovascular, liver, gastrointestinal, skin diseases, pain, psychiatric disorders, cachexia, cancer, chemotherapy-induced nausea and vomiting, among many others."

insights have blazed this trail for the last half century. Pessimism doesn't fuel such single-focused dedication.

Curiosity does.

"Our brains produce two hundred to three hundred anandamide-like compounds, most of which no one has looked at. When you sit around with your friends, are you a photocopy of any of them? If I see my granddaughter running toward me, I feel happy. Why is that?" What he is asking is: Could cannabis be the chemical link that translates the objective reality of the child rushing toward him into the subjective feeling of happiness?

And then he reveals his big theory: "Why the hell is the body making this many compounds at the same time? Why doesn't it make just five compounds? We have two to three hundred anandamide-like compounds in our brain, and their levels and ratios are different. Is it just possible that the interplay of these compounds causes the differences in our personalities or has something to do with our psychological setup? We know almost nothing about the chemistry of our personalities. Our body produces compounds that regulate every physiological system, so why not our personalities? People discovered the major neurotransmitters in the 1930s and '40s, but here's a new system, and we should expect new things to be discovered."

Of course, this is simply a theory, but it's as riveting as it is inconceivable that something in this much-maligned plant could actually hold the key to unlocking the brain chemistry of emotions.

According to Ethan Russo, it's generally wise to heed Mechoulam's hunches. "A great scientist doesn't just figure out the how, but the why, and Mechoulam excels at this. To outsiders it may seem that these three hundred chemicals he's discussing are extraneous, but one of his guiding principles is that nature doesn't waste energy. There must always be a rationale behind the energy the body expends to make these things, and his passion has been to uncover that rationale."

Or, in the words of this self-identified pessimist, "The anandamide story may continue well beyond what we know today. Why are we sorry? Angry? Happy? I don't know, but one has to prove a theory. It's not a big deal. For the next fifty years I need something to do."

Chapter 6

THE WORLD'S LARGEST HUMAN TRIAL

Tel Aviv, Israel

Not only is Israel the nucleus of cannabis research, but the country also has twenty thousand human subjects participating in the world's largest state-run medical cannabis program. Over the last two decades, this program has won support from citizens, government officials on the right and left, and religious leaders (who have, incidentally, declared cannabis kosher). "In Israel, the government takes a role in ensuring quality and safety of the product, and supports research to further the understanding of the plant's medical benefits," said Amanda Reiman of the Drug Policy Alliance. "In the US, the government has actively prevented research from taking place and has threatened municipalities that attempt to regulate quality and safety with criminal prosecution." Seeing this program in action turned me into a believer about the power of medical cannabis once and for all.

The program sprouted up in 1995, when a subcommittee in Parliament recommended that the government allow the severely ill to have access to medicinal cannabis. The decision was not taken lightly. Israel moved cautiously, fearing that it might threaten its relationship with the United States or violate the United Nations Single Convention on Narcotic Drugs. That treaty, ratified by 185 nations in 1964, aimed to stop drug trafficking across borders "by coordinated international action" and bound individual countries to outlaw "narcotic" drugs (yes, cannabis was defined as a narcotic) except for medical and scientific purposes. Article 49 of the treaty allowed countries to gradually phase out coca-leaf chewing, opium smoking, and other traditional drug uses, but insisted that "the use of cannabis for other than medical and scientific purposes must be discontinued as soon as possible."

But with Mechoulam at the bow of scientific study, and with cannabis representing a low-cost solution to so many medical problems that have no other remedies, Israel took cautious steps forward. At the start, only one doctor in the entire country was allowed to grant licenses, and he dispensed them stingily, granting only sixty-two over the course of ten years. Cannabis was also designated a medication of last resort, meaning that patients must have exhausted all other forms of treatment before being allowed to use it. The cash-strapped state was also unwilling to take on more work and cost, so it insisted that the first five licensed patients grow their own meds—a hurdle that quickly proved insurmountable, as desperately ill people are not good gardeners. The list of applicable conditions was initially limited to asthma, AIDS wasting syndrome, and vomiting and pain associated with chemotherapy. Today, the conditions are still restricted—unnecessarily so, say advocates, who also criticize the government for banning paraphernalia like bongs and grinders—but have been expanded.*

Patients now pay a fixed price of $100 per month regardless of how much cannabis they use. The starting dosage is 20 grams (0.75 ounce) per month, but patients can get more depending on their affliction—42 grams (1.5 ounces) is the average monthly dose. That price is inexpensive by Western standards—but key to the

---

*The expanded list includes chronic pain, orphan diseases (i.e., diseases and conditions that affect only a small number of people and for which few pharmaceutical drugs are developed), HIV, fibromyalgia, anorexia, multiple sclerosis, Parkinson's disease, malignant cancers, and Crohn's disease (but mystifyingly *not* irritable bowel syndrome).

program's success is the fact that two Israeli insurance companies partially cover reimbursement. (Holland and Israel are the only countries where insurance covers medical cannabis.)[1] A handful of public hospitals have even purchased Volcano vaporizers for patients who can't afford to buy them. Patients can request individual mouthpieces and balloons.

Today, twenty doctors can legally prescribe cannabis, and eight tightly monitored grows distribute it on-site, through home deliveries, and in small dispensaries and hospitals. Interestingly (and smartly), all patients must undergo training about which strains and which forms—baked goods, joints, oils, or tinctures—best treat their conditions before starting treatment. They are also advised on how to optimize dosages, reduce side effects, and monitor potential drug interactions. "It doesn't matter if you've used it for forty years, you get the same training as someone who's never touched it," says Mimi Peleg, who directs cannabis training at the state's largest distribution center, MECHKAR. "People always start out laughing at me, but by the end of the training they're not laughing anymore. They're grateful. I show them how they're probably wasting ninety percent of the cannabis they've been using. The average Israeli smokes with tobacco and never leaves the cannabinoids in their lungs long enough to be fully absorbed. You need a minimum of four seconds, especially with CBD, which takes longer to absorb." Note to US medical marijuana programs: because cannabis is not a "single bullet" approach to illness, and because strains vary widely from location to location, education is crucial. Effective treatment requires more than sending a patient to a pharmacy to pick up pills or to a dispensary to buy bud.

Still, the Israeli government didn't exactly embrace this program; until 2009, it treated it the same way it treats its Dimona nuclear reactor—by pretending it isn't there—and only 1,800 patients had enrolled. Officials didn't want Israel to be known as the Amsterdam of the Mideast, and they preferred experimenting with production and distribution without the eyes of the world watching. Most Israelis were unaware of their country's program until a documentary called *Prescribed Grass* aired on national television and blew the lid off that secret. For that, they have Zach Klein, the documentary's director, to thank.

Zach began exploring medical cannabis when his mom, Lea, was diagnosed with early-stage breast cancer. Over Friday-night Sabbath supper she broke the news to her family and explained the chemotherapy regimen she was embarking on. Strangely, she added, her oncologist had whispered something to her as she left the office: "Try to find some hashish. It will help you with the chemo." She fixed her gaze on Zach and asked, "Who here can find me some?"

Zack delivered a few grams to his mother, but Lea declined partaking. The antidrug commercials on Israeli television—very much like the Reagan-era "this is your brain on drugs" egg-frying-in-a-pan ads that blanketed US airways in the 1980s—still resonated, and she worried about the plant diminishing her mental acuity. So Zach tracked down Professor Mechoulam, who had recently been awarded the country's highest prize for scientific achievement, at a lecture and asked him, "Is it true that cannabis won't harm the brain? Does it really protect it?"

The professor flashed him a watery-eyed smile. "Didn't you hear my presentation?"

The evidence the professor laid out lit a fire under Zach, and he drove to his mom's apartment that night to share the news and a joint. A few puffs and her nausea abated; in time, sleep was restored. Then, in a stroke of bad luck, she broke her hip. The opiate-based pain meds she was prescribed sunk her into depression, so she switched to cannabis. Pain ameliorated, depression lifted.

Stirred by his mother's experiences, Zach set out to make a film about the common plant with uncommon healing properties. But there was little to shoot other than scientists synthesizing chemicals and injecting them into rats. Zach back-burnered the film, but his interest in the plant led him to Tikun Olam, the country's only cannabis farm at the time.

Tikun Olam is impressive on many levels, including its carefully crafted public image. Even its name, which in Hebrew means "healing the world through compassion, kindness, and justice," speaks to a higher purpose. It became internationally famous in 2012 by announcing it had engineered the first CBD strain that delivered all of the healing but without the "unwanted side effects"—that is, the high. In fact, Tikun Olam didn't originate the first CBD strain, but the media couldn't resist the story of a "highless" marijuana. Nor could it resist regurgitating the myth that the growing operation was started by Dorit Cohen, a biology teacher who retired to grow an herb farm in her home but switched to cannabis once she learned about its medicinal powers.

I met Dorit—she is a quiet, pleasant woman, but she is not the brains behind this operation. It was her son, Tsachi, who masterminded Tikun Olam's ascent from small grow of fifty plants in his family's home overlooking the farming village of Safed to the largest cannabis operation in the country—an eight-acre industrial garden of greenhouses, trimming machines, and different huts for baby and mother plants. Zach was so taken with Tikun Olam that he joined the operation. His first job was driving cured plants two hours away to Tel Aviv, where they were distributed to patients out of Tsachi's apartment.

Two notable aspects about the Cohens also struck me: they are an orthodox religious family, and Safed, where the operation is headquartered, is the center of Judaism's mystical Kabbalah sect. This didn't strike Israelis as odd, but the incongruity of Hassidic men trimming weed in their black hats, black coats, and side curls, davening before the plants, delighted me. In fact, farmhands play religious music for the plants (personally, I think the plants might

be happier with Bach or post-*Yellow Submarine* Beatles) and
there's a synagogue on the property where the community gathers
to pray. Rabbi Shimon Bar Yochai, a legendary Kabbalah mystic,
is buried on a nearby hill, where his spirit guards the farm from
harm.*

Thanks in large part to Sanjay Gupta's documentary *Weed*,
Tikun Olam's strains are today among the most recognized in
the world. Each is named after a dead patient. Eran Almog—the
namesake of a wedding dress designer who battled cancer for seven
years—supposedly contains a whopping 29 percent THC. Avidekel
was named for the father of one of Tikun Olam's founders; with 16
percent CBD and only marginal THC, it is a star among CBD
strains.

Tikun Olam provided Zach Klein with the setting and characters he needed to begin his film. By the time shooting began he
had also ascended to the role of Tikun Olam's minister of information. That position made him Israel's first legally designated
joint roller (he possesses a "license to roll a dangerous drug"); he
was subsequently granted a second license to chauffeur plants to
industry trade shows, where he would position them next to pharmaceutical companies' products and then educate passersby about
the medicine that grows in the ground and can't be patented.

Over two years Klein convinced patients and the country's top
scientists to participate in his film, and the narrative crystallized.
He sold a rough cut to Israeli's largest television network, Channel
2, but the network balked at including the story of one PTSD
patient in the final cut. His recovery was so extraordinary, they
said, no one would believe it.

---

* I was refused official access to the farm. The government once freely permitted
reporters to visit, but after the BBC, CNN, the Associated Press, Reuters, and
the *New York Times* descended on Tikun Olam in November 2012, media
access has been denied. Instead, I was treated to a Skype tour. Note to government
apparatchiks: digital technology renders travel bans irrelevant.

The patient in question was a policeman who had witnessed the 2002 Passover massacre, in which a suicide bomber disguised as a woman exploded a massive bomb in a hotel where 250 families had gathered to celebrate the Jewish holiday. This cop's unit was first on the scene, and the carnage—30 dead, 140 wounded, limbs strewn atop tables—was trapped so firmly in his memory that no anti-anxiety medication could eradicate it.

When he first skulked into the dispensary, this ex-cop wore his cap slung low over his eyes, as if hiding. He spoke in a hushed whisper and couldn't maintain focused attention. He hadn't worked in four years, had dropped his friends, and was barely speaking to his wife and family. He was quite literally missing in action. Zach handed the cop a joint but he brushed it away. "This is a drug."

"Your psychiatrist sent you here because this is the treatment of last resort," Zach reminded him. "There's nothing more after this."

Begrudgingly, the cop smoked half of the joint and then left. Ten minutes later a woman charged into the dispensary. "I'm his wife," she announced. "What have you done to him? For the last ten minutes he's been sitting in the car laughing. He hasn't laughed in years. *What's going on here?*"

The officer continued his cannabis treatment. A month later, his psychiatrist called Zach. "He's talking to his family. They went on holiday; he hugged his daughter; he even sat through a Passover Seder." He sent other referrals, but after the seventieth patient, the Ministry of Health clamped down and ordered him to stop. They were concerned that word would get out and that the demand for cannabis would exceed the supply.

I ask Klein why he thinks so many doctors are resistant to cannabis. He answers with a story about Ignaz Semmelweis, a nineteenth-century Hungarian gynecologist. In Semmelweis's hospital, women were dying of infections after childbirth. Semmelweis noticed that when he washed his hands before a procedure, fewer infections occurred, so he suggested that everyone in his department do the same. His colleagues derided him as crazy and eventually drove him out of the hospital. "This is the story of medicine," Zach concludes. "A lot of doctors are convinced they know everything. Others are so overwhelmed that new ideas, even simple ones, can be too much."[2]

Prescribed Grass aired November 19, 2009. The following day the Ministry of Health was barraged with so many calls it spun into crisis mode. At first it threatened to shutter Tikun Olam and import its supply of cannabis from Holland, but the Dutch rebuffed the Israeli request. Holland couldn't produce enough to satisfy a foreign market; besides, the cost would have been pro- hibitively expensive for average Israelis. The Israelis retreated and then sanctioned seven other grows to compete with Tikun Olam to meet the burgeoning demand. The program has since exploded and now serves over twenty thousand participants from all sectors of Israeli society.

Three months after the documentary aired, Zach received a distressed call from Inbal Sokorin, head nurse at the Haradim nursing home, one hour south of Tel Aviv. She had an extremely agitated patient with dementia whose family had just secured a cannabis license for her, but Inbal had no idea how to treat her. "I don't believe in this, but since you made this documentary why don't you come here and show us what to do?" she huffed.

They discussed the issues confronting her patients, but what they didn't discuss was her growing frustration with geriatric care in general. "I used to sit here and ask myself, 'What am I doing?'" she confesses to me once we've settled into her cubicle at the back of this surprisingly cheerful facility. "We were giving a lot of medication but there was a lot of suffering. We had to fight with patients to give them blood, to put in a feeding tube. By Jewish law you have to fight for life until the end, but I was asking myself, 'Why do we want them to live if they want to die?'

"Every day I'd come in and say 'Good morning' to one patient, and she'd growl, 'What's good about this morning? Last night I asked God to take me and now all I see is *you*.'" Inbal has a passion for her work that causes her avid, jet-black eyes to dance even when recounting its difficulties. The room gets palpably warmer when she smiles. But her conflict was real, she assures me. "I believe in nursing. I know I can help people and educate them. But we were fighting for life and no one was happy."

Zach presented Inbal with research findings about how cannabis can calm people with dementia, and then showed her how to store, administer, and dose cannabis flowers, all of which contravene the protocols of a traditional medical setting.[3] One doctor warned her against going forward. "Be very careful. All of the cannabis patients are going to end up psychotic. It's a very dangerous drug and you're going to have a big, *big* problem." But the initial reactions of a few patients proved him wrong.[4]

She introduced Zach to the dementia patient whom the staff had nicknamed Tiger because of her constant roar. Her antipsychotic medication, olanzapine (Zyprexa), was creating miserable side effects including spasticity, stiff limbs, and a constant twitching of the mouth.

Zach handed her a joint, but her unyielding hand muscles didn't allow her to grasp it. With Inbal's permission, Zach jerry-rigged a bong from a plastic water bottle (remember that old trick?), took a breath, and blew the smoke into Tiger's face. After two inhalations her screaming quieted. Zach asked for her hand and she gave it to him. "The anxiety and fear melted from her eyes," Inbal recalls. "I wouldn't have believed it if I hadn't seen it."

That night Inbal couldn't sleep. She was excited and confused. "I'm not religious, but if I were I would say that God spoke to me that night. And what he said was: 'I'm giving you hope, Inbal, but it's not going to be easy.'" Her approach to nursing was about to be upended.

Zach continued treating other patients at Haradim with cannabis. He secured a Volcano vaporizer and instructed the staff how to use it. One patient, Moshe Roth, became an international poster boy for medical marijuana thanks to his soul-stirring appearance in Gupta's *Weed*. A Holocaust survivor, Roth was tormented by nightmares, which made him so cranky and irritable that his marriage had all but disintegrated. One daily joint at eleven a.m. took away his fear and anxiety. Sleep returned, as did his wife, and he began to write and paint again (chickens are his theme. After he fled the Nazis he hid in the chicken coop of a French farmer for a year).

Another ninety-seven-year-old woman was so thin (seventy pounds) that she looked like a *shablul*, says Inbal, a snail, shrunken and coiled upon herself. She was refusing food, so she was being force-fed with a nasal tube, which was inserted into her nostril and threaded into her stomach. She felt imprisoned by this tube, and it was so painful the nurses were forced to restrain her hands to prevent her from yanking it out.

Instead, a few sprinkles of cannabis in her morning porridge stimulated her appetite so that her weight rose by almost half, to 105 pounds. Today she's off the feeding tube and is taking daily cannabis capsules to maintain her taste for food. Almost all elderly patients prefer capsules to smoking. "Nurses like them because they are easier to count out and store," says Inbal. "The elderly, they were born to capsules."

Inbal began tracking dosages, strains, and five conditions that commonly affect the elderly: spasticity, pain, agitation, loss of appetite, and depression (which includes trauma and Holocaust-related PTSD). She consulted with Hebrew University professors, who counseled her not to use THC for those who didn't enjoy feeling high. "Professor Mechoulam said to me that THC can affect short-term memory, which can be beneficial at times and detrimental at others. If they don't like getting high, they get CBD strains.

"But patients suffering from life, they get THC."

By tracking over one hundred patients, Inbal and her team confirmed the following:

- Cannabis, if administered gradually, produces no side effects. If there is no improvement, treatment is easily stopped with no withdrawal symptoms.
- Once appetite is stimulated, nutritional absorption rises to normal range. Swallowing is easier and spasticity is reduced.
- For acute conditions, smoke, not vapor, heals more powerfully.

Inbal knows that medical practitioners object to this last finding, but lung irritation concerns her less than providing the quickest analgesic relief.

"Of course, it's not good to smoke all the time, but if you have a strong, sudden pain and you smoke immediately"—she claps her hands, *chik chak*—"the pain is reduced.

"Physicians are doubtful, but sometimes I have to remind them that they are practicing the art of healing."

It's not difficult to see why traditionally trained doctors resist using an herb that is smoked or baked into a cookie. "Take one-quarter of this ginger snap twice a day" is not a prescription that many doctors feel comfortable making. Doctors prefer single bullets that come in finely dosed pills, and mistrust anything that hasn't passed the muster of clinical trials. The concerns are well founded, but Western medicine's unilateral approach to healing dismisses much of the knowledge that other cultures have accumulated for centuries. This dismissal is not because the other systems don't work, but more because Western medicine doesn't yet understand how they work. Acupuncture is a prime example.

The American Medical Association dismissed acupuncture as voodoo until scientists discovered that poking a needle into the skin commands an endorphin to shoot out an internal opioid that stops pain.[5] Our arrogance blinded us to centuries of statistical data culled from hundreds of thousands of patients that enabled Chinese doctors to map hundreds of pressure points. In dismissing centuries of data until they could "prove" it, Western physicians overestimated their own competence.[*]

Cannabis has been the victim of the same Western hubris, but since Israel now operates what is effectively the world's largest human trial, I figured there must be one specialist who had wide hands-on experience and could share anecdotal evidence about the drug's effectiveness. Luckily, Dr. Bereket Schiff-Keren picked up her phone when I called.

Schiff-Keren is a pain specialist who has prescribed cannabis to over 1,500 patients at Tel Aviv's massive Ichilov Hospital. Before I could get into her office, however, I had to first confront a highly agitated woman pacing the hall outside. She was rail thin and had a loosely draped scarf around her hairless scalp. When she learned that I was scheduled before her, her face creased with anxiety, so much so that I ceded my position in line.

Schiff-Keren later informed me that the woman, once a nurse in that very hospital, had terminal lung cancer and had refused

---

*Ethan Russo also points out that the key indication of good health in Ayurveda is balancing three elements: ether, fire, and water. These ideas can be easily translated to modern science but rarely are: Ether is the central and parasympathetic nervous systems; fire is thermogenesis, heat production, and metabolism; water refers to thermotaxis, heat regulation, and the formation of preservative fluids like synovia and mucus. They are more rudimentary terms for similar functions that science has vindicated as long-standing truths.

chemo and radiation. "She's going to die and she accepts that. But she also has terrible pain in her shoulder and chest where a massive tumor has invaded. Bales of narcotics didn't work, so she came to me for cannabis. Her oncologist didn't suggest it; she came of her own accord, and I'm treating her. She needed a refill and she wasn't happy about waiting."

Bereket has a quiet, gentle voice, but she's fearless, a quality that she demonstrates every day by driving her motorcycle through Tel Aviv's snarled traffic. For over a decade she has prescribed cannabis despite shifting government policies and the opprobrium of fellow doctors. "It has made me mistrusted by some of my colleagues," she says. "They think it's a kind of antiscience. Most doctors say we don't have enough evidence yet, but my patients need results. If there comes a woman like this, thirty-five kilos, you saw her? She was very thin. She wasn't happy about waiting, but she's not happy whatsoever. Pain makes you unhappy."

Herein lies the difference between a researcher and a healer. One lives strictly by the scientific method. The other sees human beings begging for relief, which makes denying treatment difficult, if not cruel.

Dr. Andrew Weil once told me that of all modern medicine's accomplishments, one of the least advanced areas is pain relief. Does Schiff-Keren agree with this assessment?

"Absolutely. It wasn't until World War Two that people became aware that pain is a disease of its own. Until then, pain was considered a symptom of something else and would be alleviated once the something else was treated. But John Bonica [an anesthesiologist, chronic pain sufferer, and the founding father of pain management] showed that pain is a disease of its own and that we should treat it *in addition* to the disease. And sometimes treating the disease is impossible. For example, ninety percent of incurable cancer patients live in pain. Alleviating it is the least we can do for the terminally ill."

What about those contending with the small pains of aging? Some naturopaths insist that you're not treating the source of the illness if you simply treat the pain.

"One of the things that keeps people alive is activity, and pain is very limiting. Enabling a person to go to work, have a family life, walk—walk!—sex, helps people to feel fulfilled in their lives. Chronic pain is common. Half of the people in their 'golden years' suffer joint or muscle pain, which is usually an outcome of degenerative joint diseases, osteoporosis, and those sorts of things. And now that life expectancy is getting longer, aging people want to be productive and enjoy their lives . . . and, I don't find cannabis treats only certain pains effectively. It treats every pain."

Every pain?

"Every pain." It works well with neuropathic pain, which causes a burning sensation along the nerve routes that makes your limbs feel as though they are on fire from the inside out, and with other pains as well. Unlike opiates, which block pain, cannabis seems to do two things: distract from it and alleviate it. And cannabis can be safely combined with other drugs: opiates, anticonvulsants, antidepressants, and anti-inflammatories. "Cannabis works with all four. It's not as strong as opiates, but every day I have patients telling me it works," Schiff-Keren says. "For me, the science is the cream on the cake. Patients telling me that it works, that counts more."

You are a very unusual doctor, I say.

"Yes, I am. Most doctors wouldn't say this. But fifteen hundred patients over ten years have taught me that cannabis is useful in most cases."

So at the risk of sounding facile, is cannabis a miracle medicine?

"It's a miraculous drug, yes. It's terrible because people are so prejudiced and frightened. But I stopped being frightened a long time ago, because the patients told me it worked."

Chapter 7

SNAKE OIL OR CANCER CURE?

Bodega Bay and Los Angeles, California

Being in Israel among this elite echelon of scientists made it clear that there is so much more within cannabis than meets the eye. It's no big surprise that the plant is useful for insomnia and pain, but bone healing? Traumatic brain injury? Diabetes? Just as the ancients observed that cannabis can treat dozens of unlikely illnesses, research, when it is allowed to occur, is elucidating the mechanism of how some of these things work. The initial results are far from conclusive, but the implications are mind-blowing—especially with illnesses such as chronic obstructive pulmonary disease (COPD) and cancer. Yes, lung disease and cancer, and no, I was not stoned when I wrote that last sentence.

Keep reading.

When Dr. Donald Tashkin, professor emeritus of medicine at the David Geffen School of Medicine at UCLA, began studying how cannabis smoke affects lung function in the 1990s, he presumed that it would lead to diseases similar to those elicited by tobacco, as both plants emit many of the same gases and tars when burned. In fact, cannabis actually contains 50 percent more benzopyrene—a cancer-causing agent—than tobacco does. But after three decades of NIDA-funded studies, Tashkin, now in his seventies, concluded that marijuana smoke doesn't contribute to COPD; it has the opposite effect, at least in the short term, drastically opening the airways to allow more air into the lungs. "The effect is comparable to a classical dose of an inhaled bronchodilator," Tashkin told me. "We also found that cannabis inhibited experimentally induced asthma."*

Another report published in the *International Journal of Cancer* in 2014 came to a similar conclusion. "Results from our pooled analyses provide little evidence for an increased risk of lung cancer among habitual or long-term cannabis smokers," the authors wrote.[1] And a 2009 Brown University study concluded that those who had a history of smoking weed possessed a much lower risk of head and neck cancers compared with subjects who did not.[2]

Make no mistake: smoking pot won't prevent lung, head, or neck diseases. But some element of the smoke appears to protect the lungs from damage. "THC is anti-inflammatory, and inflammation is necessary for COPD to progress," Tashkin hypothesizes.

"Marijuana contains the same carcinogens as tobacco smoke, so it should be a risk factor for lung cancer—but it isn't," Tashkin reiterated. "Studies in cell cultures and animal models have shown that THC inhibits the growth of glioma, thyroid, prostate, breast, and lung cancer—you name it. It causes cells to die off before malignancies develop, and there's less sprouting of new blood vessels that metastases need."

I have read those sentences repeatedly, and each time I come away scratching my head: Why hasn't this extraordinary information trickled down to the public, or at least been investigated

---

*Folk medicine has recorded this effect for centuries. Sitting in a cannabis smoke–filled room was long considered by Indian doctors to be an effective asthma treatment. What does appear to correlate with symptoms of bronchitis—namely cough, phlegm production, and wheezing—is the ash produced from smoking a joint (or any substance, for that matter). The ash accumulation can be somewhat ameliorated by using a bong, which traps ash in water, or a vaporizer.

in humans? Why have most mainstream news organizations ignored it? And why is NIDA spending millions more scrutinizing the "dangerous" aspects of secondhand cannabis smoke when the firsthand smoke might actually be beneficial?

The anti-inflammatory story is still unfolding; these protective effects of cannabis aren't seen only in the lungs. Gary Wenk, a professor of psychology and neuroscience at Ohio State University, has been studying aging and Alzheimer's disease in animals for over thirty years. He also tests experimental drugs for pharmaceutical companies, so he is one of the few Americans who possesses a DEA license to study the plant without having to run the bureaucratic gauntlet. Wenk and his entire research lab are so convinced of cannabis's power to slow the degeneration in aging brains that they come to work wearing T-shirts proclaiming ONE PUFF A DAY!

After a decade of experimental research, Wenk has concluded that a single daily puff bathes the brain in protective anti-inflammatories. Early evidence also suggests that people who smoked pot when they were younger have lower rates of Alzheimer's later in life. "These studies teach us that our brain's own cannabinoid system is necessary for us to maintain the processes that prevent the decline of our minds," Wenk told me from his office in Columbus, Ohio.

While one puff a day is no cure for Alzheimer's, there is a possibility that it might forestall its onset. "All we can say at this point is that it slows aging in the brain," says Wenk. "The real secrets to youth are out of our grasp, because the only known way to stop cells from oxidizing is to stop eating or breathing. THC crosses the blood-brain barrier [the tight scrim that guards the brain from most chemicals carried in the blood] and it has the same addiction rating as coffee," Wenk says. "So in the future we may be wearing patches that release these drugs all day. It has never made scientific sense as to why it is a schedule I narcotic, but science was never part of the law."*

The prohibition on controlled scientific studies plus willy-nilly state-by-state legalization has created a Wild West of medical cannabis use, ungoverned by federal laws or regulations. It is increasingly common for parents who have kids with seizure disorders or cancer to pick up and move to medical marijuana states, or to find treatment information from Facebook, which is riddled with public groups named "Cannabis Cures Cancer!" "Cannabis Oil Success Stories," or "CannaKids," and dozens of secret, invitation-only sites as well. Parents who venture into this uncharted territory are now known as "medical refugees," and they must usually operate without guidance. It's a lonely and vulnerable position to be in. They'll either get lucky and find a practitioner who knows what he or she is doing, or they'll run into some cannabis cowboy trying to make a buck—and if things go wrong, the results can be fatal.

*According to Wenk, who is also the author of *Your Brain on Food*, two additional nutritional changes can decelerate biological aging. First, restrict calories to 1,500 a day. "My rats on calorie-restricted diets, their hair doesn't fall out, their eyes don't fog with glaucoma, they get fewer tumors, their kidney's don't fail, they're smarter. . . . It's astonishing, there's so much evidence." But calorie restriction is no fun for humans. Instead, Wenk suggests inverting the way we consume food. "Eat everything—meat, gluten, dairy—but eat less of it and take your biggest meal at the beginning of the day," he says. His mantra? "Breakfast like a king, lunch like a prince, dinner like a pauper."

Second, eat more purple and dark-colored fruits and vegetables. They are both high in antioxidants, which scavenge the body for free radicals and put the brakes on aging. Certain orange foods, like turmeric, do the same. Indian elders have fewer incidents of Alzheimer's than their Western counterparts in part because they eat a lot of this anti-inflammatory spice that apparently also causes new brain cells to flourish. The NIH is currently investigating turmeric (but is still largely snubbing cannabis).

The first hint of the plant's tumor-terminating properties appeared in a 1974 Medical College of Virginia study launched to uncover the damages cannabis inflicted on the immune system. Instead of hastening the death of mice implanted with lung cancer, breast cancer, or leukemia, cannabis actually slowed tumor growth and extended the rodents' lives by one-third.[3] The DEA squelched that study for twenty years until some disgruntled researchers leaked a copy to the national media, which covered it halfheartedly.

Inquiry on cannabis as a tumor assailant went quiet until 2000, when Dr. Manuel Guzman, from Complutense University, injected cannabinoids into cancer cells in the brains of rats. The results were mind-boggling: cannabinoids triggered cancer cells to commit suicide—a condition known as apoptosis—and prevented blood vessels from feeding tumors. (The media ignored that story as well.) Guzman told me that further inquiry has shown that administering cannabinoids orally, especially in conjunction with the drug temozolomide, is more effective than injecting it into cells directly—cannabinoids are homebodies; they don't like to travel far when injected. But when taken orally, they surround certain types of tumors and annihilate them. Guzman, like all responsible researchers who don't want to be branded as pot docs or quacks, is quick to warn that cannabinoids have been studied only in a handful of tumors (brain, pancreatic, skin carcinoma and melanoma, and breast, primarily).* Moreover, cancer in mice (average weight: less

---

*Other researchers have learned that CBD is a potent inhibitor of breast cancer cells, metastasis, and tumor growth. Backed by NIH grants and with a license from the DEA, Dr. Sean McAllister, a biologist and pharmacologist at the Pacific Medical Center in San Francisco, reported in 2007 that cannabidiol kills breast cancer cells and destroys malignant tumors by switching off the ID-1 gene, a protein that appears to be a cancer cell conductor. This gene makes a brief cameo appearance during human embryonic development, but turns off thereafter. In breast cancer and several other metastatic cancers, the ID-1 gene gets turned on, causing malignant cells to invade. McAllister postulates that CBD's ability to silence the ID-1 gene could be a breakthrough anticancer medication.

than one pound) is far less complicated than it is in humans, which is why so many drugs that succeed in rodents fail in human trials.

That 1974 Virginia cancer study lodged in the mind of a Canadian man, Rick Simpson, back when the results were first announced. Over the years he wondered why he hadn't seen any more about it, but he assumed it was probably just another false lead in the battle against this cunning multiheaded scourge.

Then, twenty-three years later, after falling from a high ladder at work, Simpson suffered a brain injury that caused an earsplitting ringing in his ears, "about the same as having a lawn mower running in your living room," he said. "They tried every possible drug, but nothing worked. It got so bad I wanted to shoot myself."[4]

He was taking 1,000 milligrams of tegretol, a seizure-disorder drug with powerful side effects including terrible bouts of dizziness, loss of balance, and cloudy thinking. Desperate for a less overwhelming treatment, he asked his doctor about ingesting concentrated cannabis oil. His doctor tsked away the suggestion, so Simpson unearthed some old hippie recipes that used naphtha (aka paint thinner) to extract THC—just as the Denver dabbers use butane—and began to render the high-potency oils himself.

In a few weeks one daily droplet of oil quieted the ringing in Simpson's ears and also lowered his blood pressure and restored his health, he said. A few years later when melanoma patches appeared on his face, he covered them with the oil for four days before having the skin biopsied. The tests came back negative and Simpson began crowing about the "medicine that Big Pharma doesn't want you to know about."*

Taking his message wider, Simpson made a documentary,

---

*One popular conspiracy theory accuses Big Pharma of holding back cancer cures because there is more money to be made by not curing a disease but treating it partially. I'm less cynical—or more naive, depending on your point of view—about this industry's bad intentions. The mechanisms of many diseases remain elusive.

Run from the Cure, which demonstrated his extraction methods and recommended ingesting a walloping one gram a day of indica "hemp oil" to treat any and all of the two-hundred-plus varieties of cancer and tumors. This ninety-day one-treatment-fits-all regimen was to be followed by a maintenance dose of one gram a month for life. No one knows where Simpson came up with these dosages and protocols, but that didn't stop word from spreading. Today the Internet is crawling with videos of converts claiming to have cured their cancers with Simpson's oil. For those unfortunates for whom it doesn't work, well, we don't hear from them, do we?

In 2009, Canadian Mounties raided Simpson's house in Amherst, Nova Scotia, confiscating over 1,600 plants and issuing an arrest warrant for possession and trafficking. He was in Europe at the time and has been on the lam ever since, but his story has made "Rick Simpson Oil," or "RSO," a worldwide brand.

RSO offers hope—at times, false hope—to desperate people, many of whom forgo traditional treatment in favor of cannabis oil. I met one such fellow while reporting in Florida. He had a quarter-size patch of skin cancer on his leg but was uncertain if it was basal or squamous cell (the latter is more life-threatening) carcinoma or melanoma (the latter is scarier, as it more easily spreads to other organs), since he hadn't seen a doctor for diagnosis. He was painting homemade RSO on the patch with no treatment plan or medical supervision. He didn't believe in doctors (evidently he believed more in YouTube videos), and I cautioned him against the go-it-alone-pray-for-a-miracle approach.

Dr. Donald Abrams, surely one of the most procannabis oncologists in the United States, became very agitated when I asked him about the wisdom of replacing chemo or radiation with cannabis oil. "I find it sad and very devastating," Abrams told me. "The number of patients doing this is growing weekly, and it is nothing more than idealist utopian promotion that has some ugly unintended consequences." In other words, death.

Simpson doesn't sell oils and he gives the formula away for free. His goal, he says, is not profit but to spread the cannabis oil gospel to anyone who'll listen. No one knows if it works consistently or on what types of cancers, but thousands of people have sworn that it does. What is known is that squaring off with fatal diseases, especially with unproven, unregulated plant medicines of varying strengths and qualities, is risky. It's especially fraught in an un-regulated environment where there is no way to discern the quacks from the healers, as many voyagers into the new world of cannabis have discovered. Angela Ryder is one of them.

Around Thanksgiving 2012, Angela's ten-year-old son, Chico, came tearing out of the bathroom, excited about the alien growth in his throat. "Hey, Mom, look at this!" he said, opening his mouth to show her his engorged tonsil. He thought it was kind of cool. When Chico left, her husband, Paul Ryder (bass player of the English alt rock band Happy Mondays), turned to her and mouthed, "Cancer!" Angela rolled her eyes—Paul is a notorious hypochondriac. A virus had been snaking its way through the household, so it stood to reason that their youngest son was next in line.

Two weeks later, Angela spotted a lump protruding from the side of Chico's neck. It looked like a swollen gland, so they visited a nurse practitioner at the local CVS pharmacy. "You don't think it could be a tumor, do you?" Angela asked the nurse.

"Oh no."

"How can you be certain?"

"I've studied medicine. These antibiotics should do the trick . . ."

Five days later, the lump on Chico's neck had ballooned to the size of a bonbon, so they headed to the doctor, who prescribed a different antibiotic. But it's odd, he said, a throat infection doesn't typically appear on only one side of the throat—both sides are normally swollen. Let's run a test for mono.

"Good news!" the doctor's assistant said when she called in the results a few days later. "It's not mono!" But Angela was not relieved. Chico was now puking uncontrollably and his heart was racing. Something was very wrong. Next stop: a head and neck specialist who biopsied the tonsil for lymphoma.

When those tests came back negative the specialist was at a loss. We don't typically see tumors in the mouths of children, he said. People who smoke and drink, yes, but not in a child.

On December 20, Chico was still throwing up. He couldn't eat. Angela took him to another specialist, who took one look at the scan and called an oncologist stat. "Christ!" she said. "They biopsied the wrong tissue." There was a tumor hidden behind the tonsil, pushing it forward. The oncologist told Angela that the hidden tumor was so large it was constricting Chico's carotid artery, which was making his heart rate go haywire.

Eventually they identified the tumor as "rhabdo" (rhabdomyosarcoma), a malignancy of the soft tissue that affects just three hundred kids in the United States each year. It's so rare and a cure so unlikely to ever turn a profit that pharma companies have never developed a treatment for it. But there was no time to worry about such existential problems. The tumor was advancing so quickly that Chico's airway would be cut off in ten days. "We're starting chemo and radiation this afternoon," Angela was told.

It was her fiftieth birthday. She texted the news to her husband, rushed home, packed Chico's bag, canceled her party, and plunged forward into the dark.

After twenty-one days of chemotherapy, Chico's tumor shrank and his heart rate stabilized. But forty-three long weeks of chemo frazzled the nerve endings in his feet. Walking was so agonizing that he was confined to a wheelchair. Twenty-eight radiation treatments desiccated his salivary glands and left his mouth and gullet a rash of burning chancres. Swallowing was so excruciating that he was fed through a plastic feeding tube inserted into his stomach. His weight plunged almost in half, from 110 to 65 pounds. His white blood cells all but disappeared.

Angela was desperate to ease her son's pain, but the oncologist warned her that almost anything—herbs, supplements, even vitamins—could interfere with the treatment. Still, she couldn't just sit by and watch Chico suffer. A naturopath gave her glutamine to eliminate the mouth sores, and Marrow Plus, a blend of Chinese herbs, to stimulate white blood cell production, and after relentless lobbying, her oncologist agreed to try them. The glutamine healed his mouth and three days of Marrow Plus gave the white cells a lift from which they never fell. The oncologist was so impressed that he began mentioning both supplements to other patients.

The only treatment that didn't work was Marinol, the synthetic cannabis. Chico was relentlessly nauseated. When a home nurse recommended the real thing, Angela persuaded the oncologist to go along. But no irritating smoke, he insisted. Only edibles or vapor.

Angela had no experience with pot, so her first visit to a dispensary felt furtive and a little exciting, like sneaking into a sex shop. The workers laughed when she showed them the recommendation written on a proper prescription pad—"pot docs" in Los Angeles rarely submit anything so professional. The owner's mom had passed away from cancer so he was sympathetic and offered her a sample of every edible on the shelves. "See what he likes, then come back and get more," he said.

Confusingly, many of the packages weren't labeled for THC content, so at Angela's request the budtenders marked them for her: three stars for strong, two for medium, one for weak. Dosing in this manner was more than a little fraught, but in the end it didn't matter, because Chico couldn't hold them down anyway. Finally, a friend loaned them a Volcano vaporizer. Sucking on those giant vapor-filled bags provided her son with relief. "It was all completely baffling but I was going with the flow," recalls Angela.

The more Angela learned about cannabis as medicine, the more questions arose. She plowed through medical abstracts, but the language of chemistry was blindingly arcane and dull. Blogs were riddled with misspellings and typos, which didn't inspire confidence. The cannabis cancer "community" is also riven with internecine disagreement—true believers railed at Angela for "killing her son with chemo." The comments were hurtful, but she knew that the only thing that chemo killed was Chico's tumor. The side effects were rough but her son was alive.

On Facebook, Angela discovered cannakid celebrities like "Baby Sophie" and "Brave Mykayla," whose tumors shrank after using oil. At conferences, their parents take the stage to share their stories and beg the government to stop treating them as criminals, while their cannakids pose for photos with other sick babies. Angela was convinced that medical marijuana was worth a try, but she had no idea where to find oil to treat her son. None of these potent concentrates were available at her dispensary, so she turned to Facebook, where she learned that buying cannabis oil online was as tricky as trading penny stocks. Prices varied widely, as did quality.

One Facebook friend led Angela to a maker of good repute. The Ryders plunked down $3,300 for sixty grams, which arrived in three unlabeled plastic pots. The consistency was tarry, as it should be, but it reeked of alcohol, not the type you drink but the kind you keep under the sink. A slip of paper indicated that it had been tested at 80 percent THC—powerful stuff. She dipped a Tums into the oil and gave it to Chico. After a week he said two words she hadn't heard in six months: "I'm hungry." In the ensuing weeks, his appetite improved and things were looking up—until one member of her Facebook support group, Cannabis

Oil Success Stories, raised an alarm. The oil should smell fragrant and herbaceous, he warned her, and insisted she get it tested pronto. She did, only to learn that the oil was just 58 percent THC, one quarter less potent than advertised, and had been extracted with isopropyl alcohol.

"Isopropyl is rubbing alcohol. Is that bad?" she asked the chemist at the lab.

"It's poison," he responded. "Especially if it isn't all cooked off, which this isn't."

"Shit."

"Oh, and instead of sixty grams you only got forty."

Angela's initial foray was not unusual. Internet scams are growing as the word of this mighty oil spreads. One site is selling cannabis paste with the word "cure" in its name, made from industrial hemp of an unknown origin, taking advantage of confusing nomenclature in an unregulated market.

"It's a huge rip-off," says Dr. Russo. "The cost is exorbitant and God knows what toxins are in there because they use what's left over from hemp processing in countries like China or Romania and they don't have the same laws about pesticide use that we have. It's super-concentrated, so you're super-concentrating those toxins too. I don't trust any of it and I don't think anyone else should, either."

So many unwitting people have been duped by false or substandard "hemp oils" that Rick Simpson released a 2014 video warning about a group of "hemp oil hucksters" falsely claiming to be led by his grandson. They were creating fake domain names and MoneyGram accounts to which worried patients would wire money and receive nothing in return.

Finding quality medications proved elusive until the television host Ricki Lake, who was at the time producing a documentary about medical marijuana, led Angela to a Bay Area collective called Aunt Zelda's.

The very name conjured a character out of *Tales of the City* in Birkenstocks and a dirndl skirt stirring a cauldron of cannabis oil made from a recipe in the *Whole Earth Catalog*. But the owner, Mara Gordon, turned out to be more mad scientist than Anna Madrigal. Mara was a process engineer who had worked for Safeway and General Electric before a botched surgery and the twenty-six medications she was taking turned her into a chemical zombie. In 2011, a friend made her some magic brownies that eased her pain and brought her unexpected pleasures. Soon this fifty-something Jewish grandmother was devising her own recipes, blending flowers into her Aunt Zelda's carrot cake recipe (the large quantity of olive oil in carrot cake speeds cannabinoid uptake into the bloodstream) and sharing slices with other baby boomers whose bodies were falling apart.

It didn't take Mara long to see that the alternative-healing world of cannabis was ripe for reinvention. At a 2011 Hempcon conference, she surveyed heavy users about why they were smoking every day. The answers gave her pause. "This one had a football injury that never healed properly, that one was so painfully shy that he couldn't leave his house. So many people had medical issues but didn't know they were medical," she said. "They didn't want to be smoking all the time. They wanted their lives back." But all had the same question for her in return: "How do you make this oil?" So rather than delivering her prepared lecture, she told them to take out their pens and follow her instructions. "Like the adage says, 'Give a man a fish, you feed him for a day; teach him to fish and you feed him for life,'" she said.

Mara isn't warm and fuzzy. The most alternative aspect about her is that her career as a cannabis consultant makes her a healer in California and a criminal in most of the other United States. She has treated thousands of patients since 2010, and in Northern California, where cannabis oil is becoming an accepted adjunct to chemotherapy, more than a few oncologists refer patients to her.

Mara immediately switched up Chico's regimen, giving him CBD in the morning to lessen his mental fog and THC at night to get him to sleep. "Taking THC and CBD together for this illness is like having two accomplished cooks in the kitchen," she told me. "They get in each other's way." And then she made Angela toss the medicine made with isopropyl alcohol. "Why would anyone mix poison into this magic plant?" she asked.

Aunt Zelda's collective was nothing like the granola rustic village I had envisioned. It was far less exotic. The collective was housed in a condominium that backed onto a golf course in suburban Walnut Creek, about an hour north of Oakland, a sterile enclave of cul de sacs lined with minivans, straight out of the opening scenes of *Close Encounters of the Third Kind*.

On my first visit I found Mara and her husband, Stewart Smith, in their spotless galley kitchen decarboxylating (frying) a fragrant strain, aptly named Pepe LePeu, in organic coconut oil. The room smelled sweet and grassy, like a Thai restaurant in a hay field. Mara beams an infrared thermometer at the green mush, ensuring that it is heated to 219 degrees Fahrenheit, the ideal temperature to infuse the oil without degrading the cannabinoids, terpenoids, and flavonoids. Once the oil is bright green and the flowers are toasted brown, she announces that it is ready to be drained.

"How can you tell it's ready?" I ask.

"It's like matzoh balls. After a while you just sort of know when it's done."

Mara is part librarian, part compounding pharmacist, part strict disciplinarian, who discovered that she has a passion for treating cancer patients with cannabis products. At the time of my initial visits in 2013, Aunt Zelda's was treating a rash of "glios," many of them children with glioblastoma, a devastating brain cancer that oncologists call "the Terminator." Glios on chemotherapy typically live for fifteen months; left untreated they're gone in a quarter of that time. Mara has been treating some glios with cannabis in conjunction with chemo for an odds-defying three years. Dr. Nicholas Butowski, a neuro-oncologist at the University of California, San Francisco, one of the physicians who refers patients to Aunt Zelda's, suspects that the oil somehow interferes with the way tumor cells divide and proliferate. What Mara does understand is that there are clues within the data that haven't been assessed, and therein lays her opportunity. She is building a database to match the compounds within the plant to the diseases they treat, so that people who don't have the luxury of waiting ten or twenty years for clinical trials will have some evidence on which to base their treatment decisions. Some people have criticized Mara and others like her as being little more than well-meaning amateurs, but when asked what qualifies her to dispense these meds, she throws her arms up in exasperation: "Who the hell else is going to do it?"

A reasonable question to which there is no reply.

Every day Mara and Stewart welcome a parade of neighbors, most of whom arrive in bright track suits, wide-brim visors, and those oversize plastic sunglasses favored by the Bengay brigade and rap stars. Today the visitors have come to inspect a newly arrived batch of "Cookies," the Girl Scout Cookies strain. There's also much buzz about AC/DC, one of the newer "highless" CBD strains that promises to ameliorate the aches and common ailments that make mortality a hot topic among this crowd. The sight of grandmas sniffing weed is deliciously incongruous, but in retrospect I'm not sure why it struck me as odd. A plant medicine that is a balm for aging and bestows a few moments of happiness— what's not to like?

One visitor, Jim, belongs to the Medical Marijuana Club at the Rossmoor senior community center, home to ten thousand retirees down the road. The club's first meeting in 2012 attracted just five members; it's now up to fifty, but Jim still can't understand why the room isn't packed.

"Last month a couple wandered into a meeting and asked, 'Is this the Church of Latter-Day Saints?' We said, 'Boy, are you in the wrong place. This is the medical marijuana club.'"

"Oh, we'd like to hear about that," they said, and even though Mormons are euphoriant averse, they sat through the entire meeting, rapt.

Jim and his wife, Mary, both septuagenarians, rely on Mara and Stewart for guidance. Jim doesn't trust Internet sites, and his allopathic doctors—most of whom have been trained to see marijuana as a use disorder—have little idea of how or what it heals. Like many suburbanites of a certain age, Jim doesn't fancy himself a cutting-edge kind of guy, yet every so often he realizes he is an unintentional pioneer.

When he went to the emergency room with a burst diverticulum, the intake nurse asked him if he used any drugs.

"Medical marijuana," he said.

"Smoke or vapor?" she asked, referring to her computerized checklist. He was impressed that a hospital would ask that question. After his treatment and upon release, he was given Marinol. "They weren't worth a damn, but at least the hospital was progressive enough to offer them. If I knew then what I know now I'd have said, 'These are fine, but Cookies are better.'"

In 2014, Mara and Stewart sold the condo and moved their operation north to Bodega Bay, the moody waterfront town where Alfred Hitchcock filmed *The Birds*. They live on Bay Hill Road, the same road that Tippi Hedren's character, Melanie Daniels, speeds along in her Aston Martin convertible in the movie's opening scenes. Stewart has converted a garage into a production facility and has taken the reins as master oil maker, and Mara serves as patient consultant. Most of her days are spent talking: to growers across the state in search of promising new strains, to researchers around the world (the United Kingdom, Spain, and the Czech Republic) in search of the latest clues and treatment protocols, and to testing labs to verify the cannabinoid contents of her preparations. She occasionally trains nurses to treat the endocannabinoid system and offers enterprising patients tutorials in organic oil making. But mostly she guides them toward using the stuff successfully themselves.

Mara has some neat tricks to enhance the efficiency and soften the side effects of cannabis oils. Eating certain types of mangos before taking THC quickens the uptake into the brain—that's an old bit of hippie lore that science has vindicated. Citicoline, a supplement that's sold in health food stores, fortifies memory and abets the brain's "attentional processing." "It's like plugging in the router when the memory Wi-Fi goes off," says Mara. "I give it to some patients [but not cancer patients, as there are some counterindications] who suddenly stop finishing sentences when they start on the oil."

It's not easy interviewing Mara without interruption. Patients call constantly, inquiring about dosing, side effects, and storage, and today she's fielding all their questions. On occasion she lets me listen in on a few consultations (with the patients' consent, of course).

Jenny is a grandmother with cervical spinal syndrome, which makes her shoulder feel as if it is being crushed in a hot vise. For seven years she's been on a brain-muddling regimen of methadone and Neurontin, a pain and antiseizure medicine, and she wants off.[5] Mara has created a concentrate of high-CBD Cannatonic to

---

* Side effects of Neurontin include drowsiness, dizziness, loss of coordination, tiredness, blurred/double vision, unusual eye movements or shaking (tremor), swelling of the hands/ankles/feet, signs of infection (such as fever, cough, persistent sore throat), depression, suicidal thoughts/attempts, changes in mood, thoughts about harming yourself, unusual fever, swollen glands, yellowing skin/eyes, unusual tiredness, dark urine, change in the amount of urine, chest pain, rash, itching/swelling (especially of the face/tongue/throat), severe dizziness, trouble breathing.

lessen her inflammation and lessen the pain. But Jenny, seventy-three, needs some answers.

Jenny: "Is Cannatonic an indica or sativa?"

Mara: "'Indica' and 'sativa' are antiquated terms—sort of like 'Democrat' and 'Republican.' They don't mean that much anymore. [That's true. Though the terms are used around the world as a guide to effects, years of crossbreeding have rendered the terms meaningless. More accurate descriptions are "narrow leaf" and "round leaf" varieties.] What it has is terpenes—pharmaceutical-grade essential oils that are probably more responsible for directing the high or the effectiveness of the treatment."

Jenny: "I don't want to be stoned. I took a couple puffs off my son's vaporizer a few years ago, and [she begins to cry] . . . I am no longer myself . . . I'm sorry . . . I don't want to get emotional . . . I'm just in so much pain . . ."

Mara gently reminds her that the drugs she's taking can create confusion and then goes into a convoluted explanation of cannabinoids and receptors. Why, I ask, doesn't she simplify the science for easy consumption?

"Sometimes the elderly like to do research to make it as complicated as possible, so they don't have to admit they're using marijuana," she tells me.

Next up is a woman from Pennsylvania whose five-year-old daughter has a rare genetic form of muscular dystrophy. She weighs thirty-nine pounds. The story is heartbreaking, but the conversation revolves around the mechanics of treatment, including how to best store the medicine. "Treat it like a fine olive oil. Sunlight and heat are its enemies," Mara counsels.

The obvious question is why Mara doesn't save time and just include instructions in the packages she sends out. "By law, we can only mail the meds within California. This couple has family in the state but how the meds travel from there . . . we don't know [sly smile]. These people don't have time to wait for the laws to catch up, so we send instructions separately as a precaution, just in case the package gets waylaid . . ."

By afternoon, Stewart comes in with a few syringes of gooey Pineapple Kush oil—the rewards of his day's work. When he's not looking I surreptitiously squeeze two quinoa seed–size droplets onto my finger and rub them across my gums. Its concentrated grassy essence briefly parches my throat. When I tell Mara what I've done her eyebrows raise and she insists I spend the night. After much back and forth, I climb into my car to drive back to San Francisco. As I pull away I hear her scream, "If it's too much for you, come back! You can always sleep in the spare bed."

That droplet was about one hundred times more powerful than a joint. *I can handle this*, I think, and for an hour I do—the only effect is an unquenchable thirst. But by the time I hit the Golden Gate Bridge, every mirror, every engine, every car in front and behind and to the side of me, not to mention the water, the sky, the lines on the pavement, is vying for my attention. To pay the toll I have to dial a number on my phone, which requires a Herculean feat of multi-tasking focus. The only solution is to silence the radio, hug the right lane, and crawl home like a grandma behind the wheel. The lesson? Don't toy with concentrated cannabis oil. It is powerful stuff that deserves a lot more respect than "just pot."

When the Ryders returned to England in the summer of 2014, Angela realized for the first time that there was no legal way for her to get her son's medicine into the country.

Fear of arrest led her to a network of underground makers, primarily in Scandinavia and Holland, who distribute oils to patients in need. One Dutchman, Nol van Schaik, leads a Facebook group called "Adopt a Patient," a service like Tinder that matches

people in need with an excess of what the Dutch call "MediWeed."*
The site accepts no ads or personal posts and offers no treatment
advice, and it is filled with heartbreaking pleas from ill people
begging to be adopted.

Even if you succeed in connecting with a maker, you'll soon face
the problem of mailing the oils across borders. One mom in Britain
ordered three shipments from abroad. The first slipped through
customs but the second package arrived empty with an official
letter warning her that she'd be prosecuted next time if caught. A
few days later the third shipment mysteriously arrived at her home.
The woman thought that some low-level official somehow understood the gravity of what was at stake and made an allowance.

But for every kindhearted soul who bends the law to help the
sick, there are more dubious players who may be sneaking less
pure formulations between the regulatory cracks. And if their
medications turn out to be tainted, or fail to deliver the dosages
they claim, the results can be, at the very least, sickening.

One company had been producing an oil made from industrially farmed hemp that may have come from China or another
country with loose environmental regulations. The problems with
industrial hemp are twofold: (1) Hemp is not cannabis, which
means it has less of the healing terpenes, flavonoids, and powerful
concentrations of cannabinoids. (2) Hemp extracts metals, pesticide
solvents, and even nuclear toxins out of the earth to regenerate the
soil; it was planted near and around Chernobyl after the facility's
deadly meltdown in 1986. These days it is planted around factories
that manufacture computer parts, in order to absorb the effluent
containing lead, molybdenum, cadmium, nickel, selenium, and
other noxious heavy metals.

---

*Holland has one licensed distributor of MediWeed, the pharma company
Bedrocan. All of its four strains are registered as drugs, available by prescription
and reimbursed by the Dutch national health insurance. Coffee shops are
entirely different entities.

An alarm was sounded in the medical cannabis community when one distraught mother posted in a Facebook group that her twenty-one-month-old epileptic daughter was rushed to a hospital with severe diarrhea after ingesting "hemp oil" of an unknown origin. They believed it was produced by the aforementioned company. When the oil was sent to a Colorado lab, the resulting test appeared to confirm that it was tainted with some of the same heavy metals listed above.

Just days later, however, the lab repudiated its own findings. A technician had made an error, they said, and a preliminary version of the results had been released accidentally. Although the lab concluded the oil was "safe," the retraction raised eyebrows and concern in the medical cannabis community.

Months later, an executive from this hemp oil company sent samples of its products to Brandon Krenzler for his eight-year-old daughter, the aforementioned cannakid, Brave Mykayla. Thank you very much, Krenzler replied, but Mykayla—who had been successfully treated for leukemia—was not responsive to CBD oils; THC concentrates in combination with chemo worked better for her. In spite of this, the company honcho showed up at the Krenzlers' Oregon home and presented them with $2,400 worth of oil. He asked if Krenzler would consider selling it to other families with sick children, but Krenzler declined. He also promised Krenzler a generous cut if he would allow them to rebrand their product "Brave Mykayla Oil."

Krenzler again demurred, but accepted some of the oil as a gift, which he tried on Mykala and himself. Both were beset by crippling constipation, cramping, and nausea. "Maybe I dosed it wrong," Krenzler thought, and asked two other parents with sick children to try it. One mother was forced to rush her epileptic son to the emergency room, where he was diagnosed with impacted bowel. His diet hadn't changed, so she blamed the oil. The other parent said it caused her daughter to vomit and did nothing to help her seizures.

Krenzler called the company, demanding they provide testing records, import records, and production records, "so we could prove that their product was not making us sick."

Krenzler told me his pleas went unheeded.

Worried about impurities and the composition of the oils, he sent unopened samples to a local lab in Portland to verify the accuracy of the cannabinoid content listed on the label. The results, according to Krenzler, showed the oil contained hundreds of times the .03 percent THC allowed by US law, which made it illegal to ship across state lines. When Krenzler posted the results online to warn families about the risk of federal prosecution, the lab informed him that it would no longer support its own findings. "They told me they had been threatened with legal action. At one point they even denied they had tested the product, even though I was holding their report in my hand," he says.

Is it a coincidence that two labs in different states mistakenly came up with damning results? Yes, just as it's possible that the threat of a crushing lawsuit prompted their retractions.

This emerging world of industrially produced hemp oil smacks of another oil—snake oil—that was sold by grifters until the Food and Drugs Act of 1906 regulated medicines and their formulas. Prior to that, doctors sold their own homemade medicines to patients without being subject to standards or quality controls. The Food and Drugs Act was aimed at stopping the abuses of charlatans who'd swoop into a town and make audacious claims before audiences that were planted with shills proclaiming the miraculous benefits of these snake oils. Once people bought their elixirs the peddlers would move on, never to be heard from again. And those gullible people? Well, they're still around today, congregating on the Internet, defenseless because the government cannot regulate a market it deems illegal.

Meanwhile, Chico Ryder is in remission. As of this writing, he has gained twelve pounds, is doing physical therapy to get back on his feet, and is attending school three days a week. He's still taking Aunt Zelda's oil.

Chapter 8

BUDTENDERS AND SINSEMILLIERS:
INSIDE THE DISPENSARY

Denver, Colorado

In February 2014, one month after recreational cannabis became legal in Colorado, Governor John Hickenlooper announced a projected $60 million tax windfall. A few months later at a Democratic Governors Association dinner in Washington, DC, Hickenlooper warned his fellow lawmakers of the "risks" of moving too quickly to legalize. "It's not a panacea," Hickenlooper said in an interview. "It's not going to solve your revenue problems." No one paid him any mind. In fact, the state ended the year with a $76 million boost from the combined tax and licensing revenue of cannabis, more than double that of alcohol.[1]

Money is only one measure of the changes that have come quickly to what is now aptly termed "the industry." Adam Dunn still runs HoodLamb, but he is also Professor Dunn, teaching cultivation, infusion, and hemp at Clover Leaf University, "the nation's only cannabis university that is approved, regulated, and licensed by the Colorado Department of Education's Private Occupational School Board." Derek Cumings, the hash oil maker, has been made a principal in Incredibles, which is pumping out forty thousand Mile High bars a month in a dozen flavors. Sales are still being impeded by lack of cannabis oil, so Derek is building an indoor grow and extraction facility to keep production flowing.

Regulation has pushed Incredibles and many other mom-and-pop start-ups to behave more like responsible businesses by measuring and labeling the THC content of their products. Until then, many had been manufacturing products with no information whatsoever—a mix of negligence, inexperience, and a lack of state-issued guidelines.

Dixie Elixir's business had also quadrupled. In 2010, cannabis-infused edibles and drinkables represented less than 10 percent of Dixie's sales. By 2014, this segment had climbed to 50 percent of their market. Tripp Keber, Dixie's CEO, was busted for possessing a small amount of cannabis in Alabama. The cops mistook the cigar he was carrying in his hand for a blunt and pulled him out of line as he entered a music festival in Gulf Shores. He broke open the cigar to prove his innocence but *oops!* they came across a few milligrams of cannabis concentrate in the form of mints in his pocket. I called Tripp to remind him that he denied using in our initial meeting. He laughed. The bust bought him some cannabis credibility, which he realized while taking a business meeting with Willie Nelson after a concert in Newark, New Jersey. "Willie suffered and has been penalized because he's been arrested a half dozen times. That we now have in common," he said, with not a trace of irony.

The froth produced in legal cities such as Denver, Seattle, and Vancouver is just the beginning. In the vastness of the Internet, where laws have no geographical jurisdiction, it's clear that legal weed is not only here to stay but is driving all manner of new enterprises, from the electronic dab rigs to slim stash cases that hold a vape pen, an extra oil cartridge, a USB charger, plus a lighter and rolling papers (why has it taken so long to invent such a necessary accessory?). Big cultural transformations are happening now too. MassRoots.com, founded in 2013, has over 775,000 users and serves as a Facebook-like network for cannabists around the world. Ganja.girls is an Instagram photo stream of young women in scant panties and knee-high "weedsocks" sucking on lasciviously large bongs. OK, these images are not subtle, but they're not pornographic, either—the vibe is more *Girls* than *Girls Gone Wild*. Depending on your perspective, ganja.girls is either another example of the same-old male-dominated exploitation of women—or a postfeminist embrace of a substance that is less aggressive than alcohol and more tempered by tenderness. In either case, it's another signal that the tsunami of change is unstoppable.

It's the dispensary, however, that is releasing cannabis from the cultural aspic in which it has been preserved for forty years. Whether you indulge or not, the dispensary experience is not to be missed. On your first visit, you'll find yourself in a state of giddy confusion as you take in the dizzying array of edibles, drinkables, topicals, concentrates, infused products, and perfectly manicured buds on offer. Then comes excitement once the budtender, if properly trained, guides you to products that will deliver the high you desire. In higher-end establishments, each strain of flowers will be labeled with cannabinoid content, which will either mean nothing to you or, if you're well versed, provide clues about the arc of your high. The days of consumers buying whatever some guy has in his backpack are coming to a close, and not a minute too soon.

If you're Sicilian American, as I am, and saddled with a low anger threshold, or if you are even the slightest bit political, the initial exhilaration will be followed by fury. You'll understand how the citizens of East Berlin must have felt after the Wall fell and they flooded into an electronics store in the West: Total wonder and then rage about having been kept in the dark for no comprehensible reason. In the dispensary you too will inevitably ask, "What was all that prohibition fuss about?" Why has the United States spent trillions of dollars trying to annihilate this plant, suppressing all the technology, ingenuity, and science that surrounds it?

But stick with the giddiness—it's much more enjoyable.

Dispensaries in flashier cities have a more tricked-out sense of style. San Francisco has Sparc; with its modernist, minimal lines, it is a study in Scandinavian restraint. Its free extract tastings draw enthusiastic crowds that make the place feel more like a happy hour than a store. The Apothecarium sits at the other end of the design spectrum. Flock wallpaper, marble countertops, fresh-cut flowers, and an oversize chandelier create a chic-yet-olde-world-drugstore-meets-saloon ambience. When you're handed the leather-bound menu that lists selections, the experience takes another turn toward the elegant. There are no lines and no crowds, so the purchasing experience is unrushed and relaxed.

Denver Relief, where I've volunteered to intern for a few days, reflects the modest handsomeness of the city itself. It's a small operation that purveys quality cannabis grown in its own indoor facility—Colorado law requires every dispensary to grow 75 percent of its own weed so that law enforcement can more easily track and prevent it from being "diverted" into the black market. More like a private club than a full-service health center, Denver Relief keeps its quality and prices high and patient count low (a modest three thousand) to ensure it has enough top-shelf bud to go around. Recreational sales came online a month before my internship commenced, but the owners are holding back on selling recreational cannabis to ensure their medical patients are served first.

The building itself has all the flash of a small bank branch. It's a squat brick structure nestled between a hair salon and an urgent care center on an up-and-coming block along Denver's Green Mile. By city ordinance, dispensaries must be one thousand feet away from a school, candy store, or other area trafficked by children. There are no cannabis leaves or Cheech and Chong photos in sight, no hawkers dressed in joint costumes to lure customers indoors. Even its logo, a sterile green cross, is subdued and serious.

"Our goals when we started were to be good neighbors, to progress the industry, and to have excellent product. Everything else fell into place," Kayvan Khalatbari, one of the cofounders, tells me. "We did all these things we didn't have to do to be a good face for the industry. We put ourselves on the books every chance we got. We started a dialogue with the city. Everyone else was taking advantage of loose laws. We were saying, 'Let's act right now as if we are regulated and see where that takes us.' People trusted us."

As did I, which is why I wanted to work behind their counters. Unlike meetings I attended in Amsterdam, where conversations about sensitive topics flipped into Dutch, at Denver Relief I was invited to ask questions and afforded free access to all aspects of the operation. "We have nothing to hide," Ean Seeb, Kayvan's business partner, assured me. The only caveat was that I stay within Colorado law, which meant that as a nonresident I could not touch the plant, nor could I work directly with patients. I was assigned to trail the head budtender, Scott Yoss, as he made his rounds between the dispensary and the indoor grow, where he moonlighted as a cultivator.

There are worse ways to make a living.

In dispensaries geared to pushing product, your first interaction with a budtender might go something like this:

"What do you have today?"

"Oh man, you gotta try the____."

"Is it good?"

"It's fire, man."

"Oh yeah?"

"Yeah, it really fucks you up."

Denver Relief operates on another level.

Scott is behind the counter counseling Petra, a young woman who uses pot to blunt the pain of her menstrual cramps, but who also appreciates the smooth high of carefully grown, well flushed, neatly trimmed bud. Scott is presiding over a "side by side" of two hybrid indicas, counseling Petra to let her own nose guide her to the best strain for her pain. While his method is of dubious scientific merit, his enthusiasm is infectious, another indication that I wasn't in a Dutch coffee shop anymore.

"This is our eighty-day Bio-Diesel," Scott explains. "Last year *High Times* voted it one of earth's strongest strains. It has ten days more on the vine, which also creates a longer experience in the system. My first joint of this eighty-day beauty and I was high for four hours. The extra ten days changes the plant's chemistry. Even the flavor tastes more medicinal."

Scott, professorially handsome in his designer frames and trimmed beard, nabs a thumb-size bud from a glass Mason jar with his forceps and offers it up for appraisal. "The extra time also makes the bud open more." He squeezes the tongs to burst the oil sacs and places the sappy sample a half-inch below Petra's nostril.

"I get a whiff of asphalt plus a Band-Aid plastic strip on the inhale," he says. Petra nods vaguely, a little befuddled and maybe a little impressed. Even though she's a resident of Boulder, a onetime hippie outpost that bills itself today as "the city nestled between the mountains and reality," she's never heard a spiel like this.

"The Q3 doesn't show as well," he continues, popping the seal on another jar. "It's got a purple cast, but the nose is mild. The flavor is citrusy, and the high? It reminds me of sunshine." She whiffs and a discussion ensues about storing pot to prevent it from drying out. Scott recommends reviving dry buds by placing them in a jar covered by a damp cheesecloth secured with rubber bands. "One day should do the trick."[*2]

The final strain is Durban Poison, which Scott describes as "smelling like the bottom of my grandmother's purse." Petra takes a deep belly breath.

"It smells less musty and more minty to me."

"I know what you mean," Scott reconsiders with a smile. "My grandmother always kept a roll of Certs in her purse."

Petra opts for Bio-Diesel, an "elite" tier, which sells for $70 a quarter ounce ("premium" tier costs $60 a quarter ounce and "special" is $50 a quarter ounce). Wielding his forceps—it is illegal to touch the meds—Scott carefully weighs out the buds on a digital scale. Protocol also discourages pouring buds out of jars, as sudden jolts can dislodge trichomes. He tips the buds into a tamper-proof, child-resistant opaque bag—"Some of our competitors charge customers three dollars for the bag, that's pretty crass"—then slides that into another paper bag as required by law, and escorts her out the door.

"Great sales job," I remark once he's back.

He shrugs. "It sells itself."

At thirty-six, Scott is the city's first (albeit self-anointed) sinsemillier, a role he takes as seriously as does a sommelier in any top-drawer restaurant. Since high school, Scott has honored the plant with the same respect that his brother, a sommelier and wine instructor

---

*This is a dubious solution. As Michael Backes reports in *Cannabis Pharmacy*, when marijuana is dried, its oils lose volatility, and its aroma and potency diminish forever. Moisture cannot revive dried oils, but it can create mold. Best is to store cannabis in a glass jar in a cool, dark place with a Boveda moisture packet taped into the lid. Refrigerators work best for short-term storage; for longer bouts, freeze buds. Never refreeze once thawed.

with the International Wine Guild, affords the grape. The difference is that until recently Scott's passions made him a criminal
while his brother's elevated him to a connoisseur.

Presiding over the counter at Denver Relief is more than a job, he
says—it's a privilege. His twenty-year relationship with cannabis has
helped him grapple with a depression that ran so deep that "down
was up to me," and tending to the buds has provided him with unforeseen career security. "When I go to work, I don't worry about
being raided, because these guys have crossed all t's and dotted all i's
six steps in advance," he says. For forty-three hours of work a week,
Scott earns $450, plus health benefits and a 50 percent discount on
all meds. The law allows him to purchase two ounces a day. Denver
Relief offers him a 75 percent discount on two ounces a month.

Like wine, beer, and coffee, the language of cannabis connoisseurship can sound riper than a moldy cheese—we've all endured
fussy baristas intoning about the "wine and earth notes" in those
"single-estate shade-grown beans" cultivated on some finca in the
mountains of Nicaragua. On the other hand, Scott's discourse is
expanding a lexicon that has been held back by eighty years of prohibition. I don't agree with or even understand all of his apprais-
als, but no matter—establishing a language of appreciation beyond
stoner- and science-speak is an advance whose time has come.

Before manning the counter, all new budtenders at Denver Relief
must train for a week, learning the law, the house rules, and what
strains best treat the more common medical conditions. Newbies
must also secure a $250 "support badge," which the state requires
of any worker in a dispensary, grow, or packing facility, and submit
to a federal background check, which includes fingerprinting and
a criminal record review. Outstanding bills or warrants or past
crimes eliminate you from the running.[*]

---

[*]This is a contentious issue in other states, California especially. Growers
who have been busted argue that they should not be banned from the industry
today for past activities that were considered crimes during the drug wars.

Denver Relief employs forty full-time workers, most of whom are CEUs: college-educated unemployeds. Their average age is thirty-one, one indication that dispensary work is usurping waiting tables as a "bridge" profession. Statistics bear this out. When Colorado's first recreational marijuana shops opened in January 2014, the state had 6,593 licensed industry workers. Five months later, that figure rose to 9,641, about the same number of Coloradans employed in law enforcement. At a marijuana-related job fair in March 2014, the crowd was so large that applicants stood in line for three hours. By the day's end, organizers were turning people away. "With this type of industry and the money that's coming in, this is the place to be right now," said one job seeker who waited for two hours, résumé in hand. [3]

It has taken Denver Relief six years of bootstrapping to establish its good name. The business launched in 2008 with a half pound of pot, $4,000, and a memorable phone number: 303-420-MEDS. Ean was a real estate broker who, in his spare time, had been connecting patients with growers seeking to increase their patient counts. Kayvan was a co-owner of a restaurant called Sexy Pizza; Adam, their third partner, was a grower. All three knew that their current career paths were leading nowhere. Ean was bored. Kayvan had a degree in architectural engineering but found working in a firm soul-withering. He was thirty pounds overweight and surrounded by colleagues who spent their days complaining about wasting their lives. The one thing they didn't know at the time was each other— they had all met one week prior to launching the company—but they shared a vision of owning a legitimate cannabis business that would never be used as B-roll on Fox News.

Those were heady times, rich with possibilities and fraught with unknowns. Colorado had decriminalized cannabis before creating any laws to regulate it, which meant that businesses were operating without guidance as to what was legal or criminal. On January 1, 2009, the three men gathered at a bar and assessed their possibilities.

"We had no money so we couldn't just sink $150K into a dispensary," Kayvan tells me. At thirty, with his radio-smooth voice, handsome Persian features, and deep intelligence, Kayvan is among the most eligible bachelors in the industry. "I had used all my IRA and 401(k) to start Sexy Pizza and I was renting out my house and camping in a tent in the backyard. I was flat out of money, but my credit was still good . . . it was ruined by Denver Relief eventually, but that's another story."

They secured a telephone number, Ean designed a logo in Microsoft Paint, and they placed a three-line advertisement amid the sex ads on the back page of the local alternative weekly. It simply said "303 420 Meds . . . Denver Relief. We deliver."

Thus was established Denver's first door-to-door cannabis delivery service.

Deliveries began in the sweltering summer of 2009, when temperatures averaged 105 degrees. Kayvan took phone orders in his beat-up truck with no AC and with the windows rolled up so he could hear the customers. Since the law was as yet unwritten, they established their own rules, the first being that all initial patient contact should occur in public, at a Starbucks or a gas station, to preclude trouble.

Adam was the first (and last) of the three to break protocol when an unknown customer gave him a sob story about being wheelchair bound and unable to leave the house. When Adam rolled up to his driveway the guy tipped himself into the front seat and pulled a gun, hijacking the car along with patient files, cash, a credit card reader, and product.

Adam eventually got back the car, but the cash and cannabis were gone forever. So was his laxity about rules. The first month they earned $10,000; by month four they were pulling $50,000. They paid taxes (the IRS categorized their business as "wholesale, non dairy") and within a year, they signed a lease on the dispensary.

The design of Denver Relief is free of flourishes, and security was built into every aspect of the building. The walls separating patients from the inner offices are webbed with Kevlar to block a stray bullet, just in case. The roof is wrapped in industrial-gauge barbed wire to prevent thefts. There are panic buttons beneath registers. Steel doors separate rooms, windows are made with bulletproof glass, and surveillance cameras record every trans-action. Only a small amount of product is kept on premises, and when not on display it is stored in a large safe within a locked room. A wooden ceiling hides the massive airflow ducts, while rows of Ona Gel, a Canadian room freshener that scents the air with "Fresh Linen," line the shelves. "We cut the stink to be nice to our neighbors," one manager, Mike Davis, explained to me.

From its start, in July 2010, Denver Relief's cannabis was twice the price of other dispensaries', but it was guaranteed free of pesticides, mold, or mildew, and powerful. One strain is raised entirely under wide-spectrum LED lamps that promise to conserve energy and increase yield. "Lost crossed" strains are older varieties that have been crossbred with newer strains to increase hardiness, potency, or medicinal qualities, similar to the way French grape varieties were hybridized to match the growing conditions of the New World. Once Denver Relief in-stalls greenhouses in the parking lot behind its warehouse, "sun grown" flowers will join its top-shelf offerings.

"People are starting to understand the contrast between great and average marijuana," says Kayvan. "It's similar to beer. Ten years ago, craft beer was just starting to gain popularity, but now the micro-brew market is taking up more room. People have tasted good beer and they're willing to pay more for it. In our business people are building massive grows to increase efficiency and lower the price, but you can't grow connoisseur quality in that environment. They'll be Coors. To grow great marijuana you have to grow small batch. That's why you'll find the finest cannabis in the basements of certain growers scattered around the country. In the future, people will build small rooms that have ideal conditions for certain strains." Sort of like *reservas privadas*.

There's one additional feature in Denver Relief that stands it apart: a donation box. Kayvan mentors two foster kids and matches every dollar patients contribute to their educations from his own pocket. He also sits on the board of the Colorado Symphony Orchestra, which, when I visited, was planning a controversial fund-raiser sponsored by local cannabis industries in support of a program, "The High Note Series." Ean donates time to the Denver chapter of the Jewish Anti-Defamation League and occasionally hosts a lunchtime lecture series. One recent topic was "Is Medical Marijuana Kosher?" ("Is the Pope Catholic?" was Ean's answer.) This is not cynical do-gooderism. Both believe that philanthropy is essential to enlarging the foundation of compassion that the medical cannabis movement was built on.

Future dispensary owners take note.

Scott Yoss got serious about expanding his cannabis vocabulary when his older brother, Matt, prodded him to put words—"tarry," "grassy," "fruity," "fuelly"—to certain smells. An understanding of the grape has deepened Scott's admiration of the bud; it has also attuned him to the finer points of presentation. Just as the base of a wine bottle has a notch that allows a server to show the customer a label when the wine is poured, Scott grips open jars from the bottom to give patients full olfactory and visual appreciation of their meds.

Scott's next patient is Nancy. She presents her ID and state-issued "Red Card" at the intake window and her patient record pops up on Scott's screen. It includes her age (forty-four), condition (insomnia and anxiety), and past purchases.

Scott greets Nancy and explains the dispensary's different promotions: "Smokeless Mondays" entitle her to 10 percent off vaporizing accessories and edibles. Tuesdays and Sundays are "heavy bag" days, which include 4.2 grams of flowers rather than the standard 3.5 grams. On "wax weekends," patients get 50 percent off their first gram of hash. Colorado's exacting laws even prescribe the way that specials can be offered. "I can say, 'Buy six for the price of five' but not, 'Buy five and get one free,'" Scott tells me.

In the dispensing area, Nancy sees jars of indica lining the shelves on the left, sativas on the right, and a small selection of edibles, drinkables, topicals, vaporizers, transdermal patches, candies, and cannabis-covered lime chili peanuts hanging in the center.

Nancy is a self-employed nurse who has steered clear of pot for the last twenty years. A few weeks ago while sipping a latte at a cafe and debating whether to take the Xanax her doctor prescribed for the anxiety that keeps her awake at night, she logged on to Leafly.com, a sort of Yelp for cannabis, and read a customer-generated review claiming that Denver Relief had "some of the best bud in the world." Leafly also offered her "nug porn" (insanely close-up photos of flowers) and strain reviews, while her GPS informed her that she was just steps away.

This is her second time in the dispensary and she has come loaded with questions. Now that she has finally sorted out the difference between a sativa and an indica, she's noticed that they don't always work as advertised. The indica she bought to help her sleep made her mind spin instead. It's too bad she can't remember the name of that strain.

"No problem," Scott tells her. He checks her last purchase and guides her toward a Ghost Train Haze. "It's larfy, but it's some of the stoniest marijuana I've smoked."

"'Larfy'?"

"Lacking Any Real Flower. Or as some of the kids call it, Little

Raggedy Ass Fucker. It has a beautiful flavor, like pineapples, and it has true medicinal qualities. It's a lesson to never judge a bud by its structure. She may be an ugly girl, but she's a great kisser."

And what about weed candy? Nancy wants to know. One friend told her that five milligrams will make her snooze like a baby.

Eating pot is like taking another drug, Scott explains, which is true but causes confusion, especially among older patients. He doesn't go into specifics about the way THC, when eaten, is processed by the liver and turned into another metabolite, Delta-11-THC, which causes a different effect on the mind and body. But he does inform Nancy that most edibles (1) take one and a half to two hours to kick in, (2) have effects that last four to eight hours depending on dose, and (3) can knock you on your ass if you take too much. He advises her to start small (three to five milligrams) on a full stomach and patiently observe the effects. She can always increase by two milligrams a day until she finds a suitable amount. This is called self-titrating.

"We also have these OMG Medicated Drinks, which enable cannabinoids to get into the system fast because they're absorbed immediately into the bloodstream rather than first routing through the stomach. One bottle hits in a record fourteen minutes and lasts three hours. If I drink a bottle and eat a fifty-milligram edible I will hallucinate."

Nancy looks confused.

"Like many drugs, cannabis is a medical substance that can be exploited as recreation," he offers.

Scott also points out the transdermal patches by Mary's Medicinals. They come in THC, CBD, 1:1 ratios, and other assorted "flavors." Scott has tried both the 1:1 THC-CBD combo and the "sativa" formulations and was impressed with how "buzzy" they were—whether this description is nuanced enough for a former nurse is another topic. "The physical patch itself is made by Dow Chemicals, so it's designed to help the cannabis absorb into the skin quickly, in about twenty minutes," he reports. Nancy is intrigued (as am I) with the idea of mixing and matching "delivery systems," but ultimately decides to stick with something she can "smoke at ten p.m. and get knocked out."

"What do you like about coming into a dispensary?" I ask Nancy as Scott packages her selections.

"I haven't smoked pot in years and before it was like, you buy an ounce in the park and you had no idea of what you were getting," she says without hesitation. "Now it's more scientific. I can see what I'm buying and I love the education I'm getting.

"Two, I don't feel like a criminal. I'm not! Three, Xanax is the only thing my doctor has to offer for anxiety and, as a recovering alcoholic, I don't want to take pills that might be addictive."

She pauses for a moment. "And seeing how normal this is has made me question . . . When I read things like, 'The brain doesn't stop growing until you're twenty-five,' well, if that's true, maybe we should be talking about changing the liquor laws first."

The dispensary is the cannabis classroom of the post-prohibition era.

Nancy's purchases—one hash oil cartridge for her O.penVape pen plus her flowers—come to $120. Since her bill tops $100, the dispensary covers the $2 debit card fee. Scott bags her goods, then escorts her back into the middle area.

It's an elegant way of personally bidding each patient adieu, but it also ensures that no one removes the medical ID sticker and patient number on the premises, which would violate the law. "Getting in and out of the dispensary is like a pilot getting a series of clearances to take off or land," notes Scott. "Here, you need the Red Card, government ID, and patient ID to enter. If you remove the labels and attempt to resell it once you've left, it's just like you're selling prescription drugs, and you're a criminal."

One afternoon Scott and I gather in the backyard of the Arts and Crafts home that his brother Matt shares with his wife, Patty. At my request Scott has prepared a "flight" of six strains for us to sample and discuss. Describing cannabis as "a potent piece of medicine" is as clumsy as "killer bud" is vacant. I'm curious to see if we can arrive at a consensus about the flavors of the different strains before getting so wasted we can't speak. A lot of people would consider this exercise fussy and adding an unnecessary complication to something as simple as enjoying well-grown weed, but I believe that the more precisely the vaporized resins can be articulated, the more accurately we'll be able to discuss their effects on the tongue, body, and mind.

When Matt kicks off a wine-tasting class, he brings in thirty-three stereoisomers (liquid scent molecules) and asks students to associate each with a word. "Saying the word creates a neural pathway in the brain and improves your ability to categorize and identify other smells that are similar but not exactly the same," he tells me. We'll see.

First up: Chem Dawg. Scott slides it out of its plastic joint holder (another simple yet long-overdue invention that enables joints to be carried without being crushed and thus prevents them from turning pockets into ashtrays), and sparks it up.

Matt is instantly struck by the effect, which is stronger than the flavor, and hesitantly takes a second hit. "I think it's a lot of cucumber."

I've never heard of any cannabis described as cucumber and I say so.

"In wine we say that if you think that that glass of burgundy smells like burned shrimp shells, goddamn it, it smells like burned shrimp shells," says Matt with a smile. "Everyone has an individual relationship to smell and taste."

"Well, I think this tastes earthy, like fresh mud after the rain," I offer. Patty is uncertain, so rather than struggling to find middle ground between dirt and cukes, we move on to the next strain, Lemon Diesel, the name of which we all agree, fits the citrusy taste.

"It's like Lemon Pine Sol," says Patti. "The previous one was more like pencil shavings."

"Yes!" agrees Scott. "Pencil shavings and cardboard."

The third strain, Bio-Diesel, causes Matt to pronounce, "Cinnamon, maybe with some bark or sawdust."

"That sourness and spice, that's the diesel," adds Scott. "It's fuelly, or like road tar or asphalt."

Asphalt? Sawdust? One thing is clear: the flavor descriptions of wine are more sensual than those of cannabis.

Next up is OG 18, which Scott says is "sweet butterscotch on the inhale but leaves the room smelling of burned rubber bands."

"That's the same way I describe a South African Pinotage," says Matt. "It has a gamey character to it, like you're roasting an antelope on the plains. But I taste peppermint on the exhalation."

"Yes, she's delicate, not brutish," adds Scott. Hey, guys, I pipe in, there's a whopping difference between peppermint and smoldering rubber bands!

"Burned rubber is the smell it *leaves behind* in the room," Scott clarifies. "But yes, the flavor of the smoke on the exhale is more eucalyptus. It's very . . . green."

Matt, sensing my frustration with the free-form nature of this exercise, reminds me that precision isn't the point. "In France there are 475 terrains, plus an amazing number of producers outside of those regions. Each terroir grows a different variety of grape, but the local soil and microclimates also contribute to the unique taste. And that's before anything even hits a barrel to age."

"That's how experts keep their jobs," I say. "They're never able to arrive at consensus!"

"And that's the best part about it!" says Matt. "It takes a lifetime to learn about the three thousand strains. That's why cannabis and wine are both so compelling. They are living things, so always changing. You can never learn enough."

I see his point, which is finally one thing we can all agree on.

At the conclusion of the tasting, Scott explains that despite our differing opinions, we did successfully identify the broad notes of each category. The first two strains he selected for their "woodsier" flavors, which our descriptions touched upon. The second pair was more sour, which we nailed as citrusy. The third pairing included two sweets, which we missed, probably because it's impossible to disassociate taste from effect, and by that time the judges were cross-eyed. The conclusion: Tasting wine is easier. With cannabis, you can't spit it out.

Monday is a slow day. In the long gaps between patients trickling in, the staff places orders, restocks shelves, and prepares some well-stuffed, perfectly formed pre-rolls. At closing, the scales are cleaned and leveled, the keyboards air-gunned to remove any stray "shake," floors are mopped and vacuumed, and keypads, door switches, and arms of chairs are swabbed with Lysol.

The staff gathers outside in a nearby parking lot for an after-work "shifty." Smoking on the clock is verboten and results in immediate dismissal. When a joint of Durban Poison comes around, Ean politely refuses. "I've got enough anxiety right now," he says. "Sativa won't be much help." He's referring to his wedding, which is coming up next month on the fifty-yard line of a football stadium in Ann Arbor, Michigan, his fiancée's hometown.

(Here's how Abbie, Ean's fiancée, told her family she was dating a dispensary owner: "Hey, Mom, I just met a great guy! He's fifteen years older than me and owns a really great marijuana dispensary."

Silence.

"Oh, and he's Jewish."

"That's great, dear.")

Fan's statement reveals a lot about how cannabis literacy dovetails with self-awareness in the new world. He assesses his own mental state, and because he knows that the "energizing" properties of Durban Poison can exacerbate anxiety, he declines that strain. This is radical in American medicine, where "health" is generally outsourced to doctors. The notion of a patient identifying a condition, then choosing a botanical medicine that can't be patented or owned, and self-medicating? That's precisely why Dr. Grinspoon calls cannabis the true people's medicine, and why pharmaceutical companies find it threatening.

There's no question that a climate-controlled room with artificial sunlight bathing regimented rows of plants is one of earth's most unnatural environments. Brandon Kennedy, the CEO of the largest cannabis-oriented venture capital firm, Privateer Holdings, once described an indoor grow as "a bank inside of a prison filled with toasters that constantly need to cool down." I saw what he meant once inside Denver Relief's sprawling brick bunker, which had 1,200 plants crammed into 5,000 square feet with aisles so narrow I had to step one foot in front the other to proceed.

A single harvest churns about eighty pounds of bud every thirty-five days, which places the value of this inventory at any given moment at $350,000. Even with the additional 20,000 square feet of greenhouses they're planning to add, Denver Relief's operation will still be considered small to midsize. At the moment, grows occupy about 4.5 million square feet in Colorado, the equivalent of seventy-eight football fields, and the state's warehouse vacancy rate is at an all-time low.[4] "This industry has come on so fast that initially I was uneasy—it seemed like a fad," says Brad Calbert, the president of the Colliers International brokerage. "Supply is deficient, demand is excessive, and capital is abundant. Make that cash."[5]

The illumination in the Denver Relief greenhouse is as bright as an operating room—five hundred times the strength that's recommended for reading.* A high-power carbon air-filtration system keeps the humidity level low to discourage the growth of indoor microorganisms. The system changes the air thirty times an hour—sixty times the rate in a modern home. Carbon dioxide (CO_2) levels are four times natural levels, to boost plant growth. Every system, including surveillance, is connected to the mobile phone of the master grower. Should an evening snow suddenly drive down the temperature indoors, alarms sound. According to one 2012 study, the electricity used by these grows is sucking up a shameful 1 percent of the nation's annual wattage.[6]

The environment inside the grow is significantly more inoculated than that of a hospital. Visitors must remove their shoes at entry and wear protective booties to avoid traipsing in potentially destructive creatures, such as the dreaded spider mite, the full horror of which can be appreciated only though the lens of an electron microscope. This hirsute micromonster affixes to the underside of leaves and sticks its proboscis into a plant's veins to suck them dry. Another scourge is powdery mildew, a floury fungus that spreads so quickly it can wipe out a grow in two days if unchecked. Pestophobia is the reason well-designed grows are subdivided into smaller rooms. If one area becomes infected, the devastation is easier to contain. Losing an entire harvest can cost millions and destroy a business.

Scott serves as an assistant to Noah B., a former schoolteacher, and Kayvan's younger brother, Hassan. The four of us spend the morning snipping yellowing leaves to make tomorrow's scheduled reaping go faster. We deposit the dead leaves into black garbage bags, which Hassan holds up to a security camera for the control

---

*Colorado offers a power subsidy to new businesses, reducing Denver Relief's electricity bill to $6,500 a month.

board to monitor. Law requires him to weigh each bag before affixing an infrared tag that tracks every gram of garbage.

Securely transporting the flowers is akin to moving gold bars. To preclude diversion into the black market, plants are weighed five times: after they are chopped; after they are dried and cured; after they are bagged and refrigerated; and before departing for the dispensary. The state requires the driver to chart his route—if he changes course, insurance won't cover any trouble, should it occur. Once the shipment reaches its destination, the bags are again weighed to ensure nothing was lost along the way.

Tomorrow is harvest day, which means one-third of this grow will be sacrificed in the morning. The plants have been snoozing for the last twelve hours in total darkness (not even a flashlight is allowed), and the three growers and I have gathered in the dark to pay our last respects before a blaze of one thousand sulfurous lights jolts these snoozing plants into one final burst of resin production.

Under the glare, the differences between strains is breathtaking. The tawny leaves of Girl Scout Cookies appear reptilian in their rigidity, giving them a prehistoric cast. Unlike most cannabis varieties, the buds of Cookies are the same size near the light and below the canopy. They are dense and wrinkled like the folds of a shar-pei's neck. Outer Space buds grow as long as a banana and as thick as a twenty-ounce soda bottle. They are so spectacular they beg to be displayed whole under glass. Tomorrow ten freelance trimmers supplied by the Hemp Temps employment agency will set to work snipping excess leaves, which will be used for oil production. Each trimmer earns twelve to fifteen dollars an hour depending on his or her skill level. (Hassan calls the skill distinction "bullshit. The best trimmers are those who learned on illegal grows because they had to do their job steadily and quickly.") Besides trimmers, Hemp Temps also provides master growers as well as "confidential consumers," who surreptitiously drop into dispensaries and supply "detailed intelligence based on their visit to the assigned location" to owners. In other words, spies.

If fighting mites or mildew excites you, if staying atop ever-changing regulations doesn't feel like herding cats, if, at this very moment, you are contemplating moving to a legal marijuana state to open a dispensary and cash in on the greenrush, don't sell the house quite yet. The obstacles to success are many.

For every Scott Yoss, there are a hundred underground "experts" who may know a lot about growing illegally but who know nothing about navigating a tough new regulatory environment. "Our idea is to bring in the best practices from other industries," says Kayvan. "Budtenders should have great retail skills. Cultivators should have managed massive greenhouses with vegetables or flowers, or have a horticulture degree. It's easier to teach someone to grow marijuana if they know how to grow other plants than it is to show an underground grower how to manage a large facility with big automated systems. We had one grower who, if you disagreed about something, would say, 'Fuck it, I'm going to cut down all the plants.' So now we generally preach, 'Don't hire within the industry.'"

You also need a high tolerance for running an all-cash business. Financial institutions that many American businesses rely on—PayPal, Swipe, Square, not to mention credit card companies—shun the cannabis trade. Doing business with an illegal enterprise is still a crime under federal law. Banks are no exception.

The final disincentive? Because cannabis businesses fall under an obscure area of the federal tax code, the law doesn't allow them to deduct operating expenses, such as rent, salaries, or equipment costs. This means they could be paying a federal income tax upwards of 70 percent.

It's a good thing they sell a product that quells anxiety.

At the conclusion of my stint at Denver Relief, I quietly cornered Scott and Ean separately to inquire about purchasing some of their product. The answer was politely and firmly delivered: "No dice!" Scott made the excuse that since he smokes about a quarter ounce a week of flowers and a third of a gram of hash, he doesn't have a lot of slack. Ean more forthrightly told me that if he were to sell to an out-of-state visitor without a Red Card he could lose his license and livelihood. Both recommended I visit another shop down the road that allows recreational sales. I'm probably one of the few Americans to have worked in a dispensary and not been allowed to buy cannabis there, a minor inconvenience for me but an excellent sign for the future of the industry.

N.B. In 2016 Ean and Kayvan sold their cultivation and infused products licenses to Willie Nelson's company, Willie's Reserve, and their store to Terrapin Care Station. They now run Denver Relief Consulting.

PART III

FUTURE WEED

Chapter 9

DESIGNING YOUR HIGHS

Los Angeles, California

One of the problems of the current world of weed is the lack of diverse opinions within it. Advocates have been occupied fighting prohibition and all that comes with it for so long that stoner culture, which is still dominated by young guys in hoodies or old guys in hoodies who act like their younger counterparts, have hijacked the conversation for a half century. As we enter the post-prohibition era, new voices are emerging, and they are countering the received wisdom.

Michael Backes is one such disrupter. Rather than joining the chorus of those who claim that cannabis is harmless in any amount and in all circumstances, he takes the more epicurean position that it is currently oversmoked and underutilized. Backes is itching to spark a new debate about how the plant can responsibly fit into a society that doesn't outlaw or demonize it. He's convinced of cannabis's untapped potential, but he's unconvinced that stoners will be leading the way to uncovering it.

"It's not macho to take massive amounts of THC," he told me over a beer near his loft in downtown Los Angeles's Arts District. "It's not a mark of pride. But thanks to prohibition, our conception of the correct cannabis dose today is based on how much we can withstand. It's Seth Rogan hitting the bong or Snoop Dogg and Wiz Khalifa smoking all day long. It's so dumb."

The post-prohibitionist argument, as he frames it, goes something like this: For thousands of years, humans raised cannabis to complement human chemistry. But in the last half century, breeders have thrown this complement out of whack by selecting plants with massive amounts of THC. Cannabis merchants and growers don't view this as a problem, as it's more lucrative and efficient to grow plants that are smaller, more productive, and pack a bigger wallop. But in terms of creating the most pleasurable, *interesting* highs, and reaping the maximum therapeutic benefits, superweed may not be the answer.

"It's a general truism that nine percent of the pot smokers are smoking fifty percent of the pot, just as nine percent of drinkers are drinking fifty percent of the booze," Backes told me. "But the Bronfmans didn't sell moonshine when alcohol prohibition ended. They sold Seagram's. The marijuana moonshiners want to sling weed and they want more people smoking a gram of wax or an eighth [of an ounce] a day because *that's a business*. But judging pot by THC levels alone is like judging the quality of a cognac by its alcohol content. Who needs Gaston Briand if you've got Everclear?"

It's a reasonable point, one that's more often made by prohibitionists who twist it to say that today's powerpot is more dangerous than the weed of the past, and this is why we should keep it illegal. But Backes isn't worried about the unproven dangers of a relatively benign plant that has never killed one human being. He's an advocate who welcomes regulation, and he believes that the pleasures of pot can be enhanced by understanding the science of how it works. He has absorbed research from around the world, studied ancient uses, and combed through the three hundred patents that GW Pharmaceuticals has secured over the last fifteen years in its quest to bring Sativex to market as an FDA-approved whole-plant cannabis pharmaceutical.

As a founding member of Phytecs, the first company devoted

to making plant-based medicines and nutraceuticals to treat the endocannabinoid system, he is also confident that the plant can be used to produce revolutionary medicines and nuanced designer highs. "My job is to figure out where all this is going in the next five years," he says. With his black-frame glasses and pressed shirt, Backes is more egghead than pothead. Unsurprisingly, he doesn't come from the ranks of the cannabis movement. He spent most of his career in film, as a technical consultant on the Spider-Man series and supervising the computer graphics for the control-room sequence in *Jurassic Park* (several characters in Michael Crichton's books are admiringly named Michael Backes).

Like many in my generation, Backes smoked when he was young, quit as his paranoia increased with stronger plant genetics, and returned to it again in middle life when a friend recommended it to reduce the frequency of his hemiplegic migraines, which are accompanied by visual auras, withering pain, and nausea that no conventional medicine could address. A paper by Dr. Ethan Russo exposed him to two radical and counterintuitive ideas: (1) low doses could be more effective than larger doses, and (2) the obsession with THC was blinding users to the other powerful minor cannabinoids and terpenes that very likely determine the trajectory of every high.[1]

"Microdosing" didn't eliminate his pain, but it did work as a prophylaxis—it slashed the frequency of attacks from several a week to one a year. This stunning outcome inspired him to eventually cut back on film work and cofound the Cornerstone Collective in 2008, an "evidence-based" dispensary of three thousand members. Cornerstone operated in an intentionally nondescript office with no signage, and it sourced rare strains grown by connoisseur growers. It was among the first organizations to collect and share information about which strains best treat specific illnesses, and it embraced mold and microbe testing to minimize health risks to its members. It shunned plastic packaging in favor of glass, because plastic, according to one study, interacts with the plant's naturally occurring solvents to form carcinogens such as formaldehyde.[2] After five and half years, Backes severed his ties with the collective to author a book, *Cannabis Pharmacy*, and to set up Phytecs.

Backes may be a pioneering post-prohibitionist, but he has always enjoyed dancing on the cutting edge. He imported a plasma TV from Japan years before there was HD-anything to view on it. The technology was so compelling he just had to have it. He experimented with other psychoactive substances but now avoids them because they "grab too much bandwidth." He had a brief flirtation with an esoteric tonic of wild Changbai ginseng that cost $500 a pound. "It makes the price of a truffle look like a tomato," he says. "It's pure energy. I used to go through a bottle a month."

Pot provided a similar thrill when he was growing up in 1970s Tucson. He inhaled some of the legendary landrace strains that slipped across the Mexican border—Kona Gold, Panama Red, Big Sur Holy Weed, Thai Stick, Zacatecas Purple—and their smells and flavors are ingrained in his mind thanks to his eidetic memory. This idiosyncratic gift of recall was once mistakenly called a photographic memory—Teddy Roosevelt, Sergey Rachmaninoff, Abbie Hoffman, and the film director Guillermo Del Toro also have it in common. But Backes's memory is more Proustian; it allows near-total recall of sounds, tastes, and, significantly, smells. This rare ability to catalogue scents is why "noses" in the perfume industry are paid handsomely to blend essential oils into blockbuster fragrances, the finest of which leave lasting emotional impressions. It also gives Backes a unique competitive advantage in his new-found profession.

"Give me twenty strains and chances are I could name fifteen of them," he says without bluster. "It's practice. I'm not trying to be Robert Parker, and wine experts may be full of it anyway—they've blindfolded some of them and the results were not pretty—but I can honestly remember just how different Kona Gold was." A smile cuts across his face as the scent recollection of Kona Gold filters back into his consciousness. "Kona was the best high. It smelled piney like a Christmas tree and the high was like that moment on LSD when you're filled with a suffusion of joy and diamond clarity before you start tripping.

"That's why it cost $200 an ounce in 1979 [$700 in today's dollars] and came in a redwood box. People sit on pillows in monasteries for years to get to that. That's the goal with cannabis and it has been lost over time. Most people, thanks to prohibition, don't even know it's gone."

Microdosing also inspired Backes to vary the amounts he used for pleasure. He was soon mixing and matching dosage and delivery methods (smoking or vaporizing plus edibles) to potentiate specific moods, be it clarity and focus, creative idea generation, deep relaxation, or emotional connection in sex.

In tribal times, drug journeys were shaped by shamans who knew how to avoid treacherous routes and guide followers safely into other dimensions. The finest shamans don't act on superstition. They draw on a centuries-old body of systematic knowledge, and their techniques are honed and refined over time. Backes's cannabis intelligence is drawn from botany, chemistry, neurobiology, and hundreds of anecdotal reports, a rare set of skills that so impressed me that I anointed him my unofficial shaman.

When I was growing up, a joint rolled was a joint smoked down to the roach. We continued smoking stupid no matter how potent pot became. But to get interesting highs that don't knock you flat, twenty-first-century cannabis should be consumed in a twenty-first-century way. Backes says dose control is key.

Dose is one of the few ways that cannabis mirrors alcohol. One or two drinks can act as a social lubricant; five can make you socially disconnected. Aspirin is another example. At 600 milligrams, aspirin reduces pain and inflammation. At 100 to 160 milligrams, it unclogs arteries.[3] The relationship between dose and effect wasn't firmly established until Dr. Mark Wallace at the University of California, San Diego, injected capsaicin, the ingredient in chili pepper that burns, into the arms of volunteers and then treated them with varying doses of cannabis. At too low of a dose, subjects got no pain relief. A moderate dose provided excellent relief, but too high of a dose actually magnified the pain. The conclusion? Cannabis is so dose specific that large and small amounts create opposite effects.[4]

"Because it's nontoxic there's been no guidance and that's a problem," says Backes. "With tequila, someone might say, 'Don't drink five shots or you'll be unhappy.' No one says that with pot. They think that once you reach a certain level of psychoactivity you'll automatically know when to stop. You won't.

"A lot of people say they stopped smoking at some point because it made them paranoid. What's making them paranoid is an overdose of THC. Reduce that and it goes away. It took me a year to figure out to smoke a match head instead of a bowl." Binge smoking or oversmoking is yet another unforeseen result of prohibition, he contends, just as binge drinking became the norm in the 1920s and '30s, when drinkers would stockpile and guzzle as much grain alcohol as they could because they never knew where their next batch was coming from. "I can't help think that while science is undermining the prohibitionists' ability to support the lies about the dangers of cannabis, the dabbers are doing their best to keep it illegal," Backes says.

The second key to taming today's pot is understanding the role that the lost molecule, CBD, plays in modulating the high. Without it, aficionados claim the plant has morphed from something that produces a complex and subtle enhancement—think wine—to a powerful fuel, like grappa. CBD is often misidentified as the "high-less" weed, but in my experience it creates a subtle, warm feeling—

more of a flat "mid" than a rip-roaring high. This uninspiring semihigh is why growers in the 1980s and '90s bred CBD out of the plant. If the strains didn't send them flying, they would chuck the seeds to ensure they didn't produce another bum crop. It's why today's potent pot is often misconstrued as "great."

The problem with THC-only pot is that it's not what nature, in her infinite wisdom, intended. THC is a tricky chemical. It can be trippy, imparting sunny feelings of joy, but too much can create a trifecta of unpleasantness: paranoia, anxiety, and nausea. Here's why: When administered together, THC and CBD play Rock 'Em Sock 'Em Robots in the battle to fill receptors. But THC is much more adhesive than CBD; it's Superglue compared with CBD's old tape. THC usually lands first, but CBD will run interference, which tempers THC's effects. Even though they are often described as antagonists, they are more like old lovers. Yes, they fight, but overall they get on best when they're together.

One of CBD's less regaled attributes is its ability to dampen anxiety. One Brazilian research team demonstrated its usefulness in overcoming stage fright. It's a well-known dictum that people fear public speaking more than death; but when the subjects of this 2011 study were given CBD before taking the stage, it decreased their discomfort, anxiety, and sweating, and calmed their heart rates.[5]

To support this contention, Backes reminds me of this often-forgotten bit of cannabis ephemera: The Beatles, Charlie Parker, Carl Sagan, Bob Dylan, Allen Ginsberg—all the artists, writers, and thinkers that extolled cannabis for its creative fuel—weren't imbibing 25 percent THC. Their smoke was 4 or 5 percent THC, and it very likely contained an equal measure of CBD.

"When Dylan turned on Paul McCartney, Paul asked his assistant to follow him around and record the flood of ideas that cannabis was triggering. If he had smoked that amount of today's pot he'd have been on his back. Those creative highs had nothing to do with the stony Cheech and Chong highs. In California right now you can't find anything under eight percent THC, and that's twice as strong as what they were smoking." Perhaps the real act of creativity lies in knowing how much to use to get you where you want to go.[*]

According to Backes, educated Californians are using cannabis more as a precision instrument than a sledgehammer. The key words here are "education" and "precision." You need to know how much to take and how to deliver it into the body. The professionals (mostly in the film industry) Backes knows use a smidgen to open the spigot of creativity and help them get out of their own way. Larger doses are reserved for revising or going deeper into material. Other execs in high-pressure industries are substituting a low-dose 2.5-milligram edible for an afternoon cocktail to soften the rougher edges of the day and maintain calm. Those are far more noteworthy ways of using cannabis than just smoking until you can't stand up.

Athletes are also toying with dosages and delivery methods to contend with the rigors of training. Avery Collins is an ultramarathon runner who uses a smorgasbord of edibles to help him through his 120-mile-a-week workout. One ten-milligram edible makes a thirty-mile trek along the mountain trails in Steamboat Springs, Colorado, tick by. After a run, he'll soothe sore muscles with a topical salve that reduces inflammation. He reserves a joint for parties and other social occasions as an almost quaint, old-world pleasure. Oh, and he has never competed while high for fear of jeopardizing his integrity or his focus. "Cannabis is a mental enhancement for me, not a performance enhancer," he says. "I need to hold on to my determination. I don't want to see all that training wash away in one day."

---

[*] The Sanskrit Vedas counsel passing the chillum (the vertical pipe that Indian sadhus are often pictured cupping in their palms) three times and stopping for a while before taking in more.

Backes's deep understanding of the endocannabinoid system helped explain another mystery that had been confounding me: tolerance. Although my grower buddies were imbibing all day, it turns out that they're not getting as high, because their receptors are filled to the brim.

Wake-and-bakers say that their tolerance reduces side effects, such as loss of coordination and short-term memory. It's confusing how smoking more can reduce unwanted effects, but it was demonstrated in a little-noticed 1993 study by Dr. Miles Herkenham,[6] a principal investigator at the National Institute of Mental Health.

To understand tolerance, it's useful to understand the way dopamine, the neurotransmitter that stimulates the brain's "happy" center, works. Other drugs, including heroin, cocaine, amphetamines, alcohol, and nicotine, make us feel well by pumping up production of this pleasure juice, which titillates the brain's reward receptors. Heroin is so addictive because the brain quickly learns to treasure that pleasure and maximizes the amount of dopamine it produces. This, in turn, drives us to take more heroin, until the body requires those elevated levels to maintain homeostasis. If the body doesn't get its fix, a physiological storm moves in and certain systems go berserk, making addicts in withdrawal suffer cramps, diarrhea, and other wretchedness.

We know a lot about opiate addiction because the dopamine neurotransmitter system was discovered in the 1970s. But cannabinoid receptors weren't identified until the 1990s, and scientists simply assumed that cannabis worked in the same way—and they trumpeted their mistaken assumptions to the world. Their errors helped solidify some of the unfounded myths about cannabis addiction.

In his experiments, Herkenham gave mice different levels of

radioactively labeled synthetic THC for two weeks. The strongest doses were "the equivalent of smoking a thousand joints a day," Herkenham told me. At first, the superstoned mice were catatonic, so docile that the scientists could arrange their tiny limbs in different yoga positions with no resistance. But after a few days they noticed that the mice hit with the highest doses began to regain motor control more quickly.

When the scientists dissected the mice's brains, they saw those exposed to extreme THC had the fewest available cannabinoid receptors.[7] The body, in its infinite wisdom, had reduced the number of receptors that THC could bind to so the animals couldn't get as high.*

"Down regulating" cannabinoid receptors is the body's way of placing a ceiling on every high. It also explains how heavy users can smoke all day and go about their business, while more casual users would be drooling had they consumed the same amount.

And the reason cannabis causes virtually no withdrawal? There are no receptors in tissues that trigger withdrawal symptoms, just as there are no cannabinoid receptors in the brain areas that control the heart or lungs. "That's one of the nicest things about working with cannabinoids," Herkenham told me. "You can give ten thousand times a typical dose and it won't kill the animal." Or a human.

But here's the possible bad news: the effects of long-term down regulation are as yet unknown. If you're supplementing the body's main regulatory system with a large supply of THC in dabs, for example, and your body isn't producing as many endocannabinoids, there's a chance that you could tip your body into a state of

---

*In fact, the most highly dosed animals had the greatest decrease in receptors (up to 80 percent), the lowest-dosed animals had the lowest reduction (up to 50 percent), and the middle-dosed group exhibited an intermediate reduction (up to 72 percent), as shown in the previously cited study by Angelica Oviedo, John Glowa, and Miles Herkenham.

endocannabinoid deficiency. This is speculative, but other neuro-transmitter systems have diseases associated with deficiencies: dementia in Alzheimer's disease is correlated with a loss of acetyl-choline; parkinsonism is associated with low levels of dopamine; and depression is associated with low levels of serotonin.[8] Why should the endocannabinoid system, which has the greatest recep-tor density of all, be the exception?

As to what those unforeseen effects of down regulation might be, it's anyone's guess. There haven't been any longitudinal studies, but I have found that people who oversmoke for years on end do seem to exhibit some form of cognitive dulling. They lose some of their brightness and become disconnected from their inner lives (canna-bis takes away dreams, which might explain this disconnection).

These issues are the same with any substance, and the conse-quences differ depending on the drug. The writer Adam Hanft published an unforgettable article about the contributions anti-depressants made to the financial crisis of 2008. He found that prescriptions for Lexapro, Prozac, and Seroquel, the drugs that so many white-collar professionals rely on to fight off depression and power through their days, spiked in the years leading up to the recession and possibly numbed the ability of the managers to assess risk.[9] In other words, derivatives look really good if you don't care about the results. I'm not drawing a parallel between cannabis and antidepressants, but as we learn more about how the ECS functions, we would be reckless to ignore what we know about dose, tolerance, and what it means to smoke smart. Sorry, stoners. Post-prohibition means it's time to get real.

To understand how to think about designing highs that can change your mind or mood in certain desired directions, you need to understand terpenes. These powerful smell molecules, the most common of which are key components in lemon, pepper, lavender, and pine, create the pungent aromas of fresh bud (see the terpene chart at the end of the chapter). We're not talking mild aromatherapy here. Terpenes in cannabis occur in pharmaceutical-grade concentrations. When dried and heated, they combine to form a chemical cascade that may direct the trajectory of the high.

"THC increases how fast terpenes cross the blood-brain barrier," contends Backes. "Kona Gold, Panama Red, Acapulco Gold, all these great seventies genetics that got you beautifully high had lower THC content than strains today, but they had a lot of terpenes." In other words, THC determines how wide the door to the brain opens; terpenes are the different paths that are illuminated once you walk through.

From a sheath of papers Backes unfolds a chromatograph that compares the terpene content of two strains, Bubba Kush and Lemon Haze. Both have comparable levels of THC, between 13 and 15 percent, but their highs are different thanks to their terpene mixes. The peaks and dips of the lines resemble the "Random Hill" profile on a stationary exercise bike, but they zig and zag in opposite directions. Bubba Kush has a higher concentration of myrcene and linalool, two terps that cause relaxation. Lemon Haze is richer in pinene and limonene, making it more uplifting and clear.

Although I've used the words "indica" and "sativa" throughout this book, they are not reliable indicators of the stimulating or sedative qualities of one strain. In fact, the best indicator of whether a strain will bring you up or down is its terpene profile. "Once you start to know the different terpenes and how they work, you can more reliably predict the effects," says Backes.

At this point, reading the terpenes is more a forecast than a road map to each high because of a complicated interplay of chemicals known as the entourage effect. The entourage effect is best understood in musical terms: Individual instruments produce lovely sounds on their own, but the majesty of a symphony can be realized only when all the instruments play together. Terpenes are the violins and flutes, and only when they mix with other cannabinoids can the symphonic complexity of the high be realized. This also explains how cannabis has outfoxed pharmaceutical companies in their attempts to isolate and patent single-molecule medicines. The sum of cannabis's chemical parts is greater than any one of its individual components. Just as with certain celebrities who walk the red carpet, the major cannabinoids need their entourages to function optimally.

Those of us who live in illegal states smoke what our dealers bring us and hope for the best. But Backes and other pioneers of the new cannabis era are hoping to combine terpenes to engineer effects that are more predictable. GW Pharmaceuticals is breeding plants that are high in one minor cannabinoid called THCV, for example, that retards appetite and may work like a diet pill. A natural, plant-based product that gets you skinny and makes you feel happy? Now there's a business!

But it's a ways away. In the meantime, I ask my shaman what he might recommend for crisp, transparent highs that will also relieve the stiffness of my lumbar and cervical spine, my occasional insomnia, and the other indignities of aging.

For physical issues, he recommends low-dose aspirin, eighty milligrams every day for inflammation, and a high-CBD cannabis strain to ease the pain.

To sleep, I'm to take a vapor hit or two one and a half hours before bed—that will allow the high to fade in time to allow the metabolites that encourage sleepiness to kick in. And he recommends a low-dose edible just before I hit the pillow. The effects will come on after an hour, which should carry me through the night.

"To counteract morning fuzzies, eat two tablespoons of almond butter before bed. That keeps your sugar level even so you wake up sharp. For some, slow-morning starts are age related, for others it's insulin resistance. In either case it works like a charm.

"For your high, a pinene-enhanced narrow-leaf variety appears to intensify psychoactivity and eliminate memory deficits. It's not much guesswork, because you are very specific: whereas most people are just getting stoned, you want to get high. A sublingual candy once a day will also extend the length of a high," Backes tells me. "I always make sure to have THC in a ratio with CBD that works for me. And remember, microdosing promotes hyperfocus and avoids bounce-back."

Bounce-back?

"The endocannabinoid system loves balance. If you hit yourself with a big dose, your body's going to try to balance out, so the system will swing back in the other direction. It's like riding a seesaw. Two people of the same weight can balance but if some big guy jumps on one end, the little guy on the other end is going to lose his teeth. When you dabbed, you got hit in the teeth.

"What you probably want is something that goes up and comes down smoothly without a peak. Personally, I don't want an intense high. I want a gentle onset, a long-lasting effect, and then something that just disappears."

Lester Grinspoon learned forty years ago that everything he knew about cannabis was wrong because of official lies. Now that science has refuted the lies, the fog is lifting. Guiding the high is the next frontier.

Backes turned out to be a superb shaman, but he wasn't, alas, a guru: microdosing and mixing delivery systems (one five-milligram edible plus one or two hits on a joint) is an excellent way to eke out different nuances from a high, but it didn't curtail my vomiting response. Nor did specifying the origin of the strain—puking occurred with buds from California, Colorado, and homegrown East Coast varieties, too. A bong, a joint, a pipe—every method of smoking except for vaporization—brought it on, and sometimes after just two modest hits.

Nor did "set and setting" make a difference. This term, coined by Dr. Timothy Leary, explains that all drug experiences are shaped by mind-set as well as physical setting. My eruptions occurred under diverse conditions—alone, in small groups, once at a dinner party I was hosting in my own apartment. Believe me, when the host of the party disappears abruptly into the bathroom for twenty minutes and emerges ashen-faced, his credibility as poster boy for the New World of Weed is shot.

My adverse reaction, as I learned in talking to other users, isn't all that uncommon. It just hasn't been properly addressed in the literature. Something else in the plant was triggering it, as Dr. Brian Becker, an integrative physician who runs a dispensary in Tucson, Arizona, explained to me. Becker suggested that a component of certain sativa strains that I favored could be bombarding the "chemoreceptor trigger zone" (CTZ) in the medulla oblongata of my brain, an area that's also packed with cannabinoid receptors. His solution, if I wish to continue using pot (which I do), was to switch to an indica strain with a different terpene mix, or to find something with an equal ratio of THC and CBD. "CBD is your life raft," he told me.

Nice idea, Doc, but I live in the old world. Even if people in New York knew what CBD was, such a specific strain was almost impossible to obtain. It wasn't until I read a blog post by Dr. Allan Frankel irresistibly titled "How to Extend Your High from Two Hours to Six" that I found one of the life rafts that Becker spoke of.

Frankel is a warm, possibly brilliant, and at times volatile character—like many people on the forefront of cannabis exploration, he's an outsider who has battled the authorities, as well as his own demons. Marcus Welby he's not.

For thirty years Frankel was an openly procannabis internist with a busy practice on Wilshire Boulevard in Los Angeles. But he ran into trouble with the Medical Board of California for prescribing OxyContin to his girlfriend without keeping clinical notes (sin

#1) and then popping some of those opioid painkillers himself (sin #2). When the board got wind of his ethical breeches, it suspended his medical license for fifteen months. Sympathetic cannabis advocates portray Frankel as a victim of pot politics, but medical professionals across the board assured me he was sloppy, perhaps not thinking clearly, and in clear violation of medical ethics. In the service of my investigation, I suspended judgment and paid him a visit.

Frankel has since reinvented himself as a $175/hour consulting cannabis physician. He has absorbed an enormous amount of information from botany, chemistry, and medical studies, which led to the invention of a concentrated whole-plant spray that works like Sativex but is far less expensive—270 sprays of Sativex costs about $700 in the United Kingdom, where it is sold, whereas an equivalent amount of Frankel's formula sells for about $200. Frankel claims that his formula includes all of the terpenes and compounds that occur in nature and is easy to use—a few spritzes under the tongue, and it hits the bloodstream in fifteen minutes. Some people call this a joint in a bottle. Frankel refers to it more grandiloquently as his Golden Oil.

Frankel's oil is designed to appeal to doctors conversant in the post-prohibitionist world of receptor medicines. It is prescribed in precise milligrams rather than grams, which is standard in medical practice. He brags about the successes he's had with weight loss, certain psychiatric conditions, and even some cancers. A half dozen patients I spoke to supported his claims, but frustratingly he hasn't documented his findings, so there's no objective evidence by which to evaluate them. Mavericks, especially in the weed world, are not always organized.

But here's where his system really succeeds. The meds are calibrated on a psychoactivity scale of one to ten. Number one is almost all CBD, with just a smidgen of THC. Frankel recommends every smoker keep a bottle in the medicine chest as an antidote to uncomfortable THC moments. Numbers seven and above are high in THC and used for severe sleep disorders.

"People don't usually come to me with problems like yours," he told me when we met in his Santa Monica office. "They're more like, 'I have cancer that's eating my face.' And, I would prefer you use the term 'overmedicating' to 'overdosing.' 'Overdose' is such a loaded word."

For one of those bell-ringing clear highs Backes had extolled, Frankel suggested number five, which has CBD and THC in equal ratios. "Do you want to be more focused, smiley, feel less moody, happier? Would feeling awesome for six hours be acceptable over being stoned for two?"

Who could say no? I opened wide and lifted my tongue.

Two sprays and thirty minutes later, a warm fizzle spread through my body. I was energized yet grounded and clear. The high wasn't nearly as enveloping as smoking—it was more of a gentle, warm kiss that even allowed me to read. It's what awesome feels like.

And it's efficient. A joint sends 80 percent of the cannabinoids up in smoke; a pipe, 50 percent. With extracts like Frankel's you get 100 percent absorption. Extra bonus: oral spray is no scarier to use than a minty breath spray. "Anyone who isn't comfortable smoking a joint for their medical health—that's my niche," Frankel says.

Not only are the sprays less frightening for the inexperienced, the extracts have no odor and come in small brown bottles that make them undetectable when traveling. So I carried home a few bottles and offered them to my ninety-four-year-old mother, who hasn't had a full night's sleep in ten years but who refuses tranquilizers or sleeping pills because they make her dizzy and prone to falling. Believe me, this is a woman who abhorred marijuana, but before I could finish explaining how the extract is produced, she was pumping some into her mouth. The first few nights were a bust, but by the end of week one she had a few delicious nights

of uninterrupted sleep and was noticeably more peppy during the
day. And then, out of nowhere, her caregivers stopped the meds.

"Why on earth did you stop?" I asked them.

"She's just not herself. She's running around, washing dishes.
She's almost giddy, and we're afraid she might fall."

I was left, as I seldom am, speechless.

I liked the Frankel system. I enjoyed the clear high that came with
no adverse side effects. But it's impractical if you're not a Californian,
since US law forbids shipping cannabis meds across state lines. I
was back to square one until I stumbled upon what turned out to
be another life raft, the Plenty vaporizer.

Until the Plenty, vaporizing technology left me (and many users)
unimpressed. Sure, vaporizers are convenient and fit neatly into
a pocket, but their temperature controls are unreliable—you can
often taste burning plant along with the vapor, which scratches the
throat. Plus, they just don't deliver a satisfying high. You take off
but you never soar.

The Plenty is neither convenient nor sexy, and it definitely attracts
attention. It requires an electrical outlet, and it looks like a hybrid of
a Black & Decker drill and a Flash Gordon ray gun. But don't let its
clunky appearance fool you. The Plenty unleashes a generous draw,
a full aromatic burst of flavor, and a sunny high with far less face-
punching cognitive disturbance than you'll get from a joint.

This power tool for cannabists is the brainchild of Markus
Storz, half of Storz & Bickel, the same German company that produced the Volcano in 2001. For over a decade, the company has
successfully marketed its devices to the worldwide medical community, while maintaining a strict silence about what herbs its
machines vaporize so as not to run afoul of strict American import
laws. Both Storz and his partner, Jürgen Bickel, shun publicity and

have never revealed themselves to be cannabists. They needn't. The way their inventions coax flavors from the plant makes their proclivities abundantly clear.

Unlike standard-issue vaporizers that use conduction heat only, the Plenty blends conduction with convection to deliver a higher quality of satisfaction. Conduction is created by a small heating element (an internal oven, as it were); convection moves the hot air away from the heat source. This combination makes the Plenty the world's first precision vaporizer, because the temperature can be accurately controlled. It can reach 420 degrees Fahrenheit (wink), but the coiled mouthpiece ensures a cool draw.

In the same way digital technology has disrupted the "delivery system" of the cable television or music businesses, advanced vape technology could alter the way people have smoked for centuries. A vaporizer high is qualitatively different from a smoking high. It leaves users feeling less tired, forgetful, disoriented, and nauseated. Many smokers complain that it isn't the sort of face slap they are familiar with, and they are correct. There is less cognitive interference than one gets from smoking a joint or a bowl, simply because terpenes and cannabinoids melt at lower temperatures than those required to burn the plant. What's more—and this is crucial—smoking includes tars and toxins, the culprits responsible for couchlock and other adverse reactions, very likely including vomiting. I have used the Plenty for ten months and never felt even the threat of nausea.

As we learn more about the inner workings of the plant, we may one day find it possible to set the temperatures of these precision vapes to extract specific cannabinoids for different effects. Once the vaporization points of terpenes are identified, these instruments may allow us to extract more limonene for mental clarity, say, or more linalool to get to sleep, or any number of different compounds that might help the sick heal. This isn't to say the joint or the pipe are dead, but science, technology, and curious minds are allowing us to tap the complex botanical factory inside this plant to produce specific effects that until now we've never been able to control.

HOW TO READ A TESTING LABEL

LAGUNA WOODS FOR MEDICAL CANNABIS

Cannabaceutical™ Facts

Blue Headband — Hybrid / Organic

Tested On: **October 14, 2014**

Total Aerobic Count	Gold	Total Yeast & Mold	Gold	
Total Entero-bacteria	Gold	Pesticides Screen	Pass	
Δ⁹-THC Max:	17.99 %	Sum of Top Terpenes	30.6	mg/g
Δ⁹-THCA	19.85 %			
Δ⁹-THC	0.57 %	Myrcene	15.3	mg/g
CBD Max:	0.27 %	α-Pinene	6.9	mg/g
CBDA	0.16 %	β-Caryophyllene	3.5	mg/g
CBD	0.12 %	Limonene	2.1	mg/g
CBG Max	1.04 %	α-Humulene	1.6	mg/g
Δ⁹-THCVA	0.13 %	α-Bisabolol	0.9	mg/g
CBN	ND %	Linalool	0.4	mg/g

Do not use while operating a car or heavy machinery. Keep out of reach of children. For medical use only. Wt.% reported as equivalent of neutral cannabinoids. Visit www.TheWercShop.com to learn more and leave your comments.

For people who enjoy reading food labels, the lab testing of marijuana is a revelation. This label, produced by the Werc Shop in Pasadena, California, for the Laguna Woods retirement community, provides an analysis of the Blue Headband strain. Is it definitive? Not as definitive as the marketers of cannabis products would like us to believe, according to the Werc Shop's founder, Dr. Jeffrey Raber. All the studies on terpenes and cannabinoids to date have been done on single molecules, but no breakdown of individual compounds can predict the entourage effect that these chemicals produce when heated and mixed. Understanding the numbers means you're not flying quite so blindly, so it's best to think of these labels as guides, not definitive road maps to your high.

The results of this test indicate that the high would be stony and likely to end in a powerful sedative crash.

Aerobic, Entero-bacteria, Yeast and Mold: These are all micro-biological screens. A gold rating passes with flying colors; silver is questionable. Bronze means trouble.

Pesticides: Any pesticides detected would "fail" and not be salable.

THC Max: 17.99 percent is powerful but not extraordinarily so by today's standards.

THCA: This is a measure of the THC acid on the leaf before it is burned and becomes THC. THCA is a strong anti-inflammatory and is not psychoactive. This percentage correlates with the amount of THC and is also a mark of freshness.

CBD Max: Coming in at 0.27 percent, there's not much here. High-CBD strains are now available in most medical markets, with ranges rivaling the high-THC plants in the mid to upper teens, and occasionally as high as 20 percent.

CBG: Another nonpsychoactive cannabinoid with some painkilling benefits. Dr. Raber calls this a good level.

THCV: This is a THC analogue that is involved in the appetite cascade, but it does not have psychoactive properties. Concentration is low.

CBN: CBN indicates if the bud is old, which this isn't.

Terpenes: The smell molecules that help determine the trajectory of the high.

Myrcene: A terpene that purportedly contributes to the couchlock and sleepy "indica" effect. Anything over 8 or 10 will potentially produce a noticeable effect.

Pinene: This terpene dilates the bronchial tubes in the lungs. It is stimulating and enhances focus. An appreciable number is present here.

Beta-caryophyllene: The back-notes in black pepper and cloves, beta-caryophyllene is in high concentration, which indicates that it will activate more receptors in the body.

Limonene: A terpene that's anti-inflammatory, antitumor, and anti-fungal. It is purported to produce feelings of clarity in some strains. This Blue Headband sample has a negligible amount.

Linalool: The small amount of this terpene indicates it may be slightly sedative, but this effect could also be overwhelmed by the larger amounts of other terpenes present.

Terpene	Sounds Like	Smells Like	Medical Use	Type of High
Limonene	*LYME-o-neen*	The sour in citrus fruits like lemons and grapefruit	Works as an antidepressant and can cause breast cancer cells to commit suicide. It has been used clinically to dissolve gallstones, improve mood, and relieve heartburn and gastrointestinal reflux.	Uplifting
Myrcene	*MUHR-seen*	The "green" musky odor prevalent in bay, thyme, and hops	Works as a sedative, muscle relaxant, hypnotic, analgesic (painkiller), and anti-inflammatory compound.	Couchlock
Pinene	*PINE-een*	Pine	Nature's most pervasive terpene is also anti-inflammatory and a bronchodilator. It is potentially helpful for asthma, and promotes alertness and memory retention by inhibiting the breakdown of acetylcholinesterase, a neurotransmitter in the brain that stimulates these cognitive effects.	Clear, bright, sunny
Linalool	LIN-a-lool	Lavender	Anti-anxiety and stress reducing. A powerful anticonvulsant that also amplifies serotonin-receptor transmission, thus serving as an antidepressant.	Relaxing
Beta-caryophyllene	*Beta-carry-OFF-a-lean*	Found in the background of black pepper, oregano, and clove	Gastroprotective, good for certain ulcers, and shows great promise as a therapeutic compound for inflammatory conditions and autoimmune disorders. Airport dogs were once trained to detect an oxide produced from beta-caryophyllene. Today those canines have been reassigned to sniff out truly dangerous items like explosive devices.	Little psychoactive effect

Source: http://www.alternet.org/drugs/same-compounds-behind-marijuanas-distinctive-stinky-smells-give-clues-about-kinds-high-youll

Chapter 10

THE FOUR ENHANCEMENTS

Inside the mind (wherever that is)

Ineffability is the hallmark of any consciousness-changing pursuit, which makes it powerful to experience but difficult to discuss. Because most of marijuana's powers are not as immediately obvious as its capacities for fun or relaxation, and because we tend to oversmoke the plant, it seems preposterous at first glance that this mere weed might be a route to higher cognitive functioning.

It's difficult not to conjure up those cartoons that feature a shaggy-haired stoner, gazing at a smartphone uttering something banal, like "Oh wow, man!" Dumbfounded by the obvious, inarticulate to the extreme, that's the perception of the cannabis user. But I have come to think that even those words "Oh wow, man!" contain a key attribute of cannabis consciousness: an expanded receptivity to the world. Cannabis opens the reducing valve that is our brain. The taste of food, the embrace of a lover, the colors of the sea—the world is more vibrant, more amplified in the enhanced state. A more intriguing question might be, "Is there more to being high than an amplified state of receptivity?"

I began to explore the idea by examining recent studies with psilocybin and people facing the end of their lives. These studies concluded that psychedelics can create powerful and permanent changes in hearts and minds. Of course, cannabis confers a far more attenuated experience than psilocybin does, and I'm not comparing them head-on. But both substances are classified as psychedelics, not because they cause hallucinations, but because, as the Greek root of the word indicates, they both reveal the mind (*psychē* = mind, and *dēloun* = to make visible, to reveal). Unlike those of psilocybin, however, the effects of cannabis are inconsistent. I've long thought this inconsistency is the primary reason that people who like control shy away from pot and veer toward more predictable substances.

Opiates lull users into a pleasant reverie. They blunt the senses, bringing relief but little palpable joy. Cocaine, meth, and amphetamines rev us up by dumping massive amounts of dopamine in the brain. They make us feel powerful, but they don't tie us to anything beyond our own temporarily bloated egos. Alcohol is socially lubricating in small amounts, but drink too much and the effects become depressive or disinhibiting, and you tune other people out. Psychedelics and cannabis (dosed properly) enhance our receptivity to other humans, animals, and maybe to something sacred. The effects of cannabis are not nearly as dramatic or life altering as those of psilocybin, DMT, or LSD, which is one reason why it is used less often in shamanic and other holy rituals.

Most organized religions make little mention of the plants that yoked humans to the divine, even though, as Richard Schultes, the godfather of psychoactive plant research, noted, cannabis "may have introduced man to an otherworldly plane from which emerged religious beliefs, perhaps even the concept of deity. The plant became accepted as a special gift of the gods, a sacred medium for communion with the spiritual world, and as such it has remained in some cultures to the present."[1]

Scholars agree that as organized religions exerted their sway over more followers, they demonized the spiritual connection between plants and people. Priests in the Middle Ages labeled plant users sorcerers or witches who relied on potions to cast spells on others. The Spanish Conquistadores brutalized *curanderas* in Mexico who used psilocybin and peyote to open doors to a secreted world. Unlike the Rastafarians and Hinduism's Shiva sect, both of which still use pot as a gateway to the divine, most Western religions shun mind-expanding substances in favor of prayer, confession, repentance, and suffering—methods of redemption that keep the flock corralled and reinforce the church's authority.

Pot famously supplies an extra measure of perspective, and perspective is very threatening to those who don't want their authority questioned.

The yoga sutras, written in Sanskrit a few hundred years before Christ, cite "herbs" as one of five methods of piercing the veil between the conscious and unconscious mind. Conventional religious scholars contend the "herbs" in question refer to everyday cooking items. But Mark Haskell Smith, the author of *Heart of Dankness: Underground Botanists, Outlaw Farmers, and the Race for the Cannabis Cup*, is fairly certain that the sutras weren't talking about cardamom. A yoga practitioner for over twenty years, Smith said a few puffs before practice guides him "more deeply into the poses."[2] Not I. Except for activities that I perform on autopilot—swimming, cycling, or skiing, say—pot has never aided my physical prowess. Nor has it ever brought me closer to God, whoever she may be.

And while neuroscience has described the mechanics of molecules' crossing certain synaptic gaps to couple with proteins to activate receptors, those explanations are far less compelling than the effects the substances yield. Science can provide a partial answer, but I have found the reports of poets, philosophers, and astronomers far more insightful about how the states of expanded consciousness *feel*.

Carl Sagan captured the many-faceted sensations of being high in a breakthrough essay he wrote in 1969 as Mr. X. "I do not consider myself a religious person in the usual sense, but there is a religious aspect to some highs. The heightened sensitivity in all areas gives me a feeling of communion with my surroundings, both animate and inanimate. Sometimes a kind of existential perception of the absurd comes over me and I see with awful certainty the hypocrisies and posturing of myself and my fellow man. And at other times, there is a different sense of the absurd, a playful and whimsical awareness. . . ."[3]

Communion with nature and with other beings, an existential perception of the absurd, a distance that yields perspective: these are the experiences that I find interesting. They are also the areas that empirical science has the most difficulty describing.

Around the same time Sagan was exploring pot, Dr. Andrew Weil wrote in *The Natural Mind* that altering consciousness was a fundamental urge in human beings, and that we use all sorts of substances to change our minds—caffeine, sugar, alcohol, tobacco, among them. Aldous Huxley and Timothy Leary had previously flirted with similar ideas, but Weil, the father of integrative medicine in the West, surveyed cultures globally and included meditation, dancing, fasting, yoga, and prayer in his methods of altering consciousness. Weil also pointed out that this urge occurs in children as well. As kids, both he and I were addicted to hyperventilating and spinning in circles, an indulgence I pursued until the age of eleven, when I succeeded in blacking out and cracking my skull on the sharp edge of a table as I crumbled to the floor. Thus I learned to proceed cautiously when altering consciousness, for it is not always possible to predict where you'll land.

But it isn't only our species that seeks an altered state. Dr. Ronald Siegel, a psychopharmacologist who was an associate research professor in the Department of Psychiatry and Biobehavioral Sciences at UCLA, posited that the urge to transcend our everyday minds is a fourth drive in humans, followed only by the drives for drink, food, and sex, and that this fourth drive is shared by all creatures. Certain butterflies get drunk by sipping on the alcohol produced by fermented fruits on vines or trees; cats get sexually charged by catnip; coffee beans drive goats into ecstatic states that frequently end with them temporarily abandoning their guard against predators and tumbling down hills. "In every country, in almost every class of animal, I found examples of not only the accidental but the intentional use of drugs," Siegel wrote. "After examining thousands of cases, I conclude that the action of an animal in seeking out intoxicants was a natural behavior in the animal kingdom."[4]

Siegel's observation, while fascinating, isn't wholly accurate as far as the motivation of insects is concerned. Newer research indicates that their tiny brains lack pleasure centers, so the "intoxication" they feel may simply be agitation.[5] Nor is their "intention" an act of free will, as the concept of agency or mind can't be applied to insects. But the human brain is far more complex. Its topography is as baffling as the way it functions. Recent theories describe the brain as an infinite number of chemical pathways—neural maps—that traverse different areas when firing. Robin Carhart-Harris, a British neuroscientist who is using fMRI technology with patients on psilocybin journeys, is one such cartographer of consciousness.

By planting microelectrodes inside the brain, he is able to see changes in blood flow and oxygen levels of different areas. But he takes this one step further by talking to patients who are tripping on psilocybin and then correlating what he sees on scans with what people are experiencing. He is literally opening a window into the mind—or, more accurately, the brain, since we have no idea where the human mind resides.

We tend to think of our brains as sponges that absorb sensory data, but the brain functions more as an editor that prunes the heaps of sensory input of our daily lives so that we can make sense of it all. In *The Doors of Perception*, Aldous Huxley compared the brain to a reducing valve that shuts out most of the information flooding into our senses. When Carhart-Harris looked at the results of his fMRI scans that pinpointed the areas that the drugs were affecting, he saw that Huxley was onto something. Psychedelics substantially reduced brain activity in the various interconnected areas known as the "default-mode network," rather than opening up the floodgates of perception.

The default-mode network was first described in 2001, and it has since become the favored metaphor by which neuroscientists discuss the structure of consciousness. In the beginning of the twentieth century, Freud described the architecture of consciousness in terms of ego, id, and superego. In the 1980s, it was left-brain/right-brain thinking. But the default-mode network is the first neural structure that scientists have actually been able to see at work.

Basically, it comprises a hub of brain activity that activates when we are at a state of wakeful rest. It's on when we are not attending to the world or to a task, and it "lights up" when we are daydreaming, ruminating, or removed from sensory processing. It's akin to what is commonly referred to as right-brain thinking. It is however, self-referential, which means it always maintains a concept of the bounded self.

Carhart-Harris discovered that blood flow and electrical activity in the default-mode network shut down significantly when people are on psychedelics. Since he was able to speak to the patients as he was viewing these neurochemical changes, he listened to them consistently describe the loss of self and the merging with the universe that occurs while tripping. When the default-mode network shuts down, activity in other brain regions is unleashed, and things hidden from view during normal waking consciousness come to the fore: emotions, memories, wishes, and fears. Regions that don't ordinarily communicate directly with one another strike up conversations.

Carhart-Harris agrees with Freud that the psychedelic state resembles the psychological condition of the infant who has yet to develop a sense of himself as a bounded individual. Psychedelics loosen the ego boundaries that separate us from the rest of the world and allow the workings of the unconscious mind to rise above the surface. They remove a filter that hides much of reality. It's possible—probable even—that cannabis does the same thing, but to a lesser extent.*

This sort of enhanced thinking can help people by relaxing the grip of our overbearing egos and the rigid rationality they enforce. By adulthood, the mind has learned to predict and anticipate the way the world works based on past experiences. Such habitual thinking saves us a lot of mental energy, since we don't have to approach every situation with what the Buddhists call beginner's mind. Rote thinking—doing things on autopilot—enables us to survive and navigate our complex environments.

Up to a point. In Carhart-Harris's view, adults pay a steep price for order. "We give up our emotional lability, our ability to be open to surprises, our ability to think flexibly, and our ability to value nature," as Carhart-Harris puts it.[6] The ego can become despotic. This becomes clear when we are depressed. The self turns inward and the uncontrollable introspection gradually grays out reality.[7]

Carhart-Harris contends that people suffering from mental disturbances characterized by excessively rigid patterns of thinking, such as addiction or obsessive-compulsive disorders, could

---

*I don't want to overstate the effects of cannabis or equate it with the power of psilocybin. The cannabis experience is hugely different than that of psychedelics, not just in terms of degree but of quality. Dr. Erin Zerbo, an assistant professor in the Department of Psychiatry at Rutgers New Jersey Medical School, clarified this: "The brain is such a complicated system with lots of parts. It's also possible that activated cannabinoid receptors in the hippocampus and elsewhere in the brain might impair memory formation [not everyone agrees that this is an "impairment"], so perhaps that alone creates the feeling of living 'moment to moment,' of going forward without knowing where you just were."

benefit from psychedelics, since they "disrupt stereotyped patterns of thought and behavior." In his view, these disorders are ailments of the ego. He also suspects that psychedelically induced disruptions could lead to more creative thinking—some brains could benefit from a little less order. Whether cannabis can take them there is yet to be proved, but there is ample evidence that it is one way of "pulling back the veil of consciousness," to paraphrase William James, to open us to a different way of greeting the world.

Even if you've never taken a substance, this less mediated way of thinking will feel vaguely familiar—we call it intuition or daydreaming. Those who are more prone to being hypnotized or who are more plugged into the voices inside their heads—and I'm not one of them—rely on intuition more than their reason-based minds. When people do something "without thinking about it," or when they are in the "flow," they're letting go of some cognitive processing and accessing some of these other, more instinctive forms of awareness.

Western culture favors rational thinking over this more mysterious or "spiritual" thought. You don't have to be a religious person to recognize this. But by stressing the rational, we sacrifice a certain amount of receptivity to the natural world around us. I'm not arguing that cannabis will help us contend with climate change or the eradication of certain animal species, but there is little doubt that it affects the way we see our place in life's grand order. This enhanced receptivity, not to mention insight, empathy, and awe, are but a few of the cognitive functions that cannabis underscores. I refer to them as the Four Enhancements.

RECEPTIVITY

Cannabis enhances our responsiveness to the world around us and inside our own bodies as well. When high, all of our senses—

touch, taste, sound, sight, smell—become *italicized*, in Michael Pollan's phrasing, as if we are capable of absorbing more color, flavor, and scent.

Increased receptivity means that we are, as the poet bell hooks put it, less amputated from our emotional lives. This may explain why more men gravitate to pot than women. Forgive the generalization, but women typically appear to be innately more emotional and intuitive than men. Men, for many reasons, favor the rational and logical over the more inward-facing side of themselves, and thus can lose touch with it. Pot, used mindfully, can reconnect them with their more nurturing aspects.

Experienced smokers don't resist these states. Like a skier coursing through moguls, they lean into them and ride them to deeper pleasures. I'm thinking in particular of two cognitive functions that pot famously distorts: short-term memory and one's sense of time. When these cognitive disruptions occur, thoughts and feelings bullet through our brains more quickly than we can process. Verbal acuity sometimes flies out the window, perhaps because we're taking in so much more. When we're more open, we're less invested in being on top of things, and this can be misinterpreted as being vulnerable, gullible, less aware—even though we may well be absorbing more than otherwise.

The first thing that nonsmokers notice when high is the short-circuiting of their short-term memories, a state I call memory interruptus. This state of thoughts darting in and out of the brain so quickly that they can't be grasped can make anyone feel just one step away from early-onset Alzheimer's. It doesn't last long, and no long-term effects on memory have ever been demonstrated. Still, it can be disconcerting when it's not hilarious, as it often is, as this snippet from the cult comedy classic *A Child's Garden of Grass* illustrates:

VIRGINIA: "Are you hungry?"

ANDY: "No (long reflective pause). Wait a minute. Did you mean am I hungry for food or am I hungry in the abstract, like hungry for knowledge or adventure?"

VIRGINIA: "What were we talking about?"

ANDY: "You asked if I were hungry."

VIRGINIA: "Did I?"

ANDY: "Yes."

VIRGINIA: "Well, are you?"

ANDY: "Am I what?"

As Sebastián Marincolo points out in *High: Insights on Marijuana*, his brilliant book that examines the benefits of pot as opposed to the detriments, and to which I am indebted for much of the thinking in this chapter, experienced users can turn memory interruptus to their advantage.

Marincolo says that memory interruptus may to some degree be caused by mind racing, which could lead to a sort of buffering problem in the brain. If you take a rapid series of photos—of athletes performing, say—the camera eventually needs a moment to save the images, and at that instant the "stream" breaks. This could very well happen with our thought stream during a high. It's less of an "impairment" of short-term memory than an overflow of input. Marincolo also suggests that the pre-synesthetic effect of the high allows for wider associative leaps in thinking, so conversations travel far beyond the original subject; this makes it hard to recollect where you started and easier to lose the thread.

But when users quiet down and allow their receptivity to increase, they can access different types of memory—associative and episodic among them. A skilled user can relax and let go of his rational mind and allow other memories buried deep in the vaults to rise to the surface. In fact, before cannabis was banned in the

United States, psychiatrists from the American Medical Association testified to Congress that memory retrieval was one of the most promising uses of the herb in psychotherapy.[8]

There's one additional benefit of memory interruptus, which is one of cannabis's greatest unheralded pleasures: it can create a more childlike way of viewing the world. This, in turn, results in a renewed sense of awe, an ideal remedy for jaded adults in need of fresh eyes.

Picture a child who's greeting the world for the first time. Everything tickles him. But for adults to experience awe, we must first forget our preconceived notions. Cannabis assists that, and it offers one additional benefit: it is gentle. It lifts us out of our everyday minds without making us lose our minds.

The writer and art dealer Mark Wolfe marshaled some of that childlike "Oh wow, man!" awareness to help him contend with some of the rougher patches of fatherhood. He discovered that cannabis, which he had been using to alleviate back pain, had one amazing off-label benefit: parental attention–surplus syndrome.

After a long day at work in his gallery, Wolfe found himself to be a dutiful, but not especially enthusiastic, dad to his three daughters. Fatherly obligations felt like chores, mostly because he was exhausted and couldn't shake off his work stress. That stress was making daily rituals like putting the kids to bed interminable. Here was a typical evening exchange between Wolfe and his oldest daughter before he rediscovered pot:

CHILD: Daddy, can you show me how to make a Q?
FATHER: (sipping bourbon and soda, staring at iPad) Just make a circle and put a little squiggle at the bottom.
CHILD: No, show me!
FATHER: Sweetie, not now, OK? Daddy's tired.

Enhancement led to this exchange:

CHILD: Daddy, can you show me how to make a Q?

FATHER: (getting down on the floor) Here, I'll hold your hand
while you hold the pen and we'll make one together. There!
We made a Q! Isn't it fantastic?

CHILD: Thanks, Daddy!

FATHER: Don't you just love the shape of this pen?

"I swear it has made me a more loving, attentive and patient father," Wolfe wrote in the *New York Times*. "I am able to become a kid again, to see things through my daughters' eyes and experience, if I'm lucky, the wonder of each new game, each new object and sound, as they do." Of course, his more task-oriented mind would prefer he use meditation or yoga to achieve these states, but the realities of modern parenthood have tempered his ambitions. "If I had a full-time staff of cooks and nannies I'd give that a whirl. But . . . my wife and I are raising multiple tots on modest incomes in a small space in a very expensive city. No time for Tantra."[9]

I stumbled upon the benefits of awe renewal quite unexpectedly when fighting the depression that accompanied a midlife crisis that didn't hit me until my fifties. I'm not big on making generalizations based on age, but I found that in our twenties and thirties, trudging up the mountain of life, our focus is forward; we're excited and challenged by life's possibilities. From our dreams we build the narrative of our selves. Somewhere in our forties we typically confront one of two possibilities. We've achieved success— material wealth, families, houses, education—but it's not all it was cracked up to be. The soundtrack to this reckoning is Peggy Lee's "Is That All There Is?" Those who haven't reached their goals must instead reconcile their shortcomings. They can stay on the path they've been treading or attempt an about-face and forge a new direction. Their soundtrack might be John Lennon's "(Just Like) Starting Over."

I got hit with the double-whammy combo platter. I had found

success as a magazine editor but I found the work dispiriting. I was spending countless hours producing publications that had no connection to my life and, in the process, time was hurtling by, leaving me in its wake. Adrift from the passions that once stoked my fires, I sank into a vortex of depression for the first time in my life. It took me months to identify it. All I knew was that some part of my spirit had gone missing.

Eventually, with the help of twenty milligrams of Lexapro (plus talk therapy and an erratic Vipassana meditation practice), I stumbled into a new path forward. But it was a years-long slog. I was lucky enough to be experimenting with cannabis at the time, and it was one of the routes that helped bring me back to myself, perhaps by loosening some of the ego lock that Carhart-Harris speaks about and reconnecting me with that state of wonder. It helped me see the world and myself anew.

I was noodling this while driving around Los Angeles on one of my several trips there. Passing through the cluttered landscape of asphalt roads, billboards, and unremarkable concrete buildings that is LA, I was struck by just how difficult it is to grasp the heart and soul of the city through a car window. Only when flying ten thousand feet above can I take in the extraordinary terrain that makes up this megalopolis between the mountains and the sea. Seeing the whole requires perspective, and that's what pot can provide: a perch from which I can stand back from my thinking and get a wider vantage than what I can normally see at close range.

As one friend put it, "Feeling more fully present is the most important first step to everything in life. If I'm in a bad mood my world feels narrower, my judgment is more cynical. I need to attend family gatherings that I know won't be that much fun, so rather than sitting back with my arms folded and being grumpy about what's going on at the table, I take a puff or two. It makes me more accessible and engaging and more in touch with the humor of the situation. By letting go of some of my mind-based judgments, I have a better time. Some people may call this an emotional crutch, but a crutch is a tool that also enables people to walk, so depending on how it's used cannabis provides a sort of freedom."

Perspective offers relief from our everyday selves, but it doesn't occur by simply lighting a joint. It took me a long time, and a lot of wasted weed, to figure out how to choose the proper strain, dose, and setting to get where I wanted to go. Ignoring these elements makes it too easy to overindulge, veg out, and ultimately lose track of your priorities. Cannabis can be a famously placating substance, which is both its great strength and failing. It makes people content to be where they are. Unlike cocaine, say, which the writer David Lenson terms a "drug of acquisition that makes users hunger for more," pot generally makes everything in front of you just fine, which can be both good and terrible. The rock goddess Chrissie Hynde expressed this best: "Smoking while vacuuming makes vacuuming better but smoking while sitting on the couch makes vacuuming harder." Complacency is one reason cannabis is seen as demotivating. If you want to get to awe, it's crucial to know how much to smoke, when to smoke, and when to skip it altogether. A bit of awe is awesome; too much can be awful.

DEEP FOCUS

Along with memory interruptus, the other common effect of cannabis is time slowdown, that pleasantly languorous experience of the hands of the clock pushing through honey. Musicians have famously extolled time slowdown, as it seems to provide them with more space between notes in which the next phrases seem to originate. Some find it heightens sound perception, so chord formations seem easier to analyze.[10]

Time slowdown induced from a strain high in pinene or limonene can create a state of extreme attention or mind racing that

Marincolo calls hyperfocus. Such extreme attention can magnify one detail of a painting until it occupies the entire frame. It also allows us to make rapid-fire associations, and neuroscience has shown that the mere fact of the brain ticking along quickly causes feelings of joy.

Here's how Carl Sagan described hyperfocus in his Mr. X essay:

> I can remember one occasion, taking a shower with my wife while high, in which I had an idea on the origins and in-validities of racism in terms of Gaussian distribution curves. It was a point obvious in a way, but rarely talked about. I drew curves in soap on the shower wall, and went to write the idea down. One idea led to another, and at the end of about an hour of extremely hard work I had found I had written eleven short essays on a wide range of social, political, philosophical, and human biological topics. . . . I have used them in university commencement addresses, public lectures, and in my books.[11]

It was his conclusion, though, that struck me: "I am convinced that there are genuine and valid levels of perception available with cannabis (and probably with other drugs) which are, through the defects of our society and our educational system, unavailable to us without such drugs. Such a remark applies not only to self-awareness and to intellectual pursuits, but also to perceptions of real people, a vastly enhanced sensitivity to facial expression, into-nations, and choice of words which sometimes yields a rapport so close it's as if two people are reading each other's minds."

Here was a great scientist expounding on matters that can't be measured but that he found immeasurably useful. Lesser minds might dismiss them because they can't be quantified.

Deep focus, or hyperfocus, also explains why certain professions, such as computer programming, attract cannabis smokers. One blogger, Corpus Callosum, explains hyperfocus hyperlogically: "Lets [sic] say you have 1000 units of brain processing power per second. Normally you could put 200 units to 5 different things thereby handling 5 things simultaneously, but on a more superficial level. Pot can let you focus 950 units onto whatever you are doing or thinking about so you can do that one thing better." Chaz Carlson, a writer at *Tech Noir,* put it in less mechanistic terms: "You are able to focus on details you might not notice before, your brain connects ideas that it might not otherwise, and you can get fully immersed in something."[12]

If there's any doubt about this, let me point out that in 2014, the FBI changed its no-tolerance drug policy to attract more cannabists to its cybercrime-fighting ranks. "I have to hire a great workforce to compete with those cyber criminals and some of those kids want to smoke weed on the way to the interview," FBI director James Comey said at a conference of the White Collar Crime Institute in Manhattan. When one conference-goer asked the FBI chief about a cannabis-smoking friend who had shied away from the agency because of the policy, Comey replied: "He should go ahead and apply."[13] Comey later recanted that comment, but the message had already been publicized around the world. Mission accomplished.

INSIGHT

Norman Mailer counseled his kids to finish their educations before they began using cannabis. The more you know, the better the flow of ideas when high, he contended. "You think associatively on pot, so you can have real extraordinary thoughts. But the more education you have, the more you have to put together . . . the more wonderful connections there are to see in the universe."[14] I cannot prove that theory, and it hints at a correlation between intelligence and better highs, which seems dubious. All the same, there seems to be some grain of truth about pot expanding the number of associative connections and, more interestingly, linking thoughts that seem to have no common thread.

In the 1850s, the members of the Club de Hashischins (*hashashin* is the Arabic word from which "assassin" is derived—more bad press for cannabis) dressed in robes and gathered at a hotel on the Île Saint-Louis in Paris to investigate the "intellectual intoxication" sparked by hashish. They suspected it was preferable to the "ignoble heavy drunkenness" of alcohol but wanted to test this exotic new substance for themselves.[15] Hash, like tobacco, was a novelty in Europe at that time; Napoleon's troops had brought it back from North Africa, and the intellectuals of the day, including Charles Baudelaire, Victor Hugo, Alexandre Dumas, and Théophile Gautier, gathered regularly to ingest massive amounts of it, which they prepared as a "marmalade." Based on their descriptions of the hallucinatory spirals they slipped into, it appears that they were spiking the hash with opium, that other popular Eastern import of the day.

Baudelaire, the most prolific writer in the group, concluded that hashish didn't spark any new ideas. He deemed it little more than a magnifying glass to the thoughts already present in a user's mind; he and I (and Sagan) will have to agree to disagree on that. But almost as an afterthought, he made one observation that caused Sebastián Marincolo to take notice: hashish made "sounds take on colors and colors contain music." Marincolo traced the connection between this 160-year-old observation and one of the oddest illnesses known to man, synesthesia, and uncovered recent findings in neuroscientific theory to explain how cannabis might trigger the type of insight that leads to creativity.

Synesthesia is a cross activation of the senses in the brain. Russ, the synesthetic character played by Matthew McConaughey in the first season of the television series *True Detective*, does a superb job of explaining his illness: "Synesthesia is a misalignment of synaptic receptors and triggers. . . . It's a type of hypersensitivity. One sense triggers another sense, like sometimes I'll see a color and it'll put a taste in my mouth. A touch, a texture, a scent, can put a [musical] note in my head." This cross activation of the senses occurs ten times more frequently in creative personalities. Duke Ellington, Leonard Bernstein, and Vladimir Nabokov were famous synesthetics, as is David Hockney. Nabokov used to cry when he saw certain numbers printed in the wrong color, a complaint that only his mother understood because she too had the disorder.[16]

The synesthetic connection to creativity makes even more sense once you understand that the brain areas that process our senses are not fixed or surrounded by firm borders. In normal brains, these areas are loosely kept apart by chemical fences that block neurons from triggering neighboring regions. But when Dr. V. S. Ramachandran, the neuroscientist who heads the Center for Brain and Cognition at the University of California, San Diego, investigated these areas further, he saw that when the inhibiting molecules malfunction, some sense signals activate neighboring regions. In less enlightened times, psychiatrists called hearing colors or tasting shapes a sort of hysteria. Today we know better.

Uncovering the mechanics of synesthesia led Ramachandran and his coresearcher E. M. Hubbard to believe that they had inadvertently opened "a window into the nature of thought."[17] This is most easily grasped by the way we use metaphor, one of our most abstract forms of thinking. Metaphor can be seen as a simple presynesthetic response. We all understand "feeling blue" seeing "loud colors" and tasting "sharp flavors," for example. And if you think that metaphors are arbitrary, they aren't. "Loud shirt" or "sharp taste" makes sense to us; "bitter touch" doesn't.

Cannabists know that when we're high, interesting links often form between unrelated concepts and events. The high famously connects certain music with deep feelings, or, in Sagan's case, explained the roots of racism via a complex statistical equation. A connection was created that had previously eluded his rational thinking. This linking of disparate ideas is one of the reasons so many people enjoy a puff before viewing art or listening to music. Cannabis allows previously unnoticed associations to rise to the surface. Some of these insights are visual, others are intellectual, and sometimes they involve all the senses.

In his 1966 essay "The Great Marijuana Hoax," Allen Ginsberg, the father of Beat poetry, detailed how smoking a joint enabled him to finally understand the motivations behind certain paintings that had always eluded him. "I first discovered how to see Klee's Magic Squares as the painter intended them (as optically three-dimensional space structures) while high on marijuana. I perceived ('dug') for the first time Cezanne's 'petit sensation' of space achieved on a two-dimensional canvas (by means of advancing & receding colors, organization of triangles, cubes, etc. as the painter describes in his letters) while looking at 'The Bathers' high on marijuana."[18]

If Sagan and Ginsberg are reliable guides to inner experience (and I believe they are, especially as they approach it from such different perspectives), then it stands to reason that pot can be used to inspire fresh insight, perhaps by loosening the boundaries that constrain our task-oriented rational thinking. Illumination, in my experience, rarely comes from drugs, but drugs can introduce users to see possibilities where previously they saw none.

Creativity, of course, occurs in many forms and crosses disciplines. I conducted a small, unofficial survey of several associates from different professions to test the hypothesis. Joseph S., a venture capitalist who funds socially progressive start-ups, told me that he uses cannabis to help him reframe problems. "During a board meeting we use our linear minds when it comes to strategy and oversight. But an after-dinner enhancement can bring other dimensions that we may not have considered. Great ideas often come out, but our rule is to make no decisions until the next day."

Alan G., an architect, was designing an urban renewal project to combat sprawl in a small Southern city. By day, his team attacked the project with plans and schematic drawings. But at night they'd take a few puffs and then explore the neighborhood and surrounding wilderness on foot, interacting with the local fauna and exploring the ways residential and commercial (and animal) behavior intersected. Rather than approaching a neighborhood solely as a grid of streets and sidewalks, his team used cannabis to help envision it more broadly as a complex ecosystem, more like a garden, in which every element plays an equal role. This more holistic attention helped new patterns emerge. In their final plan they moved backyard vegetable gardens to front yards, designed corner lots to be pocket parks with benches, turned intersections into play areas, and altered traffic patterns to accommodate the changes. The project won national acclaim.

"We were able to see how you can make a big cultural impact in a complex urban environment by a changing a few simple things," the architect told me. He envisions the day when businesses use guided cannabis workshops to explore creative problem solving. "It's in the interest of all cannabis activists in the post-prohibition era to make sure this sort of education happens safely and successfully," he says. "It could be enormously useful."

INTIMACY, EMPATHY, AND SEX

Cannabis has been vaunted as an aphrodisiac for at least three thousand years, since the Persians brought it to India and extolled the ways it boosted sensual pleasure through Tantra. It loosens inhibition, intensifies touch, and some even claim it extends the duration of orgasm—all of which enables one to get lost in an embrace.

Cannabis has shown itself to be more than just herbal Viagra; it famously magnifies feelings of communion with a sexual partner. This is one of its great powers. In my experience, it opens the door to something beyond physical pleasure: real and deep intimacy. "After a while, sex for some couples is problematic," says Dr. Nick Karras, a sexologist and the author of an unpublished book, *The Passionate High: A Lover's Guide to Cannabis*. "You tell them to drink a glass of red wine or to have a date night, but what really needs to happen is that you have to reframe what sex is. Cannabis is great for enhancing your imagination and increasing your empathy."[19]

Karras is on to something: cannabis undoubtedly expands feelings of empathy, and empathy has many benefits, not only interpersonally and societally, but also evolutionarily. The ability to imagine what another is feeling has worked to our advantage as a species. It's essential to almost every social interaction and has enabled us to advance by cooperation. It makes us sympathetic friends, good negotiators, loving parents, and responsive citizens. It also makes us fierce and strategic opponents. Without empathy, we couldn't estimate our enemy's next move (presumably Machiavelli was a highly empathetic statesman, but one you wanted to keep on your good side). Modern Western cultures that stress efficiency and technology tend to undervalue empathy, often to their detriment, and there's an explanation for why that occurs that will shortly become apparent.

One clue about the way empathy works in the brain came with the discovery of mirror neurons. In the early 1990s, Giacomo Rizzolatti and his research team at the University of Parma in Italy set out to investigate a type of brain cells—motor neurons— that transmit the electrical impulses that control movement. He attached microelectrodes to cells in a monkey's brain to see which neurons fired when the animal reached for a peanut.

The motor neurons went off as expected, but something odd happened when the monkey saw a lab assistant reach for the peanut: the very same motor neurons fired again. The scientists thought their wiring had come undone. The monkey hadn't moved, so why were his motor neurons afire? Further tests revealed that the monkey's motor neurons were "mirroring" the activity being performed by someone else.

"Mirror neurons tell us that we're literally in the minds of other people," says Marco Iacoboni, the director of the Brain Mapping Center at UCLA, and chances are they demonstrate that we're molecularly wired to take other people into account. When we see someone in pain, for example, we imitate her expression of grief without thinking. Yawning is contagious. When a toddler sees a friend crying, his tears flow almost automatically. All are the result of mirror neurons.

Some scientists think that a malfunctioning mirror neuron system may be a determining factor in autism. And since cannabis has been shown to somewhat ameliorate the effects of this disease, thinkers like Marincolo have speculated that cannabis use may stimulate mirror neurons and, consequently, play a crucial role in enhancing empathy.

Marie Myung-Ok Lee, a writer and professor at Columbia University, documented her experiments with cannabis on her severely autistic young son. J. was having three hundred tantrums a day and appeared to be in such constant pain that his only response to affection was violence. When his grandmother once attempted a hug, he struck her. Other behaviors were inexplicably odd and potentially fatal. He'd bang his head against a porcelain tub until he bled. He ate his clothing, which caused as much pain going in as it did coming out, and drove his parents to buy him edible shirts.

Marie contacted a grower, a controversial decision given her family's traditional Korean antipathy toward cannabis. After a few months of use, J. began to react to other people. He laid his grandmother's shoes out before her. When she smiled, he smiled back, and then he allowed her to hug him. One of his big break-throughs occurred one evening during supper. Typically, meals ended with plates being frisbeed against walls, so Marie and her husband would often leave J. alone to finish eating. One night, they were in another room and heard their son leave the table to go into the kitchen. Rather than the sound of porcelain crashing, they heard a mysterious splish-splashing. J. was washing his bowl in the sink and then loading it into the dishwasher—he was imitating his parents' actions for the first time. While these small acts are hardly the powerful displays of affection his parents had hoped for, they do indicate that cannabis helped create an awareness of others that had previously been absent.

In *Bowling Alone*, Robert Putnam, the sociologist who has been called "the poet laureate of civil society," points out that the most telling sign of happiness isn't wealth or health, but one's connec-tions to other human beings. Cannabis used intelligently can build bridges of connection. In fact, a 2014 study from the University at Buffalo examined 634 couples in their first nine years of marriage and found that those that smoked together were happier and less prone to domestic violence than those that didn't. One newspaper trumpeted this story with the headline "Could Smoking Marijuana Be GOOD for a Relationship?" Hyperbolic, yes, but that's one headline you'd never see topping an article about gin.[20]

PRICKLES AND GOOS

Not everyone is prone to using cannabis for inner explorations, and plenty of people deem empathy or associative thinking irrelevant to everyday life. Thinking about the way we think or feel doesn't appeal to everybody. One of the earliest and most entertaining explorers of consciousness, Alan Watts, described different personality types as prickles and goo. Prickles want rigor and precise statistics; they're edgier, introspection-averse personalities who see gooier types as hopelessly vague. Goos accuse prickles of being overly literal and cut off from inner experience. Prickles, they say, know the words but not the music. Of course, few of us are exclusively prickles or goo; as Watts said, it's gooey prickles and prickly goos, and most of us veer between these two poles.

Another way of discussing these disparities is in terms of right- and left-brain thinkers. No matter what you call them, the point is the same: the brain has several lenses through which it perceives the world.

In a footnote to *Dragons of Eden*, his Pulitzer Prize–winning book about the evolution of human intelligence, Carl Sagan postulated that marijuana suppresses left-brain activity, the ruler of our rational minds, in favor of activity in the right hemisphere, which is more inclined to favor connection and the interdependence of things. And Iain McGilchrist's magisterial book *The Master and His Emissary* sets forth a fascinating reevaluation of the right/left brain divide and how the struggle within the brain determines human consciousness. This weighty tome reads like a thriller; it's so rich with ideas I had to reread it immediately after finishing it the first time.

The concept of the divided brain entered the mainstream in the 1980s and launched an industry of scientists, authors, and marketers, all trumpeting the idea that different areas of the brain control specific senses and mental processes. The right hemisphere was considered the silent, less intelligent partner, content to preside over the gooier areas like art, music, and our inner selves, while the left hemisphere controlled the more prickly domains of rational thought. Advanced imaging technology has debunked that idea. "It's not simply 'emotion on the right, reason on the left,'" McGilchrist says. "There are plenty of both aspects in both sides of the brain."[21]

The brain is far more "plastic" than originally thought, and MRI studies of brains damaged in accidents have shattered the idea that any one hemisphere is ever in control. The brain isn't divided by function; instead, it's more a difference of perspective, of conflicting ways of seeing the world. This dual perspective enables us to see both close-up and broad versions of reality, and to think both linearly and abstractly at the same time. To illustrate this ongoing dance between the right and left hemispheres, McGilchrist relies on Nietzsche's fable about the master and his emissary, from which he derived the title of his own book.

In this story, there was a wise ruler who presided over a vast kingdom. This ruler didn't want to lose touch with the different areas of his kingdom, so he appointed an emissary to travel the kingdom to report back on what he saw. In doing so, the emissary learned about the defense systems in each realm; he understood minute problems and figured out a way to exploit the unhappiness of some locals. He also realized just how powerful he was, which enabled him to easily usurp the ruler.

Here's how this translates: the right brain, the ruler, prefers to sit back and take in the whole picture. It rules areas that preside over empathy and imagination. It also controls metaphor, which McGilchrist calls "the associations by which we come to know the world."

If the right brain provides a floodlight on experience, the left hemisphere provides the spotlight. It allows the focused attention we need to survive. It enables us to parse the mechanics of how things work: how we get our food, build our houses, make our laws. The left hemisphere dissects things into their component parts so that we can understand them. The left side also controls language, and it is largely responsible for knowledge, which is why it was originally considered the "smarter," more calculating side. Simply writing that sentence convinced me that the left brain is more important to survival, which is exactly what it wants me to think.

It was impossible to read McGilchrist's book and not wonder if cannabis stimulates right hemisphere thinking—Sagan seemed to think it did—so I contacted him through his website for further discussion. He graciously declined my invitation to talk, but unlike most of the scientists I spoke to in researching this book, he had no compunction revealing his own experience with the herb (and other substances). "I am not an expert on cannabis, and, very oddly, however much of it I take—and I have tried probably 10 times and by different routes—it does absolutely nothing for me. Nothing! A cigar does far more. Ditto in combination with magic mushrooms and ketamine, which I have also tried under supervision." (McGilchrist wrote to me from South Africa, where he was working, so I encouraged him to try Durban Poison, a native South African sativa strain, to see if it would change his fortunes with the plant. I never heard back from him.)

Still, his explanations of how the two hemispheres differ reads to me like a playbook for cannabis-induced consciousness: "The right hemisphere . . . sees things in context, it understands implicit meaning, metaphor, body language. . . . It understands individuals, not just categories; it has a disposition for the living rather than the mechanical. It experiences the connections between things. Expanded attention, which is driven by the right brain, is more connected to the broader world. It's about relationships. It allows us to stand back, to gain *perspective* [italics mine]. It is responsible for vividness of experience. It provides depth, a more 3-dimensional take on reality. It allows us to read the expression on someone's face. It helps us 'feel' music, and 'read' the tone of a conversation [*metaphor*]. It's the glue that connects us to other sentient beings [*empathy*] and enables the spiritual yoking."[22]

McGilchrist ambitiously expands his insights on the divided brain to suggest why Western society is going off the rails—and he indirectly makes an argument for embracing the sort of "mosaic" thinking that cannabis can bring about. He contends that when modern Western civilization began in the Reformation, the two hemispheres were more balanced, both in physical size and in terms of function. But as time has passed and our world has grown increasingly complex, the balance has drifted further to the left hemisphere's point of view—so much so that it now occupies more volume than the right. This reliance on rational, mechanistic thinking robs us of the ability to see life's interconnections. "Nowadays we live in a world which is paradoxical," McGilchrist writes. "We pursue happiness and it leads to resentment, and unhappiness . . . we pursue freedom but we are more monitored by CCTV cameras and . . . our daily lives are more subjected to what de Tocqueville called a network of small complicated rules that cover the surface of life and strangle the freedom we crave. We have never had more information, yet wisdom seems to be further out of our grasp. We prioritize the technical and the virtual over the real. All of our technical connectedness makes us ever more lonely."[23]

The reason we find ourselves in this pickle? Because the left hemisphere—"the Berlusconi of the brain" in McGilchrist's terminology—writes and directs the narrative of what's important to human progress. Because it governs rational thought and is in charge of language, it preaches the benefits of the rational over those of interconnectedness. And because the right hemisphere doesn't have as loud of a voice, it has more difficulty being heard.

McGilchrist is a soaring intellect who makes it abundantly clear that he doesn't oppose reason or linear thinking—he relies on it daily and couldn't have researched his book without it. It's just that he's more passionate about the more intuitive mode, and he longs for mankind to return to a more balanced view of ourselves and of the world. He echoes the concern of that other great left-brain thinker Albert Einstein, who said: "The rational mind is a loyal servant and the intuitive mind is a sacred gift. We have become a society that honors the servant but has forgotten the gift."

In addition to using cannabis to put us in touch with awe, empathy, and creative insight, it's possible that we may, in time, learn to employ it as an ambassador in the struggle between the rational and the intuitive. Perhaps this is another explanation for the plant's enduring relationship with human beings. If Sagan was correct, that cannabis temporarily suppresses left-brain perspective, and if McGilchrist is correct about the struggle for civilization being reflected in our divided brains, then, as Marincolo argues, it seems possible that this plant is one way of temporarily returning us to a more balanced state of mind (and body). If nature maintains an equilibrium inside the physical body, is it not possible that nature has also given us a plant to balance the emotional and intellectual sides of our minds?

If that's the case, I'd say that qualifies as "Oh wow, man!"

Chapter 11

THE NEXT REINVENTION OF WEED

New York City

It's remarkable just how effective eighty years of propaganda, woolly science, and high moral dudgeon can be. Americans doubt the government is capable of doing anything effectively, but it has succeeded magnificently in sowing first fear and then confusion around a generally agreeable weed. By issuing claims unsupported by evidence and twisting science to their own ends, the authorities have deflected attention from another, more interesting question: How might the components inside this magic weed be used to benefit our health and minds? This book is but a preamble to that question; subsequent generations will tackle it with much more lucidity. They'll also look back at prohibition and ask: What were they thinking?

Even after three years of immersing myself in the unfolding world of cannabis, I must admit that forty-five years of NIDA studies dutifully disseminated by an unquestioning media have made an impact. Every so often, a little voice in a corner of my mind asks, "Might your thinking be clearer, quicker, or more insightful without cannabis? Could those cannabinoids stored in your fat tissue for thirty days be causing some lingering, imperceptible effect?" Would I, as Professor Bab wondered, be more depressed "once all that euphoria wore off"?

There was only one way to find out. So before my journey ended, I made one more stop—into stone-cold sobriety.

The first leg of that expedition began in my kitchen. Above my refrigerator there's a small cabinet where I've stashed some of the souvenirs I've collected along the way.* Cabinets above refrigerators are terrible places to store cannabis. The heat emitted from the motor desiccates the oils, aging them before their time. Once terpenes are gone, they never come back. It was time to attend to that.

I spread the contents of my cupboard across my dining room table and took stock. My first response was shame. Knowing now how much labor, sweat, and risk it takes to cultivate, harvest, cure, test, and label these plant products, I felt that my collection should look more dignified. The motley assemblage of bottles and plastic pill containers had no aesthetic coherence. No self-respecting host keeps a bar this untidy.

My second response was to marvel at how many different forms this plant now assumes. In addition to a half-dozen jars containing beautiful buds, I found ampoules of golden hash oil, two crumbly blobs of water hash, and two quarter-size slabs of amber shatter. A plastic syringe contained five milliliters of medical-grade organic hash oil that I occasionally smooth on my gums. I had forgotten about a liqueur called Cannalua made by a physician in California. Made of cannabis oil drowned in Kahlua, it was surprisingly tasty.

---

* Even though the dogs once trained to sniff for pot have mostly been reassigned to bomb squads, I prefer to not take foolish chances. To transport souvenirs without incident through airports, I followed the advice of a blogger who once worked for the DEA. Lore has it that stashing flowers in a bag of ground coffee masks the smell, but like many myths, this one is not to be trusted. In fact, the terpenes in cannabis are far more powerful than those in coffee. My DEA advisor suggested vacuuming-sealing fresh buds. Also, while TSA officials are not overtly looking for illegal substances, if found, they are required to call local law enforcement, and you'll be prosecuted under the laws of that state. The US mail is another option, but it is unreliable depending on your point of origination. In my limited experience, packages mailed from California have a greater chance of arriving without a hitch; several small parcels I sent from Colorado went missing. Unsurprisingly, postal authorities in tightly regulated states are stricter about allowing illegal packages to cross their borders.

So many varieties, so little time to try them all. I taped Boveda moisture-control packs inside the tops of the jars to maintain the humidity at a steady 62 percent, the ideal level for keeping flowers fresh and mold free, and stowed everything in an antique toolbox.

Next, the instruments. In bolts of fabric I wrapped the beautiful bong that Tsachi Cohen gave me while in Israel, plus a few vape pens that I had largely abandoned. The propylene glycol used to thin the mass-market oils scratched my throat, and the middling high they delivered was never exciting enough to justify the irritation. A small dab rig that a seller at a convention gave me when he learned I was writing about his favorite plant—again unused—followed, as did a butane torch that I had loaded but never fired.

I had forgotten about my Magic Flight, but it remains one of the few compact vaporizers I like. Handmade by a group of Burning Man artisans in San Diego, this nifty wooden instrument is as small as a bar of travel soap and heats flowers with a rechargeable AA battery. It's lo-fi, low cost ($100), and it gets the job done. Back in its box it went.

I set the toolbox in a dark drawer in my study. Then, in true twelve-step fashion, I announced my decision to several confidantes. "Receptor cleanses are the best!" one friend wrote back. Who knew that the passive act of "not smoking" had been elevated to an active "cleanse"? Another assured me that my first post-cleanse high would be spectacular, reminiscent of my first orgasm. It was something to look forward to, but orgasmic wasn't the point. I simply wanted to gauge if my thinking, once free of cannabis, would be sharper.

When I began this project I focused away from politics, but knowing what I now do, it became impossible not to think about cannabis without politics, especially since the supposed solution to drug abuse has ended up being far worse and stratospherically more expensive than the problem itself. So while on my cleanse I began to explore how prohibitionists have adapted their arguments in light of the inevitable march toward legalization. The target of the scaremongering has changed: the plant is still bad, but the corporations that are plotting to push legalized pot on young kids, turn them into addicts, and usher in the decline of Western civilization are far worse. Users don't need prison, they now say, the poor things need treatment. Old messages, new twists.

"Legalization is not about someone's individual right to smoke marijuana," Kevin Sabet, the great white hope of the anti-legalization lobby, told me. "It's about creating Big Tobacco all over again." The issue isn't that marijuana kills, he says, "the issue is really about getting a small number of people rich."

Sabet, along with former congressman and OxyContin addict Patrick Kennedy, leads Project SAM (Smart Approaches to Marijuana). Project SAM's narrative goes like this: Once tobacco companies muscle their way into cannabis, they'll crank up their PR machines to downplay the health concerns just as they did with tobacco. This will result in more kids dropping out of school, more workplace and road accidents, and more psychotic episodes. "I'm not saying these things will happen," Sabet clarified, "but it greatly increases *the risk*, and this is what I'm worried about. That's why I'm trying to formulate a more nuanced social policy, something between Richard Nixon and Colorado."

Sabet's motivations have puzzled and enraged reformers for years. A former social policy advisor in the Clinton, Bush, and Obama administrations, he cofounded Project SAM in 2014. Though he presents himself more as a drug diplomat than as a drug warrior, Sabet's past reveals him to be a long-standing pot opponent. As an undergraduate at Berkeley, Sabet was leafleting and warning students against it, according to fellow classmates. He even tried unsuccessfully to have People's Park, the symbolic epicenter of the anti–Vietnam War protest movement, razed to make way for a student dorm, a proposal that was overwhelmingly shot down by his peers. Today, he's still getting off on standing well outside the popular clique.

Sabet is understandably cagey about his past as a drug warrior. In 2007, he served on the board of an organization called Drug Free America Foundation. This group is supported by the notorious antidrug crusaders Mel and Betty Sembler, who are also the masterminds behind Straight, Inc., the Abu Ghraib of drug treatment programs. In lawsuits, the victims of Straight's "rehabilitation" methods testified about being sleep deprived, gagged, and pinned on the floor for so long that they soiled themselves. When one journalist asked Sabet if he had worked for the Semblers, he flatly denied it. When the journalist later confronted him with an annual report that listed him on their advisory board, he dissembled. "I was on the advisory board along with Jeb Bush, Bob DuPont, and others for a few years—that's all unpaid." Such trademark Sabet doublespeak provokes his opponents to describe him as obnoxious or bullying. Post-prohibitionist Michael Backes calls SAM "the Westboro Baptist Church of drug policy and Kevin Sabet their Shirley Phelps-Roper."[1]

What they don't call him is dumb. I reached Sabet at his home in Princeton, New Jersey, where he lives with his wife. We spoke for about an hour, during which he laid out his arguments, calmly and rationally. He clearly believes what he is saying; the problem is that the "facts" he lays out don't add up. Consider some of his well-worn pronouncements:

Pot is stronger today and therefore more dangerous. Yes, pot is stronger, but cannabis has never appeared on a morgue report. While the jury is still out on the long-term consequences of steady dabbing, dabs are not the cannabis equivalent of crack, no matter what headline writers say.

New forms of pot, such as edibles, have caused a "huge upsurge" in the number of ER visits by people who ate too much. Edibles are no more harmful than smoking, though confusion about and inaccurate labeling of THC strength is indeed an issue. Foes quote alarmist headlines like those that appeared in the journal *Clinical Pediatrics* that reported that between 2006 and 2013 there was an "upsurge of over 147%" in children under six who ate their parents' edibles when they inadvertently thought they were candy. That sounds like an enormous jump, but it's a tiny change when the raw numbers are examined: from 100 in 2006 to 250 in 2013.[2]

Western society is better suited to alcohol because we have a longer history with it. Sound familiar? It should—it's little more than a redux of the same xenophobia that Harry Anslinger used to attack Mexican immigrants and their "loco weed" in the 1930s. An identical argument could be made against green tea: Because it's from the East and more foreign than coffee and therefore less understood, be wary.

If pot is legalized, teen use will skyrocket. Sabet claims that one in six kids will get hooked on pot, a fact he bandies about with not one shred of supporting evidence. In fact, studies in Holland, which decriminalized cannabis in 1976, and Portugal, which decriminalized all drugs in 2002, show just the opposite. Holland has the lowest teen use of any European country, and Portugal's youth have not started to smoke with abandon.[3]

The pot lobby has spent over $100 million over the last twenty years to legalize all drugs, and the anti side doesn't get one tenth of that. This extraordinary half-truth ignores the trillions of dollars the US government has spent in the last forty years to demonize cannabis. According to the Office of National Drug Control Policy, the US federal government spent over $15 billion in 2010 prosecuting the War on Drugs, at a rate of about $500 per second.

Secure and contented people aren't heavy consumers of psychoactive substances. Meaning, pot is something that intelligent adults outgrow. Older adults are the fastest-growing group of cannabists, as they are searching for more natural, less toxic, and less expensive ways of protecting their minds and bodies from the ravages of age.

And finally, my all-time favorite disputation: **There is no proof that cannabis works as a medicine.** Sabet, who has no medical training, made this blindingly tautological claim in the *Huffington Post* in 2014. Of course, there is no "proof" of the plant's medical efficacy, but that is not because it has ever failed to meet the standard of proof. Rather, the tests required to demonstrate its efficacy have never been allowed because of the schedule I restrictions.

Our conversation spooled on for over an hour, and throughout it struck me that Sabet was describing a monster that bore no resemblance to the cannabis I know. So I asked: Has he ever sampled, just once, the substance that he has spent his entire adult life battling against?

"No," he replied. "I know people are kind of interested in that question and it's kind of a fun thing but I agree with serious scholars that it's a really dumb question for policy. We don't ask cancer doctors to get cancer or we don't ask people whether they think jumping off a roof is bad idea if they've never done it. So it's kind of a weird question but I understand why you ask it. A lot of people do."

Condescension noted and the linking of cannabis to cancer duly ignored. "I don't think everything that everyone is working on is something that they have to experience themselves to be able to comment on it," he continued. "I think, you know, my PhD from Oxford, an undergraduate degree from Berkeley, working in three administrations, and speaking to the top researchers in the world has somewhat qualified me to be able to talk about this from a public policy perspective. And I actually think if you're a regular marijuana user you're disqualified from talking about the issue because you're clearly biased. It's hard for you to acknowledge that this could be a problem, hard for you to acknowledge that something you enjoy doing might not be good for your brain. I don't think we can count on an objective point of view from somebody who might be under the influence of a psychoactive substance at the time of trying to critically reason about it."

But if he is so concerned about the evils of drugs, why not fight a real slayer like meth?

"I got into this field in my early teens because I saw issues of mental health and marijuana addiction being swept under the rug. People didn't want to confront it because they didn't want to confront a problem in their family or because they didn't think it was a big deal. And in reality, some of my friends growing up did have a lot of problems with marijuana and alcohol and other substances, and that actually drew my curiosity, seeing other smart, otherwise athletic friends not reach their potential."

You can see the problem here: I am disqualified from having an opinion because I use pot, yet his opinions were based only on hearsay and the recitations of discredited drug war science. I concluded that Sabet is a man who relishes being a lone wolf, staking out the unpopular position. But it begs the question of who is funding his lonely battle. Is it Big Alcohol that fears pot will wipe away some of its market?

"Ha," he said. "We don't get any alcohol, pharma, or tobacco funding. If anything, the alcohol folks don't like what we say about their industry targeting people who drink heavily, because that's what the marijuana industry would do, too. Our funding is mainly from volunteers. We just had a summit where a few treatment centers gave us five thousand dollars.

"The National Association of Drug Court Professionals have given us money for our summit."

"How about Big Pharma? Are they backing Project SAM?"

"I'm waiting by the mailbox eagerly for the check. I don't know where people who say this get their information from."

I do. The most vocal antipot groups, Partnership for Drug-Free Kids* and the Community Anti-Drug Coalitions of America (CADCA), receive funding from federal grants worth some $90 million, and from pharmaceutical companies, who contribute undisclosed amounts.[4] So while it's ostensibly true that Project SAM receives no funds from the government or pharmaceutical companies directly, the local chapters of CADCA regularly hire Sabet at $3,000 a pop to deliver lectures and inspire the beleaguered troops in their war of diminishing returns.

Even more indicting: the two largest corporate funders of these antilegalization groups are Purdue Pharma, the maker of OxyContin, and Abbott Laboratories, the maker of Vicodin. Both of these opioid painkillers are among the most addictive drugs known to man. Opioid painkillers now cause more deaths than heroin and cocaine *combined*, according to the Centers for Disease Control. OxyContin has been linked to thousands of overdoses since it came to market in 1996.[5]

The antipot groups funded by these two pharmaceutical giants predict that legalizing cannabis will lead to delinquency, addiction, and death, yet they are conspicuously silent about limiting access to opioids. When such legislation is floated in Congress, they lobby to kill it and have done so successfully for years. They also oppose removing cannabis from schedule I.

Why? Because the profits of Abbott and Purdue (and the government funding of anticannabis groups) depend on maintaining the status quo. OxyContin has raked in more than $27 billion since 1996. Purdue has no intention of ceding market share to a mere plant that also happens to relieve pain, is not addictive, and

---

*Formerly the Partnership for a Drug-Free America, the group that produced the powerful and memorable "this is your brain on drugs" ads of the 1980s.

can be grown in the backyard. It may be an underhanded way of enforcing one's agenda, but it's not surprising given that corporations have a legal obligation to their shareholders to defend their markets.

Is it coincidental that Sabet's agenda aligns so neatly with these pharma companies' or that he argues that no plant can be a true medicine, as he did in the *Huffington Post*? One thing is certain: it makes conspiracy theories about drug companies' fear of cannabis sound a lot less like stoner paranoia.[6]

OK, so let's imagine that these vested interests run out of steam, more states vote to legalize, and the federal prohibition lifts. What will this unfettered world of cannabis look like? You don't need a crystal ball to see this future, and it looks nothing like the doomsday scenario that Sabet and others paint. The experience of other countries, plus the United States' history of ending alcohol prohibition, are fine guides to how the future will unfold.

When cannabis becomes more widely available, usage typically spikes a few percentage points, but it levels off once the curious get their kicks.[7] This is what occurred in Portugal, where that debt-burdened nation decriminalized possession of *all drugs* in quantities less than ten grams in order to move from an imprisonment paradigm to a less costly treatment paradigm. To be clear, Portugal has not legalized drug use, it has simply decriminalized it. The number of drug addicts who have undergone rehab has increased dramatically, while the number of drug-related HIV infections has decreased in kind. The country hasn't suffered an outbreak of societal pandemonium. In Colorado, there hasn't even been an outbreak of laziness. In its first year of recreational sales, ten thousand people were at work in the industry.[8]

Legalization and regulation will, of course, create new problems, but none of them, as we can see from Colorado and Washington, are unsolvable. Big Tobacco and Big Alcohol will likely swoop in and eventually come to dominate the mass market, just as they do now with beer, cigarettes, and wine. All sorts of claims will be made, with various levels of truthiness, as is the case with food supplements— but this is endemic to capitalism, not pot. Celebrities large and small will muscle into the act. Willie Nelson has formed Willie's Reserve, though no one quite knows what the company will be doing or selling. Snoop Dogg engaged Pentagram, one of the world's most established branding firms, to craft the "California cool" visual identity of his "Leafs By Snoop" range of products; Melissa Etheridge is developing marijuana-infused wine (sounds disgusting); Whoopi Goldberg has launched a line of topical rubs and bath products aimed at women suffering from menstrual cramps; even the reality TV star Bethenny Frankel is supposedly working on a strain of Skinnygirl weed that she hopes will leave users free of the munchies. All advertising and marketing will undoubtedly be restricted and reined in, just as it is with alcohol and tobacco today.

But legalization will allow researchers and others to investigate how we might use the plant to make our lives better. It will allow us to solve more vexing issues than it will create.

Take dosing, for instance. Today we almost intuitively know that one 1.5-milliliter shot of vodka has roughly the same alcohol content as a 5-ounce glass of wine (18 milliliters) and a 12-ounce bottle of beer (20 milliliters). Those standards enable everyone to moderate his or her intake without having to do any math. I can't wait for the day when a label will tell me that a 5-milligram edible is the equivalent of three hits on a joint of Blue Dream (but that the effects won't kick in for an hour and will last twice as long). It will also make some of the puzzling adverse reactions less puzzling. In the normalized world, imaginary increases in psychoses and other red herrings will take second place to real problems (mold, pesticides, inaccurate dosing and testing, maybe even vomiting) that are currently underreported because of prohibition.

Until that occurs, cannabis will continue to be the world's noisiest flower. All people, whether they use it or not, whether they are excited by or deny the science, whether they favor or abhor legalization, have an opinion about this weed. The century-long demonization has magnified cannabis to the point where it is seen as either magical or monstrous, and this is yet another distortion. Pot is peripheral to life, not essential to it. It belongs on the sidelines, not in the spotlight. I can't wait until it becomes boring and normal.

Another benefit of legalization: it will allow a culture that has been trapped in time to mature. New ideas will blossom, and those who have been marginalized can be ushered into the mainstream. This is occurring in Northern California, where the members of the Emerald Growers Association (EGA), a group of eight hundred farmers who are concentrated in Mendocino, Humboldt, and Trinity Counties, are demanding to be recognized as producers of top-tier, sun-grown organic cannabis, rather than being sidelined as criminals.

Pressing for regulation in a state that has been legally vague for two decades is a risky position. Many of the EGA's fellow cannabis farmers are dead set against coming out of the shadows to work within the system. They fear reprisal from the government, which is still raiding their grows, and they mistrust corporations, fearing they will buy up their farms and knock them out of business, just as they did with small tobacco farmers. Their concerns are not unwarranted.

But there is no future in staying outlaw. "When you're illegal, this year is always the last year," says Casey O'Neill, the chair of the Emerald Growers Association. "There's no way to plan for the future, no reason to make infrastructure upgrades." The EGA may be the only group in America that wants to pay taxes, and if they did, the boon would be undeniable. There are an estimated fifty-three thousand cannabis farmers in California, who raise a crop estimated to be worth $32 to $36 billion a year. This raises the question of what is the bigger crime: growing and taxing the sale of a plant, or asking a state that can't afford to keep its libraries open to forgo the estimated $2.5 to $3.5 billion in new annual tax revenues?

There's a larger issue at stake. In Northern California, most of these cannabis farmers also grow organic broccoli, tomatoes, zucchini, and every other vegetable that their hot microclimate will produce. But vegetables can no longer sustain small farmers or their families. Cannabis provides a "fulcrum crop," which brings in half to two-thirds of their yearly income. This steady income allows growers to join the economy, escape the black market, and pay their workers twice what a typical farmhand earns. "Small farms are part of the American dream, but the economics are no longer there," says O'Neill. "Today, we have two choices. We can levy taxes and give small farmers a subsidy, but I'm not asking for a handout. Or we can allow small farmers to grow organic, heritage strains that create dollar potential, maintain the environment, and thrive rather than subsist."*

To secure this future, the EGA is also taking unprecedented steps to protect the heritage of its growers' strains by establishing a controlled appellation system similar to that of French wine makers. In thirteenth-century Burgundy, the monks who grew grapes noticed that certain soils and climates produced wines of unique character that couldn't be produced elsewhere. The terroir is what made certain varietals of Burgundy good and others outstanding. The EGA is hoping to replicate that system once granted legitimacy, and the idea is spreading to other cannabis-growing

*Sun-grown cannabis requires few pesticides and is among the least thirsty crops grown in drought-ravaged California. One pound of beef requires 1,500 gallons of water. Almonds suck 1 gallon per nut. A bottle of wine takes 200 gallons. One avocado, 35 gallons. One eighth of an ounce of cannabis—the standard retail unit—takes a mere 2 gallons.

regions around the world. It's not unimaginable that we could see top-tier cannabis wars in the near future: sun-grown Humboldt Green versus Blue Mountain Jamaican. Take your pick!

When prohibitionists hear this, they paint a picture of a drug-induced free-for-all. They envision strain reviews next to wine reviews in the *New York Times*, chalkboards beseeching patrons to smoke up in the same way that bars encourage drinking (One recent favorite: "Has your dog died? Worried about the size of your penis? Found out your husband's gay? . . . You can numb any of these problems temporarily with the help of Booze. Remember: The more you drink the less you worry!"), or foresee the day when cannabis owns basketball the way that beer owns football. But I see a different picture, one in which a maturing market benefits from regulation and control, and in which educated customers demand pesticide-free pot, grown in small batches, and in which the profits get tied back to the local community. My forward-facing picture is based in part on the fact that Big Agriculture, Big Tobacco, and Big Pharma have fallen into disrepute, and that a sizable number of weed users are the same people who prefer organic, chemical-free food and resist popping pharmaceuticals for every minor ache and pain. They will demand that their pot is grown sustainably, cleanly, and in line with their do-gooder values.

But the other part of my picture is formed by looking back through the rearview mirror at the end of alcohol prohibition. Lifting the prohibition on alcohol in 1933 put the brakes on the anything-goes atmosphere created by speakeasies and bootleggers, says Daniel Okrent, the author of *Last Call: The Rise and Fall of Prohibition*. It established closing hours, age limits, and Sunday blue laws. It created regulations that stopped people dying from tainted slush masquerading as alcohol, and it mandated physical distance between bars or liquor stores and schools, churches, or hospitals. "Just as Prohibition did not prohibit, making drink legal did not make drink freely available," Okrent concludes.[9]

Perhaps the most radical change legalization will bring about is what might be termed the Fourth Reinvention of Pot, from sacrament to botanical medicine to intoxicant to wellness product. It may seem like a stretch at this moment to regard what Ronald Reagan fingered as "probably the most dangerous drug in the United States" as something that promotes health, but science can be denied for only so long. Once companies like Michael Backes's Phytecs are up and running and integrate empirical evidence into a viable health regimen, products that tickle the receptors of the endocannabinoid system will likely be viewed much the way vitamins or common over-the-counter remedies are today, with one significant difference: they'll be more effective. A few examples of these speculative health-altering meds include:

- THCV, which retards the appetite rather than inducing the munchies. This endocannabinoid also boosts metabolic rate, which reduces fat buildup in the liver and the amount of bad cholesterol in the blood.[10] As an estimated 40 percent of Americans are obese and diet pills are a bust, the consequences could be profound. THCV also affects cells that produce insulin. Diabetes, in all its many forms, is endemic in China and most of the West, and it will drain the US health-care system of an estimated half trillion dollars in the next decade. If this plant-derived chemical proves effective, that's a game changer.

- CBG. Achy joints and back pain are the most commonly reported medical complaints. CBG synergizes with THC to relieve pain just as Aleve, ibuprofen, and Advil do, but without side effects. Who wouldn't prefer a safer, botanically derived Advil?

- CBD. New studies are linking the long-term use of anti-anxiety meds like Xanax, Ativan, Valium, and Klonopin to dementia and Alzheimer's. It appears that a mere two milligrams of CBD may keep us calmer and protect our brains against aging at the same time.[11]

- THCA. An acid that appears on the raw leaf before it is heated, THCA is one of the most powerful anti-inflammatories known to man. According to Kymron deCesare, chief research officer of Steep Hill Labs, it has twice the potency of hydrocortisone taken internally with none of the side effects. One week of this treatment noticeably diminishes pains and aches associated with joint diseases.*

Even old weed can be useful. CBN, an oxidation product of THC commonly found in dried-out stashes left in the garage over the summer, is an excellent sleep remedy. "CBN is about six times as effective as any other cannabinoid," says deCesare. "If you light up old weed, the first effect is a yawn, next your muscles relax, then the sedative kicks in and your brain wants to shut down."

Viewing cannabis as a wellness product does not constitute some arbitrary marketing shift. Rather, it's a profound reincarnation of the plant and a negation of everything we have been taught about it in the last century of demonization. Prior to my journey, I might have said that everything you put into your body incurs some risk, but pot is less harmful than cigarettes or alcohol. After all, smoking kills five million people worldwide each year. Alcohol kills almost 88,000 Americans a year and is linked to domestic violence, brawls, car accidents, rape, homicide, and a high percentage of suicides. But science is showing that pot, used intelligently, may actually be good for you. The evidence is mounting; it's time to learn the truth.

---

*Here's a handy recipe for an anti-inflammatory THCA-infused oil that you can make at home: Grind 10 grams of top-shelf flowers in a new coffee mill. (Do not use an old one. Coffee is an alkaloid, which interacts negatively with terpenoids.) Then combine with 10 grams of olive or coconut oil—oils enable faster and fuller absorption into the intestine. The mixture will resemble corn-meal mush. Let it sit twenty-four hours. Take 1 gram of the infused material twice a day. Reduce your intake to once a day as symptoms dissipate.

We've lost a century prosecuting this war on weed, and the result has been exactly the same as every other war America has conducted during my lifetime: pointless. A decade trying to prevent communism in South Vietnam resulted in a communist government the minute we pulled out. Another decade in Afghanistan and Iraq have given birth to regional instability and ISIS, with no end in sight. Obviously, war incurs all sorts of unintended consequences, and the war on weed is no exception. What began as America's Sisyphean attempt to wipe out the plant ended up turning the United States into the world's largest cannabis producer. Trillions of dollars spent, hundreds of thousands of citizens jailed, and countless lives ruined to eradicate a plant that turns out to help kids with cancer, like Chico Ryder, or elders in Israeli nursing homes, or stressed-out executives in search of a little calm.

Why?

Whether you like weed or hate it, it's time to let science take the lead in posing new questions and answering them. As we hurtle into the twenty-first century, our on-demand lives are creating a new set of stressors. Smartphones and twenty-four-hour news cycles are bombarding us with five times as much information than we received in 1986.[12] Isn't it comforting to know that something grown in the earth can bring relief to our overloaded brains and help us confront the loneliness of our screen-based world? People are swarming into cities at a frightening pace, and this mass migration and the resulting overcrowding is predicted to continue until 2030. Isn't it reassuring to know that there's a plant that can, for a few hours, heighten perceptions so that we can more closely observe the fluttering of a butterfly's wings or find new beauty in the scent of a pine tree? Something that, when used intentionally, can help us appreciate the subtleties in our increasingly mediated, fractalized lives?

After sixty days, twice the length of time necessary to empty my receptors, I ended my cleanse. Unsurprisingly, none of the "withdrawal symptoms" that could supposedly affect heavy users when quitting—constipation, heavy perspiration, and sleeplessness—surfaced. Cannabis sobriety was, for me, as it is for most people, a nonevent of spectacular proportions. Yes, I missed the aphrodisiacal qualities in bed. I missed the relief that comes from "taking away the mind," the joyous spurts of associative creative thinking, and of course, the lovely ritual of sharing a puff with friends. But unlike a digestive cleanse that wreaks havoc on so many bodily functions and washes away motivation, the receptor cleanse caused no noticeable differences in my physical or mental acuity. The only change I observed was an uptick in my alcohol intake. Rather than one glass of wine at night I had two, occasionally supplemented by a shot of vodka or scotch. The sugar metabolized from the alcohol disrupted my fragile sleep patterns and left me with mental cobwebs in the morning, which were eventually wiped away by a jolt or two of tonic made from that other popular botanical, coffee.

So on May 1, 2015, I unpacked my toolbox and selected two sticky fingers of a Mendocino sun-grown strain called XJ 13. I pulverized the aromatic green and scooped it into my Plenty vaporizer. When the dial hit 360 degrees Fahrenheit I took three deep draws, felt the cool mist swim into my lungs, and thought, *Maybe I am hooked on pot after all*. We have a relationship, this plant and I. Some people love weed, but love is a powerful connection that can also be accompanied by aching, longing, and obsession. For me, reuniting with pot has been more like reuniting with an old friend. The relationship is flexible and it allows me to come and go as I please. It's familiar, yet full of mystery, and it's one that takes a lifetime to truly know.

Appendix

BEYOND STONED

Cannabis for Inspiration, Intimacy, and Other Adult Pleasures

When I began this book I mistakenly thought everyone knew how to use pot. I was very wrong. My generation lacked knowledge of what made the plant work and how it interacted with our bodies. The current generation is lacking information on how to best use this new, unfolding knowledge to its benefit, which is one reason I've written this book.

If you simply want to cripple your mind—to forget about yesterday, today, and tomorrow—spark up a fat joint and smoke it to the roach. If you want to use it to get creative, interesting highs that crack open doors of insight and emotional connection, that's another story. Humans have altered cannabis, but the ways we use it haven't kept pace. Here are a few twenty-first-century ways to use this twenty-first-century plant.

BEFORE

Know the dose that makes you happy.

Pot is dose-dependent and biphasic. In other words, smoke too much, and feelings of increased sensitivity can turn to paranoia, or an ecstatic journey can end in couchlock.

Mind-set: "Set and setting" refers to the way mind-set and environment can influence any journey on any substance. I'll add this: cannabis is, as Baudelaire put it, "the mirror that magnifies" what's already going on in your mind. If you're depressed, cannabis can sink you lower; if you're feeling energetic, you might get a boost. Smoke a puff or two, wait three minutes, and evaluate the direction things are heading. Stop if you've taken the wrong road.

Setting: When using cannabis to hack into or expand your consciousness, try being in a quiet place where you can control the lighting, the music, and the company. Also, marijuana tends to make whatever one is doing while smoking more interesting, but it makes switching from one activity to another more challenging.

Do what you know: Save learning new activities for another time. For me, swimming while enhanced, especially outdoors, is sensory bliss. Tennis, at which I'm less accomplished, is overwhelming. Following the ball, appraising my opponent's next move, second-guessing the angle of my racquet . . . it's all too much. So learn what you enjoy and, more important, what you don't enjoy, in the enhanced state. This is key to knowing how to be high.

Strains: The strains matter, but they are not 100 percent accurate predictors of your high, especially if your cannabis hasn't been tested. If you are affiliated with a dispensary that tests, ask a knowledgeable budtender to explain the meaning of those numbers. THC, CBD, and terpene profiles are more likely to predict the effects of the high than strain names or categorizations such as "indica," "sativa," or "hybrid." Try strains that have both THC and CBD if you can find them and note the difference. And get to know your terpenes, as they help predict the trajectory of your high.

INHALATION

Know your delivery methods.

A bong is efficient, as it delivers the largest intake to the lungs, and you will not watch half a gram go up in smoke as you will with a joint. I find coughing deeply unpleasant, so I monitor how much smoke fills the stem and adjust my inhale accordingly. When you lift the bowl out of the pipe, you will get a rush of smoke. You don't need to take it all.

Vaporizer pens are discreet and odor free; however, the mass-market oils that fit pens like the O.penVape are generally of lower quality and made with propylene glycol, which can irritate the sensitive tissues of the throat. Vaporizers such as the Pax that burn flowers are better, but the ceramic heating element burns at hotter, less controlled temps, so you are frying some of the oils before they get to your lungs, which makes the high flatter, less nuanced, and less colorful.

The beauty of a precision vaporizer like the Plenty is that the temperature can be adjusted. The vapor is cool, the flavor robust, and the high is crystal clear. Extra bonus: it's so strange-looking you are guaranteed to be the hit of any party you bring it to.

Dabbing is for more experienced smokers. If you're going to dab, be sure to try it with people who know what they are doing and be sure that they are starting you out with a small, *sesame seed–size* dose. Remember, you are smoking an extremely potent concentration of THC and cannabinoids, so this is one case where size really does matter.

My rule is simple with oil: Avoid anything made with solvent. Butane is toxic, so why risk it? Water or CO_2 processing is clean and does the trick.

A joint is, in fact, the least efficient way to smoke. About 50 percent of what you roll will simply perfume the air, which is not necessarily a bad thing. That said, there's something old-school and reassuringly simple about a joint, though I suspect they may be going the way of the roll-your-own cigarette as newer technologies come online. Still, rolling is a skill worth knowing.

When lighting a pipe, position the flame far enough away from the bowl to lightly kiss the top of the green. Do not torch the plant.

Too much fire annihilates the resins. Serious cannoisseurs prefer matches to cheap lighters, as they say they can taste the butane.

EDIBLES

Again, dosing is key. The days of Alice B. Toklas randomly dumping a handful of fried weed into brownies and you eating a square are thankfully over. Most home cooks have no idea about portions, so it's up to you to know what you're doing. Unless you're experienced and have a tolerance, five milligrams or less should be enough to create a sunny inner state. Too much and you'll be horizontal and possibly paranoid for far too long. Try a few test runs; ingest a specified amount, and wait one to two hours to evaluate. If nothing happens after two hours, you need more, but remember it will take another one to two hours to kick in. Alternatively, you can just add inhalation or vaporization to extend the high or add new textures. Oh, and by the way, cannabis doses have no relation to your body weight. A big guy can be flattened just as easily as a small woman on the same amount.

ETIQUETTE

Just a puff or two to start, then take a break. Sharing a joint or a bowl is a lovely ritual, but the tendency is to oversmoke. Best to start slowly, take a break, and then resume if you want to go further.

• Respect silence. Words don't work quite as well when stoned, although ideas and feelings can still be communicated. Sometimes pot makes me talkative and helps my emotional connection to those around me. At other times, I prefer solitude. This social/antisocial swing is difficult to predict. If uncertain, I suggest smoking one or two puffs before entering a crowd.

You'll know immediately if you need to sit in a corner or if you can dive into the group.

- Notice nuance. As Sebastián Marincolo writes: "While high, the taste of eating chocolate or drinking red wine usually is not only more intense but also more complex." Attend to these extra dimensions.
- Don't insist that others around you smoke, even if you think they'll enjoy it. Let them ask you to try it. They'll be happier if it's their choice, and you'll avoid blame should things take a wrong turn. With newbies it's good to say something like, "I can't predict your response, but chances are you'll enjoy it. If not, I'll be there to support you whatever comes up."
- Avoid mixing pot with spirits. It's difficult to avoid, given that both are seen as party favors, but I recommend keeping them distinct to really understand the difference between these two wildly different substances. Pot can be used to party, but it is a less predictable social lubricant than alcohol.

PAIN

In general, cannabis relieves neuropathic (nerve) pain, not the kind of pain that happens when you stab yourself with scissors. If something bothers you persistently, get it checked out to learn the root of the problem. If it's fixable, get it fixed. Pot won't heal it. If it's not fixable, figure out how to use pot so that it enables you to function without going into a black hole. Experiment with CBD strains if you can find them.

MAINTENANCE

- Cleanse your receptors regularly. Twenty-eight days of abstinence will scour your endocannabinoid system, and you'll get you more pleasantly high when you pick up again. Should you have trouble stopping for a month, you might want to think about how much you're smoking and why.

- Take notes. Just as recording your dreams can help you meaningfully integrate them in your waking life, writing down your insights while high can be useful for revivifying your inner life.

- Don't make it a habit. Habits are done without thinking and are not as much fun as activities that are done occasionally. Think about what you want to get from your highs and set your intentions accordingly. Fun, laughter, silliness, and joy are all fine intentions, by the way.

- Remember, the best thing about pot is also the worst thing about it: It makes everything in front of you seem OK. Don't lose track of your priorities. If you find this is happening, stop. Don't sacrifice discipline and focus. And if you can't stop, ask yourself why you can't, and maybe find some help doing so.

- And of course, stay curious and enjoy the journey. It's a brave new world of weed out there, and there's much to learn and explore.

Acknowledgments

In addition to the people profiled in these pages I am so happy to know and to thank Valerie Corral, a hero in the cannabis world, for helping end-of-life patients through their transition and for helping me navigate the history of medical cannabis in California. Al Byrne and Mary Lynn Mathre are the fantastic founders of Patients Out of Time, the first organization to hold world-class conferences for world-class scientists studying cannabis and the endocannabinoid system. Heroes. These people are heroes.

Drs. Donald Abrams, Ethan Russo, Jeffrey Block, Sunil Aggarwal, Brian Becker, Julie Holland, Jeff Guss, Erin Zerbo, Andrew Weil, Allen Frankel, Jeffrey Raber, and Lumir Hunis each spent hours explaining the chemistry of cannabis and making it comprehensible. They were always wise, measured, and available to answer questions. Roy Upton and Michael Fratis were huge helps on the botanical front.

Ethan Nadelmann, Amanda Reiman, Ted Trimpa, Joe Brezny, Brian Vicente, Christian Sederberg, and Graham Boyd were my spirit guides through the ever-changing political and legal landscapes, while Sebastián Marincolo, Jonathan Teysko, and Zach Klein served as my spirit guides in general.

For shelter, wisdom, and support: Mark Matousek, Jocelyn and Bill Zuckerman, Jack Millam and Brad Stamm, Henny Garfunkel, David Binder, and Marco Calvani were always there, as was my beloved family, Lynn Dolce and Tee Minot and Susan and Chipper Moore.

I must also thank Leslie Bocskor, Daniel Okrent, Barbara Ehrenreich, Joel Solomon, Linda Solomon, Justin Hartfield, Lea Klein, Michael Martin, Casey O'Neill and Amber Cline, Ellie Sapir, Carl Olsen, Kristin Nevedal, Richard Lee, Brandon Kennedy, Diane Goldstein, Peter Christ, John English, Josh Wurzer and Alec Dixon, Tsachi Cohen, Maayan Weisberg, Martin Lee, Nate Jackson, Riley Cote, Robert Forte, Steve D'Angelo, Andrew D'Angelo, Tim Blake, Matt Stang, Douglas Johnson, and Lindy Speakman.

And thanks to my publishing dream team: Sarah Murphy, Brian Perrin, Dave Kass, Amrit Judge, and Hannah Robinson. Milan Bozic created the year's best book jacket; my agent, Bob Levine, encouraged and sustained me through my doubts; and my two great loves, Karen Rinaldi and Jonathan Burnham, gave me the best birthday gift imaginable by agreeing to publish this book.

Notes

CHAPTER 1: BIG BAD SCARY WEED

1. J. C. Callaway, "Hempseed as a Nutritional Resource: An Overview," *Emphytica* 140 (2004): 70.
2. Ethan Russo, "Cannabis in India: Ancient Lore and Modern Medicine," in *Cannabinoids as Therapeutics*, ed. Raphael Mechoulam (Boston: Birkhäuser, 2005), www.drugpolicy.org/docUploads/Russo_Cannabis-InIndia_Mechoulam2005.pdf.
3. Roger Parloff, "How Marijuana Became Legal," *Fortune*, September 18, 2009, http://archive.fortune.com/2009/09/11/magazines/fortune/medical_marijuana_legalizing.fortune/index.htm.
4. Evan Morris, "Pot," *The Word Detective*, 2016, www.word-detective.com/2008/07/pot/.
5. Charles Whitebread, "The History of the Non-Medical Use of Drugs in the United States," *Schaffer Library of Drug Policy*, www.druglibrary.org/schaffer/history/whitebl.htm.
6. Jacob Sullum, "How Many Daily Heroin Users Are There in the US? Somewhere Between 60,000 and 1 Million. Maybe," *Forbes*, March 10, 2014, www.forbes.com/sites/jacobsullum/2014/03/10/how-many-daily-heroin-users-are-there-in-the-u-s-somewhere-between-60000-and-1-million-maybe/#2596a437eb43.
7. The information in this table, with the exception of the cannabis total overdose deaths, was compiled by the National Institutes of Health and the National Institute on Drug Abuse. No cannabis overdose deaths have been reported. See National Center for Health Statistics, "Overdose Death Rates," *National Institute on Drug Abuse,* December 2015, www.drugabuse.gov/related-topics/trends-statistics/overdose-death-rates.
8. Ronald Shaffer, "Unnamed Witnesses Say Bourne Used Pot, Cocaine at Party," *St. Petersburg Times* [Florida], July 21, 1978.
9. Patti Davis, *The Way I See It: An Autobiography* (New York: Putnam, 1992).
10. Peter Gorman, "Operation Green Merchant: An Overview," *Peter Gorman Archive*, n.d., petergormanarchive.com/green_merchant.html.

11. Daniel Forbes, "Prime-Time Propaganda: How the White House Secretly Hooked Network TV on Its Anti-Drug Message," *Salon,* January 13, 2000, www.salon.com/2000/01/13/drugs_6/.

12. Ibid.

13. Ibid.

CHAPTER 2: THE DUTCH MASTERS

1. "Hempfest: Thousands Attend Opening of Three-Day Pot Festival in Seattle Park," *Daily News* [New York], August 17, 2013, www.nydailynews .com/news/national/hempfest-thousands-attend-three-day-pot-festival-article-1.1429555.

2. "Will Banning Marijuana Sales to Foreigners Hurt Holland's Economy?," *The Week*, April 27, 2012, http://theweek.com/articles/476012/banning-marijuana-sales-foreigners-hurt-hollands-economy.

3. "Big Serious Seeds Cultivation Showdown: AK-47 Regular vs Feminised," seriousseeds.com, last modified February 2016, www.seriousseeds.com/grow-ak47.

4. Ibid.

5. Besar Likmeta, "Europe's Marijuana Capital Isn't Amsterdam," *GlobalPost*, August 16, 2013, www.globalpost.com/dispatch/news/regions/europe/130815/europe-marijuana-capital-lazarat-albania.

CHAPTER 3: THE MARTYR AND THE MILLIONAIRES

1. Paul DeRienzo, "Dennis Peron: The Marijuana Mouse That Roared," *High Times*, August 1998.

2. Michael Pollick, "A Medical Pot Pioneer's Story," *Herald-Tribune* [Sarasota, Florida], July 26, 2014, http://marijuana.heraldtribune .com/2014/07/26/medical-pot-pioneers-story/.

3. Eric Bailey, "6 Wealthy Donors Aid Measure on Marijuana," *Los Angeles Times*, November 2, 1996, http://articles.latimes.com/1996-11-02/news/mn-60512_1_medical-marijuana-measure.

4. "Marijuana Prosecutions for 2010 Near Record High," *NORML.org*, September 29, 2011, http://norml.org/news/2011/09/19/marijuana-prosecutions-for-2010-near-record-high.

5. US Department of Justice, "Uniform Crime Reports—Crime in the United States, 2000—Table 29: Total Estimated Arrests in the United States," *FBI.gov*, October 22, 2001, www.fbi.gov/about-us/cjis/ucr/crime-in-the-u.s/2000/toc00.pdf.

6. Julie Holland, ed., *The Pot Book: A Complete Guide to Cannabis* (South Paris, ME: Park Street Press, 2010), 386.

7. George Soros, "Why I Support Legal Marijuana," *Wall Street Journal*,

October 26, 2010, http://online.wsj.com/news/articles/SB1000142405270 2303467004575574450703567656.

8. Andy Kroll, "This Is How Private Prison Companies Make Millions Even When Crime Rates Fall," *Mother Jones*, September 19, 2013, www.motherjones.com/mojo/2013/09/private-prisons-occupancy-quota-cca-crime; Vicky Pelaez, "The Prison Industry in the United States: Big Business or a New Form of Slavery?," *El Diario-La Prensa, New York and Global Research*, March 10, 2008, www.globalresearch.ca/the-prison-industry-in-the-united-states-big-business-or-a-new-form-of-slavery/8289.

9. Lee Fang, "The Real Reason Pot Is Still Illegal," *The Nation*, July 2, 2014, www.thenation.com/article/anti-pot-lobbys-big-bankroll/.

10. Ibid.

11. Ralph Nader, "The Boundary-Breaking John Lewis—A CEO Who Mattered," *Cleveland.com*, December 5, 2013, www.cleveland.com/opinion/index.ssf/2013/12/the_jolting_peter_lewis_a_ceo.html.

12. Peter Lewis, "Billionaire Peter Lewis: My War on Drug Laws," *Forbes*, September 21, 2011, www.forbes.com/sites/clareoconnor/2011/09/21/billionaire-peter-lewis-my-war-on-drug-laws/#5aa8c4447575.

13. Isabel Macdonald, "The GOP's Drug-Testing Dragnet," *The Nation*, April 3, 2013, www.thenation.com/article/gops-drug-testing-dragnet/.

14. Mike Riggs, "Four Industries Getting Rich off the Drug War," *Reason*, April 22, 2012, http://reason.com/archives/2012/04/22/4-industries-getting-rich-off-the-drug-w.

CHAPTER 4: WIDGETS AND DABS

1. Sadie Gurman, "Hash Oil Explosions Rise with Legalized Marijuana," *Seattle Times*, May 6, 2014, www.seattletimes.com/seattle-news/hash-oil-explosions-rise-with-legalized-marijuana-1/.

2. Robert Connell Clarke, *Hashish* (Los Angeles: Red Eye Press, 1998), 111.

CHAPTER 5: THE ENDOCANNABINOID SYSTEM

1. Donald Abrams, "Medical Marijuana: Trials and Tribulations," *Journal of Psychoactive Drugs* 30, no. 2 (April–June 1998): 163–69.

2. Michael Pollan, "Cannabis, Forgetting, and the Botany of Desire," *Occasional Papers of the Doreen B. Townsend Center for Humanities*, no. 27, (Berkeley: Doreen B. Townsend Center for the Humanities, University of California, 2002), http://townsendcenter.berkeley.edu/sites/default/files/publications/OP27_Pollan.pdf.

3. David Jay Brown, *Mavericks of Modern Medicine: Exploring the Future of Medicine with Andrew Weil, Jack Kevorkian, Bernie Siegel, Ray Kurzweil and Others* (Petaluma, CA: Smart Publications, 2006).

4. Melanie C. Dreher, Kevin Nugent, and Rebekah Hudgins, "Prenatal Marijuana Exposure and Neonatal Outcomes in Jamaica: An Ethnographic Study," *Pediatrics* 93, no. 2 (1994): 254–60.

5. Melanie C. Dreher, "Marijuana Use in Pregnancy," The Ninth National Clinical Conference on Cannabis Therapeutics, YouTube video, posted December 6, 2015, www.youtube.com/watch?v=YWr8QDHCFos

6. Ester Fride, "Cannabinoids and Feeding: The Role of the Endogenous Cannabinoid System as a Trigger for Newborn Suckling," *Journal of Cannabis Therapeutics* 2, no. 3/4 (2002): 51–62.

7. Leo Hollister, "Health Aspects of Cannabis," from *Pharmacological Reviews*, 1986, www.druglibrary.org/schaffer/hemp/medical/hollis1.htm.

8. Pollan, *"Cannabis."*

9. Christine Del'Amore, "Runner's High Hardwired in People and Dogs," *National Geographic,* May 11, 2012, http://news.nationalgeographic.com/news/2012/05/120510-runners-high-evolution-people-dogs-science/.

10. Richard Friedman, "The Feel-Good Gene," *New York Times*, March 6, 2015, www.nytimes.com/2015/03/08/opinion/sunday/the-feel-good-gene.html.

11. Anthony Wile, "Dr. Raphael Mechoulam: The Promise of Cannabis," *The Daily Bell,* October 19, 2014, www.thedailybell.com/exclusive-interviews/35732/Anthony-Wile-Dr-Raphael-Mechoulam-The-Promise-of-Cannabis.

12. "Facts and Stats," *International Osteoporosis Foundation,* last modified 2015, www.iofbonehealth.org/facts-statistics.

13. Ken Belson, "Brain Trauma to Affect One in Three Players, N.F.L. Agrees," *New York Times*, September 13, 2014, www.nytimes.com/2014/09/13/sports/football/actuarial-reports-in-nfl-concussion-deal-are-released.html.

14. Jeanne Marie Laskas, "Bennet Omalu, Concussions, and the NFL: How One Doctor Changed Football Forever," *GQ*, September 14, 2009, www.gq.com/story/nfl-players-brain-dementia-study-memory-concussions.

15. F. M. Leweke et al., "Cannabidiol Enhances Anandamide Signaling and Alleviates Psychotic Symptoms of Schizophrenia," *Translational Psychiatry* 2, e94 (2012), doi: 10.1038/tp.2012.15.

16. P. Pacher and G. Kunos, "Modulating the Endocannabinoid System in Human Health and Disease—Successes and Failures," *FEBS Journal* 280, no. 9 (2013): 1918–43.

CHAPTER 6: THE WORLD'S LARGEST HUMAN TRIAL

1. "Why Bedrocan Is Selling Cannabis in Canada: Q&A with CEO Marc Wayne," *LeafScience,* January 26, 2014, www.leafscience.com/2014/01/26/bedrocan-selling-cannabis-canada-qa-ceo-marc-wayne/.

2. Howard Markel, "In 1850, Ignaz Semmelweis Saved Lives with Three Words: Wash Your Hands," *PBS News Hour*, May 15, 2015, www.pbs. org/newshour/updates/ignaz-semmelweis-doctor-prescribed-hand-washing/.

3. E. Aso et al., "CB2 Cannabinoid Receptor Agonist Ameliorates Alzheimer-Like Phenotype in ABPP/PS1 Mice," *Journal of Alzheimer's Disease* 35, no. 4 (2013): 847.

4. "Cannabis, Alzheimer's Marijuana Helps Calm, Restore, Harmonize," *ALZConnected.org*, October 7, 2014, www.alzconnected.org/discussion .aspx?type=carecenter_footer&g=posts&t=2147509906.

5. J. S. Han, "Acupuncture and Endorphins," *Neuroscience Letters* 361, no. 1–3 (2004): 258.

CHAPTER 7: SNAKE OIL OR CANCER CURE?

1. L. R. Zhang et al., "Cannabis Smoking and Lung Cancer Risk: Pooled Analysis in the International Lung Cancer Consortium," *International Journal of Cancer* 136, no. 4 (2015): 894–903.

2. C. Liang et al., "A Population-Based Case-Control Study of Marijuana Use and Head and Neck Squamous Cell Carcinoma," *Cancer Prevention Research* (Philadelphia) 2, no. 8 (2009): 759–68.

3. Raymond Cushing, "Pot Shrinks Tumors; Government Knew in '74," *Alternet*, May 30, 2000, www.alternet.org/story/9257/pot_shrinks_tumors%3B_government_knew_in_%2774.

4. "Rick Simpson's Hemp-Oil Medicine," *High Times*, November 30, 2013, www.hightimes.com/read/rick-simpsons-hemp-oil-medicine.

5. "Neurontin," *WebMD*, n.d., www.webmd.com/drugs/2/drug-9845–8217/neurontin-oral/gabapentin-oral/details#uses.

CHAPTER 8: BUDTENDERS AND SINSEMILLIERS

1. Sean Williams, "7 Stunning Figures That Sum Up Colorado's Marijuana Market," *Motley Fool*, March 8, 2015, www.fool.com/investing/general/2015/03/08/7-stunning-figures-that-sum-up-colorados-marijuana. aspx; Wil Hylton, "Willie Nelson's Crusade to Stop Big Pot," *New York*, November 1, 2015, http://nymag.com/daily/intelligencer/2015/10/willie-nelson-crusade-stop-big-pot.html.

2. Michael Backes, *Cannabis Pharmacy* (New York: Black Dog & Leventhal, 2014), 58–60.

3. Eli Stokols, "Welcome to America's Drug Laboratory," *Politico*, May 13, 2014, www.politico.com/magazine/story/2014/05/colorado-marijuana -americas-drug-laboratory-106624; Jesse Sarles, "Job Seekers Swarm Marijuana Career Fair as Colorado's Green Rush Continues," *CBSDenver.com*,

March 14, 2014, http://denver.cbslocal.com/2014/03/14/job-seekers-swarm-marijuana-job-fair-as-colorados-green-rush-continues/.

4. Fred Barbash, "Pot Sales Spark Warehouse Boom in Colorado," *Washington Post*, March 11, 2014, www.washingtonpost.com/news/morning-mix/wp/2014/03/11/pot-sales-spark-warehouse-boom-in-colorado/.

5. Steve Raabe, "Pot-Growing Warehouses in Short Supply as Demand for Weed Surges," *Denver Post*, March 11, 2014, www.denverpost.com/marijuana/ci_25316132/pot-growing-warehouses-short-supply-demand-legal-weed.

6. Evan Mills, "Energy Up in Smoke: The Carbon Footprint of Indoor Cannabis Production," Energy Associates, n.d., http://evan-mills.com/energy-associates/Indoor.html.

CHAPTER 9: DESIGNING YOUR HIGHS

1. Ethan Russo, "Clinical Endocannabinoid Deficiency (CECD): Can This Concept Explain Therapeutic Benefits of Cannabis in Migraine, Fibromyalgia, Irritable Bowel Syndrome and Other Treatment-Resistant Conditions?," *Neuroendocrinology Letters* 29, no. 2 (2008): 192–200.

2. Michael Backes, *Cannabis Pharmacy* (New York: Black Dog & Leventhal, 2014), 60–62.

3. S. Malhotra et al., "Effect of Different Aspirin Doses on Platelet Aggregation in Patients with Stable Coronary Artery Disease," *Internal Medicine Journal* 33, no. 8 (2003): 350–54.

4. Mark Wallace et al., "Dose-Dependent Effects of Smoked Cannabis on Capsaicin-Induced Pain and Hyperalgesia in Healthy Volunteers," *Anesthesiology* 107, no. 5 (2007): 785–96.

5. Mateus Bergamaschi et al., "Cannabidiol Reduces the Anxiety Induced by Simulated Public Speaking in Treatment-Naïve Social Phobia Patients," *Neuropsychopharmacology* 36, no. 6 (2011): 1219–26.

6. Angelica Oviedo, John Glowa, and Miles Herkenham, "Chronic Cannabinoid Administration Alters Cannabinoid Receptor Binding in Rat Brain: A Quantitative Autoradiographic Study," *Brain Research* 616, no. 1–2 (1993): 293–302.

7. Ibid.

8. Russo, "Clinical Endocannabinoid Deficiency," 192.

9. Adam Hanft, "Anti-Depressant Nation," *Daily Beast*, October 5, 2008, www.thedailybeast.com/articles/2008/10/05/did-antidepressants-cause-the-mortgage-crisis.html.

CHAPTER 10: THE FOUR ENHANCEMENTS

1. Julie Holland, ed., *The Pot Book: A Complete Guide to Cannabis* (South Paris, ME: Park Street Press, 2010).

2. Laurie Winer, "A Yoga High with a Little Help," *New York Times*, December 5, 2012, www.nytimes.com/2012/12/06/fashion/marijuana-and-yoga-pairing-up-in-classes.html.

3. Carl Sagan, "Mr. X," marijuana-uses.com, April 20, 2009, http://marijuana-uses.com/mr-x/.

4. Ronald K. Siegel, *Intoxication: The Universal Drive for Mind-Altering Substances* (Rochester, Vermont: Park Street Press, 2005), 13.

5. David O. Kennedy, *Plants and the Human Brain* (New York: Oxford University Press, 2014).

6. Michael Pollan, "The Trip Treatment," *New Yorker*, February 9, 2015, www.newyorker.com/magazine/2015/02/09/trip-treatment.

7. Robin Carhart-Harris, "The Entropic Brain: A Theory of Conscious States Informed by Neuroimaging Research with Psychedelic Drugs," *Frontiers in Human Neuroscience*, February 3, 2014, http://journal.frontiersin.org/article/10.3389/fnhum.2014.00020/abstract.

8. Janet E. Joy, Stanley J. Watson Jr., and John A. Benson, *Marijuana and Medicine: Assessing the Science Base* (Washington, DC: National Academy Press, 1999).

9. Mark Wolfe, "Pot for Parents," *New York Times*, September 7, 2012, www.nytimes.com/2012/09/08/opinion/how-pot-helps-parenting.html.

10. Anonymous, "The Effects of Marijuana on Consciousness," in *Altered States of Consciousness*, ed. Charles T. Tart (New York: Doubleday & Co., 1972).

11. Sagan, "Mr. X."

12. Matthew Klickstein, "Does Pot Enhance Your Ability to Code?," *iTech-Post*, March 7, 2013, www.itechpost.com/articles/6198/20130307/pot-enhance-ability-code.htm.

13. Charles Levinson, "Comey: FBI 'Grappling' with Hiring Policy Concerning Marijuana," *Wall Street Journal*, May 20, 2014, http://blogs.wsj.com/law/2014/05/20/director-comey-fbi-grappling-with-hiring-policy-concerning-marijuana/.

14. Sebastián Marincolo, *High: Insights on Marijuana* (Indianapolis: Dog Ear Publishing, 2010).

15. Jonathon Green, "Spoonfuls of Paradise," *The Guardian*, October 11, 2002, www.theguardian.com/books/2002/oct/12/featuresreviews.guardianreview34.

16. Marincolo, *High*, 74.

17. Vilayanur S. Ramachandran and Edward M. Hubbard, "Hearing Colors, Tasting Shapes," *Scientific American*, May 2003, http://cbc.ucsd.edu/pdf/SciAm_2003.pdf.

18. Allen Ginsberg, "The Great Marijuana Hoax," *Atlantic Monthly*, November 1966, www.theatlantic.com/past/docs/issues/66nov/hoax.htm.

19. Jasen Davis, "Cannabis and Sexology: A Coach for Couples and Canna-

bis," *Culture*, February 4, 2016, http://ireadculture.com/cannabis-and-sexology/.

20. Sarah Griffiths, "Could Smoking Marijuana Be Good for a Relationship? Less Domestic Violence Found Among Married Couples Who Use Drugs, Study Claims," *Daily Mail* (UK), August 27, 2014, www.dailymail.co.uk/science-tech/article-2735566/Could-smoking-marijuana-GOOD-relationship-Less-domestic-violence-married-couples-use-pot.html.

21. Iain McGilchrist, "The Divided Brain" (TED Talk, October 2011), www.ted.com/talks/iain_mcgilchrist_the_divided_brain.

22. Iain McGilchrist, *The Master and His Emissary: The Divided Brain and the Making of the Western World* (New Haven, CT: Yale University Press, 2012): 29–31.

23. McGilchrist, *The Master*.

CHAPTER 11: THE NEXT REINVENTION OF WEED

1. Tony O'Neill, "We Need to Talk About Kevin Sabet," *Substance.com*, January 21, 2015, www.substance.com/we-need-to-talk-about-kevin-sabet/19316/.

2. Bridget Onders et al., "Marijuana Exposure Among Children Younger Than Six Years in the United States," *Clinical Pediatrics*, June 7, 2015, http://cpj.sagepub.com/content/early/2015/06/03/0009922815589912.abstract.

3. Maia Szalavitz, "Drugs in Portugal: Did Decriminalization Work?," *Time*, April 26, 2009, http://content.time.com/time/health/article/0,8599,1893946,00.html.

4. Lee Fang, "The Real Reason."

5. Ibid.

6. Kevin A. Sabet, "California Medical Association's Decision Not Based on Public Health," *Huffington Post*, October 21, 2011, www.huffingtonpost.com/kevin-a-sabet-phd/cmas-decision-not-based_b_1024471.html.

7. Wiebke Hollerson, "This Is Working: Portugal, 12 Years After Decriminalizing Drugs," *Spiegel Online International*, March 27, 2013, www.spiegel.de/international/europe/evaluating-drug-decriminalization-in-portugal-12-years-later-a-891060.html.

8. "1,000–2,000 New Marijuana Jobs in Colorado," *Marijuana Business Daily*, May 21, 2014, http://mjbizdaily.com/1000-2000-new-cannabis-jobs-in-colorado/.

9. Daniel Okrent, *Last Call: The Rise and Fall of Prohibition* (New York: Scribner, 2011), 374.

10. Bari Adams, "Cannabis Compounds THCV and Cannabidiol Linked to Metabolic Rate," *Examiner.com*, July 10, 2012, www.examiner.com/article/cannabis-compounds-thcv-and-cannabidiol-linked-to-metabolic-rate.

11. Paula Span, "Study Links Anxiety Drugs to Alzheimer's Disease," *New York Times*, September 24, 2014, http://newoldage.blogs.nytimes .com/2014/09/24/study-links-anxiety-drugs-to-alzheimers-disease/.

12. Richard Alleyne, "Welcome to the Information Age—174 Newspapers a Day," *The Telegraph Online*, February 11, 2011, www.telegraph.co.uk/ news/science/science-news/8316534/Welcome-to-the-information-age-174-newspapers-a-day.html.